THE COOK'S ENCYCLOPEDIA OF

CURRIES

THE COOK'S ENCYCLOPEDIA OF

CURRIES

MRIDULA BALJEKAR

HERMES HOUSE

This edition is published by Hermes House

Hermes House is an imprint of Anness Publishing Ltd
Hermes House, 88–89 Blackfriars Road, London SE1 8HA
tel. 020 7401 2077; fax 020 7633 9499
info@anness.com

A CIP catalogue record for this book is available from the British Library.

Publisher: Joanna Lorenz
Managing Editor: Judith Simons
Art Director: Clare Reynolds
Project Editor: Sarah Ainley
Copy Editor: Catherine Humby
Designer: Nigel Partridge
Reference section: Mridula Baljekar and Sallie Morris
Recipes: Mridula Baljekar, Kit Chan, Rafi Fernandez, Deh-Ta Hsiung, Shehzad Husain, Christine Ingram, Manisha Kanani, Sally Mansfield, Sallie Morris and Jennie Shapter
Photography: Edward Allwright, David Armstrong, Nicki Dowey, Amanda Heywood, Ferguson Hill, Janine Hosegood, David Jordan, David King, Patrick McLeavey and Sam Stowell
Editorial Reader: Richard McGinlay
Production Controller: Don Campaniello

1 3 5 7 9 10 8 6 4 2

NOTES

Bracketed terms are intended for American readers.

For all recipes, quantities are given in both metric and imperial measures and, where appropriate, measures are also given in standard cups and spoons. Follow one set, but not a mixture, because they are not interchangeable.

Standard spoon and cup measures are level.
1 tsp = 5ml, 1 tbsp = 15ml, 1 cup = 250ml/8fl oz

Australian standard tablespoons are 20ml. Australian readers should use 3 tsp in place of 1 tbsp for measuring small quantities of gelatine, flour, salt, etc.

Medium (US large) eggs are used unless otherwise stated.

CONTENTS

INTRODUCTION

The sub-continent of India and the neighbouring countries of South-East Asia evoke mystery, magic and romance. Both regions are steeped in history and heritage; theirs is a chequered history of exciting discoveries of new lands, great empires built and destroyed, valuable allies and dangerous enemies. Central to the dramas that have unfolded in these regions are the exotic spices that have been grown here for centuries. It is carefully prepared blends of these spices that provide the mouthwatering tastes, flavours and aromas of curries.

India has long been known as the spice bowl of the world, and South-East Asia, too, occupies its own important place in the history of the spice trade.

Below: *Pork balchao, from Goa, is one of only a few pork recipes that exist in India.*

The use of premium quality spices in these sun-drenched, monsoon-fed lands was an established way of life long before traders, among them Arabs, English, Dutch, Portuguese and Spanish, came to the area, lured by the valuable spices.

Spectacular geography, fascinating ancient customs, and glorious foods all continue to draw foreigners to these magical lands. From India's border with Afghanistan in the north to the beaches of Indonesia's paradise islands in the south, this corner of the world is diverse in every respect. Just as much as the breathtakingly beautiful scenery, culinary traditions have also been influenced by geographical and climatic conditions. With vast distances to be travelled, and no means of transporting fresh produce efficiently, cook's have made the best use of the ingredients available locally.

Above: *Beef biryani is a speciality dish from the Muslim community in India.*

Besides offering fabulous flavours, Indian and South-east Asian cooking is extremely healthy. The emphasis is firmly on freshness, with a wide range of meats, fish and shellfish, vegetables and salads, together with wheat or rice as the staple. Meat and fish are served in small quantities, surrounded by inviting little side dishes, such as pickles, chutneys, salads and sambals, flavoured with fresh herbs and chillies, yogurt or soy sauce, and used as seasonings. Rice or breads in India and rice or noodles in South-east Asia form the staple diet. Many of the ingredients used in these dishes are

Below: *This rich fish curry, known as* kalia, *originates from Bengal, in eatern India.*

known for their medicinal properties. For example, there is strong evidence that garlic and fresh root ginger, two of the most essential ingredients in curries, contain properties that can help to combat heart diseases and stomach ulcers respectively.

The striking resemblance in many of the cooking and serving styles in India and South-east Asia is reflected in the ingredients used. The exquisite flavour of cardamom pods, the warmth of cumin, the sweet, mellow taste of coriander, the woody aroma of ginger and fiery chillies are characteristic flavours, adding zest and flavour to countless curries. The coconut-based curries of south India strongly resemble those of South-east Asia in taste, aroma and flavour; curries from these regions are distinguished by the curry leaves used in south Indian curries and the kaffir lime leaves used in South-east Asia.

The Indian commercial community, who emigrated to South-east Asia, added their own identity to local cuisines and customs, and this has helped to merge culinary practices. The Indian influence is strongest in Malaysia, while the cuisines of Vietnam and the islands of the Philippines have profound French and Spanish legacies. Only Thailand has remained free from colonial rule.

In India, too, foreign powers have introduced cooking styles that are still in practice today. The north continues to be dominated by Mogul cuisine, while the east has tribal and Anglo-Indian styles. In the south, Syrian Jews and French traders contributed techniques, and western India came under the influence of the Portuguese and the Persians (Parsis). The result is a multi-dimensional, colourful cuisine of richness and depth, with a repertoire of recipes that is virtually unmatched anywhere else in the world.

Culinary skills and expertise from around the world have been developed in India and South-east Asia, and the best of the resulting dishes are featured in this wonderful collection. The aim of this volume is to offer traditional curry recipes with authentic flavours and uncomplicated preparation and cooking methods. I hope it will encourage even novice cooks to get to know the delights of cooking hot and spicy curries.

MRIDULA BALJEKAR

Above: *Although mussaman curry is a Thai dish, its roots can be traced back to India.*

Above left: *Simmering vegetables in coconut milk in place of stock or water is a typical south Indian cooking technique.*

Below: *This coconut-flavoured fish curry is one of Malaysia's more traditional dishes.*

INDIA

In a country the size of India, it is no surprise to find variations in cooking styles and a preference for local produce in dishes across the regions. History and religion have both played their part in the development of cultural and culinary traditions and the shaping of eating habits. As a result, India now has one of the richest cuisines in the world.

CULTURE and CUISINE

India is a vast country, with a total area of around 3.3 million square kilometres (1.3 million square miles) and a population in excess of 859 million. It is a land of striking contrasts, with huge variations in terms of climate, geography, religion, culture and customs. All of these factors have had a powerful influence on the country's cuisine, which has emerged as one of the most rich and diverse in the world.

The country's various climates, affected by a wide range of geographical conditions, naturally dictate the types of crops that are grown in different regions. In the past, when transport and communications were poor, people had to confine themselves to the ingredients that grew naturally around them. They created a vast array of recipes, with distinct variations between each region.

Religion also played an important role in the development of Indian cuisine. Many religions exist side by side in India, with Hinduism being the indigenous faith. The Sikh and Buddhist religions are both branches of Hinduism. Islam was introduced by foreign traders, and went on to become one of the main religions of the land. Both the Hindu and Muslim religions have certain taboos as far as food is concerned. Hinduism prohibits the eating of beef: the cow is regarded as sacred because Hindu mythology depicts it as the companion of one of the most important Hindu gods, Lord Krishna. The Koran, on the other hand, prohibits the consumption of pork, so beef has become popular among people of the Muslim faith, and an excellent range of beef-based recipes is found across the country. Although pork is not generally eaten by Hindus, the Christians of Goa, on the west coast, and the warrior community in Coorg, in the South, have created a variety of delicious recipes for pork.

Cultures and customs have also had a considerable impact on Indian cuisine. Over the centuries, historical events have imposed many different cultures upon India, and the country has not only absorbed them, but has also encouraged each to flourish individually.

Below: *Hessian sacks of fresh and dried chillies for sale in an Indian street.*

REGIONAL DIVERSITY

The diversity of the food culture across the regions of modern-day India may not be as pronounced as it once was, but in a country so vast it is inevitable that long-standing traditions for produce and cooking styles have persisted.

North India

The northern states of India have been subjected to a vast number of foreign invaders, traders and pilgrims throughout history. The north, more than any other region, allows easy access into India, with the Khyber Pass providing a natural link between Afghanistan and present-day Pakistan. Groups of travellers have entered through this long, narrow pass and spread themselves all over the area. Most notable were the Moguls, who invaded India in the 16th century and ruled for almost three hundred years.

During their journey to India, the Moguls came across the much-admired Persian style of cooking, which they adapted and introduced to India. This has become known as Mughlai cuisine, and is now almost as widely eaten in the West as it is in India. Foreign travellers are also credited with introducing exotic fruits and nuts to Kashmir, where they were used to create a variety of sumptuous dishes. Kashmiri cuisine is prized for its unusual richness and varied textures and flavours, and dishes such as kormas, pasandas and biryanis are now firmly established as some of the most popular foods of northern India.

From Kashmir, the Moguls spread south and west into the Punjab, which is renowned for its tandoori cooking. Punjab is also known as the bread box of India, for the enormous variety of breads, both leavened and unleavened, it produces. Naan is the most widely eaten bread among the leavened variety,

Above: Indian housewives shop daily for fresh ingredients at the vegetable market.

Below: The huge expanse of land that is India reaches from neighbouring Afghanistan in the far north to Sri Lanka in the south.

Above: Rice is the staple food of southern and eastern India, and a plentiful harvest is essential for the survival of these regions.

while tandoori rotis, which is cooked in a tandoor, or Indian clay oven, is the most common unleavened bread.

Delhi, the capital of India, was once the centre of the Mogul dynasty. The Moguls' love of fine food, along with their exquisite taste in fine art and architecture, are so deeply rooted in Delhi that the city is now a major tourist attraction. As well as the traditional Mughlai food, Punjabi food, which includes a wonderful range of sweets (candies), has made Delhi a true food lover's paradise.

East India

The influence of Mogul cuisine is not so pronounced in the eastern region, where local styles of cooking have more of a stronghold. The state of Bengal, for example, has developed in almost total isolation despite its proximity to the northern states. Apart from some minor reminders of the Moguls' brief presence in the region, Bengal has a unique cuisine, which is famous all over India.

Bengalis have always been very proud of their produce, and have made full use of home-grown ingredients to create a fascinating style of cooking. Mustard grows extensively in the area and mustard oil is widely used as a cooking medium. Several vegetarian, meat and poultry dishes also make use of ground mustard. Coconut, another local product, is widely used in both sweet and savoury dishes. Bengalis are immensely proud of the rice grown in their soil, and of the fish found in the waters of the Bay of Bengal. Together, rice and fish curry constitute the everyday diet of the Bengali people, although the state's most significant contribution to Indian cuisine is generally regarded to be its superb range of sweets.

Calcutta, the capital of West Bengal, has a strong tradition for Anglo-Indian cuisine, which is popular among the city's Anglo-Indian community, and in the clubs and sports centres established by the British Raj in the 19th century. These eccentrically outmoded institutions still thrive in the old British manner: cocktails are served by liveried staff, and are accompanied by delicious tidbits, cooked in the Western style but flavoured with Indian spices.

The streets of Calcutta are bustling with vendors selling all kinds of tempting local and Anglo-Indian sweet and savoury snacks. Ghugni, a spiced chickpea dish served with mouthwatering relishes, is one of the favourite local dishes.

Although the food of Bihar and Orissa, two other eastern states, has not made any significant impact on the cuisine of the subcontinent, Orissa deserves a mention for its excellent fresh fish and shellfish, which it exports worldwide in large quantities.

South India

The southern states have been greatly influenced by the indigenous Hindu faith. On the southern tip of the country, however, the Malabar Coast provided easy access to the French, Dutch, British and Portuguese, as well as to a small number of Jews from Syria. The French had some influence on the cuisine of this area in the state of Pondicherry, and the Jews contributed meat and poultry dishes to Kerala. As well as making their mark on the eastern region, the British had thriving trading posts in Madras, and an Anglo-Indian community still exists in that area. Otherwise, since the Dutch had no impact on Indian cuisine, and the Portuguese were concentrated in Goa, southern India has remained free of foreign influence seen elsewhere.

South Indian food is quite different from the rich cuisine of the north. It is light and refreshing, and the sauces are enriched with coconut milk, whereas in northern India, dairy cream and nuts are used for the same purpose. The food in the south is generally fiery: the temperature here is hot throughout the year, and chillies are known to have a cooling effect on the body.

Along the coast of southern India, fish curry and rice are eaten on an almost daily basis, but there are two dishes for which South India is famous. Dosas, paper-thin pancakes made from ground rice and lentils, are filled with spicy vegetables and served for breakfast with a coconut chutney, while idlis, which are steamed rice dumplings, are eaten with spicy lentils and chutneys.

Between Maharashtra in the west and the Bay of Bengal in the east, lies the state of Andhra Pradesh, which is

Above: Numerous varieties of beans, peas and lentils are on sale in this pulse shop, along with spice mixes for cooking them.

famous for its forts and palaces, and for its unique cuisine. Mogul traditions are strong here: even though the state has never been ruled by the Muslim rulers, the last Mogul emperor retired to the capital city Hyderabad, causing a culinary revolution that influenced the whole region. Kababs, biryanis and kormas exist side by side with hot, fiery local foods and a wide variety of rice, which is grown locally.

West India

In western India lies the state of Gujarat. Most Gujaratis are strictly vegetarian and, unlike the many non-meat eaters in India who eat fish, they eat neither fish nor eggs. Their religion emphasizes the respect that must be shown to all living beings, and prohibits the taking of any life for reasons of personal enjoyment. As a result, the Gujaratis have truly perfected the art of vegetarian cooking. Fresh vegetables, lentils, beans, peas and dairy products have taken centre stage, and dairy products are abundant. People take yogurt and buttermilk on a daily basis, and use them in cooking. Breads are skilfully made, using both millet flour and maize flour (cornmeal).

The most famous culinary export of Gujarat is the vegetable- and lentil-based dhansak. About 13 centuries ago, a group of Persians fled their country to avoid religious persecution. Gujarat, being open to the sea, was the most convenient point from which to enter India. The Persians were made to feel at home here, and became known as the Parsis. They adapted the rich and varied culture of Gujarat and eventually spread further west, to Bombay.

Bombay is situated on the edge of the deep blue Arabian Sea, and it is here that the Gateway of India was built during the British Raj, to commemorate a visit by the Prince of Wales. Bombay is the capital of Maharashtra, a mainly vegetarian state with a cosmopolitan population that has given rise to a rich and varied cuisine. Bombay is probably the only city in India where food from almost any part of the country can be sampled. As well as Indian food, Chinese dishes with an Indian twist can be found in the numerous restaurants throughout this vibrant city. Fresh fish and shellfish are also plentiful in the area.

To the south of Bombay is Goa, where the lure of Indian spices brought Portuguese traders, who colonized the area. Goa remained under Portuguese rule until 1962, and the influence the Portuguese left behind has created a happy marriage between East and West. Goa's most famous export is vindaloo, which has Portuguese origins.

Below: Fisherman inspect their early morning catch on the beaches of Kerala.

PRINCIPLES of INDIAN COOKING

Until recently, no written record of Indian recipes has existed in India itself. Recipes have traditionally been handed down from one generation to another. Far from being a disadvantage, this has actually helped to fire the imagination of the creative cook, and many dishes that first started out as experiments in spice blends and flavour combinations have now become world classics.

Spices and aromatics

The key to successful Indian cooking lies in the art of blending spices and herbs, rather than sophisticated cooking techniques. The traditional Indian cook relies on instinct rather than written recipes when measuring and combining spices, and in this way unique and very personal tastes can be created. This is one reason why the same dish from one region can look and taste quite different, according to who has cooked it.

Herbs are added to a dish during the cooking time to add flavour and aroma, but spices, including those used mainly for taste or for aroma, perform a more complex role.

Spices can be divided into two main groups: those that are integrated into a dish by the end of the cooking process, and those that are removed. The spices in the first group add taste, texture and colour. Different combinations are used, and no single spice is allowed to dominate the final flavour. Useful spices in this group include coriander, cumin, turmeric and garam masala, all in ground form.

The second group of spices add aroma to a dish. They remain identifiable at the end of cooking, as most of them are used whole. Once these spices have released their aroma, their function is complete and they are not eaten, but removed from the dish before serving or simply left on one side of the plate. Examples of this type of spice are whole cloves, cardamom pods, cinnamon sticks and bay leaves. These spices can also be ground, in which case they will blend into the sauce during cooking, and will be eaten in the dish in the same way as any other ground spice.

Adding flavour

Having chosen which spices to use, you can then decide what kind of flavours you would like to create. For instance, dry-roasting and grinding flavouring ingredients before adding them to a dish creates a completely different taste and aroma from frying the raw ground spices in hot fat before adding the main ingredients. The flavour of a dish will also vary according to the sequence in which the spices are added, and the length of time each spice is fried and allowed to release its flavour.

Indian cooking lends itself to being personalized by different cooks, and with even just two or three spices, you can create distinctly varied dishes.

Below: *Spices and seasonings are what gives Indian food its unique character.*

What is a curry?

In India, the word curry refers to a sauce or gravy used as an accompaniment to moisten grains of *chawal* (rice) or to make *rotis* (bread) more enjoyable. The rice or bread are considered the main dish of the meal.

The word curry is generally believed to be an anglicized version of the south Indian word *kaari*. It belongs to the Tamil language, which is spoken in the state of Tamil Nadu, of which Madras is the capital. In Tamil, the word means sauce and it is thought that when the British were active in this area, the spelling was somehow changed to curry. Other theories suggest that the word *cury* has existed in English in the context of cooking since the 14th century, and that it was originally derived from the French verb *cuire* (to cook).

The main ingredients of a curry can vary enormously, and two highly dissimilar dishes can be equally deserving of the name. Even the lentil dish known as *dhal*, which bears no resemblance to a sauce, falls under the definition of a curry; in India, *dhal-chawal* and *dhal-roti* are eaten on a daily basis.

A vegetable curry usually consists of a selection of fresh vegetables cooked in a sauce, which can have a thick or a thin consistency, depending on the style of cooking in the region. The sauces for meat, poultry and fish curries also vary in consistency, and are all designed to be served with rice or bread. Gujarat in the west and Punjab in the north also make spiced curries using just yogurt mixed with a little *besan* (gram flour). Made without meat, poultry or vegetables, these dishes are known as *khadis*.

Above: *Most of the key ingredients needed for Indian curries are now available from large supermarkets, but Indian food stores will usually stock a wider selection.*

What to eat with a curry

In south and eastern India, curries are always served with rice, which, as the region's main crop, is the staple food of the area, and is eaten daily. Wheat grows abundantly in north India, and in most northern regions, breads such as naan, chapatis and parathas are eaten with curries and with dry, spiced vegetable and lentil dishes. In the Punjab region, however, breads made from *besan* and *makki* (cornmeal) are more usually served with curries. In western India, curries are eaten with breads made with flour prepared from *jowar* (millet) and *bajra* (milo).

PREPARING an INDIAN CURRY

While there may be no such thing as a definitive curry recipe, there certainly is an established procedure to follow when preparing a curry. Deciding what type of curry you are going to make is the first step. Choose your main ingredient, and select your cooking pan accordingly, as this will affect the ultimate success of the dish. A deep-sided pan will be necessary if the curry is to contain lots of liquid, while for fish, a wide, flat pan is needed to allow the pieces of fish to be laid flat, side by side, in a single layer.

Cooking fats

You need to decide whether you want to use ghee, which is clarified butter, or oil as your cooking medium. Traditionally, the Indian housewife would use ghee, not just for its rich flavour, but also because dairy products are believed to be more nutritious. Modern Indian families are now deviating from this practice, however, because of a growing awareness of the dangers of eating too much saturated fat. Sunflower, vegetable and corn oils will all make suitable alternatives. Olive oil is not normally used, although a basic cooking version (not virgin or extra virgin) will work perfectly well. Ghee can be reserved for special occasion dishes, if you like.

Cooking liquids

Most curries are water-based. Stock is sometimes used in Indian cooking, but it is not a common practice as meat is always cooked on the bone, and this creates a sufficiently robust flavour. Whether you use stock or water as your cooking liquid, it is important to make sure the liquid is at least lukewarm. Adding cold liquid to carefully blended spices will impair the flavours.

Adding salt

Pay careful attention when using salt in an Indian dish. Do not be afraid to use the amount specified in a recipe; even if it seems a lot, it will have been worked out to achieve an overall balance of flavours. There are now several brands of low-sodium salt on the market, which can be substituted, if you prefer.

Above: Fresh and dried herbs provide colour, flavour, aroma and texture to Indian food.

Thickening agents

Indian cooking does not rely on flour to thicken sauces. Instead, the consistency is more usually achieved by adding ingredients such as dairy cream or coconut cream, nut pastes, onion purée, tomatoes, and ground seeds such as poppy, sesame and sunflower.

Adding colour

Some of the ingredients added to curries not only determine their texture and consistency, but also their colour. In Mughlai sauces and curries, the onions are softened but not browned, which gives the dishes their distinctive pale colour. Bhuna (stir-fried) curries, on the other hand, brown the onions, making the final dishes reddish-brown in colour.

Souring agents

Some of the souring agents used in curries also affect their colour and consistency. Tamarind, for instance, darkens and thickens a sauce at the same time. Lime, lemon and white vinegar, however, will neither alter the colour of a curry nor thicken it, and a thickening agent such as coconut milk or a nut or seed paste has to be used as well. Ingredients such as dry mango powder (*amchur*), dried pomegranate

COLOURING INGREDIENTS

The depth of the curry's colour will depend on the amount of colorant used in relation to other ingredients.

turmeric: bright yellow
saffron: pale apricot
red chillies: reddish brown
fresh coriander (cilantro) leaves: green
tomatoes: reddish, if used alone; pinkish if combined with yogurt
onions: brown
ground coriander: deep brown if fried for 5–6 minutes
garam masala: deep brown if fried for 1 minute

seeds (known as *anardana*), as well as tomatoes and yogurts are all used to lend a distinctive tangy flavour to a curry, and they will also affect the colour to varying degrees.

Adding heat

The most important ingredient for achieving a fiery flavour and appearance is chilli. Although chillies were unknown in India before the Portuguese settlers introduced them in the 15th century, it is difficult to imagine Indian food without them today. It is chilli in its powdered form that contributes to the colour of a curry, and chilli powder is readily available in a range of heat levels. Always be sure to check the label carefully. If you want the curry to be appealing to the eye without scorching the taste buds, choose a chilli powder made from either Kashmiri or Byadigi chillies. This will lend a rich colour to the dish, but the flavour will be fairly mild. You can always use it in conjunction with a hot chilli powder if you prefer to give the curry some kick. Another way to achieve both colour and heat in the same dish is to combine chilli powder with fresh chillies: fresh chillies are always hotter than dried.

When buying fresh chillies, try to find the ones used in Indian cooking, rather than Mexican varieties. Those used in Indian cooking are long and slim, and are sometimes labelled "finger chillies". Thai chillies make a good substitute, and are available from Asian food stores.

Paste made from dried red chillies also gives a very good colour and quite a different flavour from chilli powder. To make it, all you need to do is to soak the chillies for 15–20 minutes in hot water and then purée them. The paste will keep well in an airtight jar in the refrigerator for 4–5 days.

Cooking a curry

Several factors will influence the making of a good curry, and one of the most important of these is the cooking temperature. The fat should be heated to the right temperature and maintained at a steady heat until the spices have released their flavour. A heavy pan, such as a wok, karahi or large pan, will help to maintain the temperature, so that the spices can cook without burning. While recipes may vary, the usual procedure is to start off by cooking the onions over a medium heat. Once the onions have softened, the ground spices are added and the temperature is lowered.

Another important factor is the chopping of the onions. The finer the onion is chopped, the better it will blend into the sauce. In many recipes, onion, ginger and garlic are puréed to make a wet spice paste, which is fried until all the moisture has evaporated, before the ground spices are added. It is crucial to follow the timings specified in a recipe for each of these cooking stages.

Adding spices in the correct sequence is also vital. While some spices take only a few seconds to release their flavour, others need a few minutes, and if you add spices that require less cooking time together with those that need more, some will burn and others will remain raw. The simplest way to avoid this is to keep to the order in which the spices are listed in the recipe, and to be very exact about following the specified cooking time for each ingredient.

Below: The secret of Indian cooking lies in the use of spices, and blending spices at home will give more flavoursome curries.

PLANNING an INDIAN MEAL

When planning your menu, always bear in mind that an everyday Indian meal features only three items: the main dish, a side dish and a staple, which would be rice or bread. Chutneys, salads and raitas can also be served to add a tangy taste.

Planning the menu

When deciding which foods to serve, consider the main dish. Is it going to be highly spiced, such as a vindaloo or a bhuna? Or will it have subtle flavours, such as a korma or a pasanda? A little careful planning will ensure that the flavours of the dishes complement, rather than compete with, each other. Choose the side dish according to the strength of the main one. A lightly spiced side dish is more enjoyable when the main dish is spicier. This does not apply in reverse, however, and a side dish with complex spicing is not the ideal accompaniment to a mild main dish.

Below: *There is no rigid structure to an Indian meal, but there should always be a good balance of dry and moist dishes.*

Dishes with a drier consistency are generally accompanied by a vegetable curry or a lentil dish. Biryanis and pilaus are traditionally served with a simple raita, although they are more usually served with a vegetable curry in Indian restaurants in the West.

How to serve

An Indian meal is not served as separate courses, with an appetizer, followed by a main dish and one or two side dishes. Although the meal will usually consist of several dishes, all complement each other and are brought to the table at the same time, with diners helping themselves to each dish in any order.

USEFUL STANDBYS

- Use bottled ginger and garlic purées (paste) rather than peeling and chopping the fresh spices.
- Canned chopped tomatoes can be used instead of fresh tomatoes, although you may need to increase the quantities of souring agent, salt and chilli to compensate for the depleted flavour.
- Canned or packet creamed coconut is a convenient replacement for fresh coconut. Use according to the manufacturer's instructions.

For entertaining and more lavish occasions, you can add other dishes to the standard three-dish Indian menu. One or two dry meat dishes, such as a kabab or tandoori chicken, in addition

to some chutneys, pickles, raitas and poppadums, with a dessert to follow, can turn an ordinary family meal into dinner-party fare.

Indian desserts

In India, a meal will usually end with fresh fruit, rather than elaborate or cooked desserts. Fruits can be served with real flair, however, and are often combined with other ingredients to create imaginative and exciting flavours. Choose one or two exotic fruits, such as papaya, pomegranate or star fruit, and combine them with everyday fruits in a fruit salad. Serve with Greek (US strained plain) yogurt flavoured with rose water and a little ground cardamom.

Indian sweets (candies) are quite heavy and are served as a snack with tea and coffee, in the same way as cakes and biscuits (cookies) are eaten in the West.

COOKING FOR A PARTY

It is a good idea to cook the curry dishes a day ahead of the party, storing them in the refrigerator until you are ready to reheat them. Accompanying dhal dishes can also be prepared 24 hours in advance, although the seasonings should not be added until just before serving. You can prepare vegetables in advance, but do not cook them more than a few hours ahead. Likewise, you can prepare ingredients for raitas a day ahead, but do not assemble them until a few hours before they are needed; the yogurt for raitas should always be fresh. Pickles and chutneys will benefit from advance preparation, but follow individual recipes for timing guides, as some will deteriorate more quickly than others. The bread dough for rotis can be made the day before. The rotis can be made 2 hours before you plan to serve them. Spread them with butter and wrap in foil to keep warm, then set them aside; reheat in the oven before serving.

Freezing curries

In today's busy world, it is not always possible to serve a meal while it is still sizzling in the pan. If you are entertaining, you may prefer to cook the curry in advance to save yourself time on the day, or you may like to cook a larger quantity than you will need and freeze some for another meal; you may even have leftovers.

Spicy food is ideal for freezing as the flavours seem to improve when the food is thawed and reheated. Most of the spices used in Indian cooking have natural preservative qualities, as does the acid in souring agents. However, you should bear in mind the following factors if cooking specifically for the freezer:

- Leave the food slightly underdone.
- Cool the food rapidly. The best way to do this is to tip it into a large tray (a large roasting pan is ideal) and leave it in a cool place.
- Once the food has cooled completely, spoon it into plastic containers, then label and chill it in the refrigerator for a couple of hours, before transferring it to the freezer. The food will keep in the freezer for 6–8 months, depending on the star rating of your freezer.

Food that you did not plan to freeze, such as leftovers, should not be kept in the freezer for longer than 2–3 months, again, depending on the efficiency of your freezer. Meat and poultry curries freeze very successfully, as do curries made from vegetables, lentils and pulses. Fish curries can be frozen, but they are generally less successful as changes in the water balance may damage the more delicate texture of cooked fish.

Thawing and reheating

It is important to thaw frozen food thoroughly and slowly. Leave it in the refrigerator for 18–24 hours before reheating. After reheating, always make sure the food is piping hot before serving. These steps are crucial in order to ensure that any potentially harmful bacteria are destroyed. If you have a temperature probe, check that the reheated food is at least 85°C/185°F right the way through before serving.

REHEATING LEFTOVERS

This method will make leftover food that has been frozen taste really fresh. The method can also be used to reheat food that has been stored for a day or two in the refrigerator.

Heat about 10ml/2 tsp vegetable oil in a wok, karahi or large pan over a medium heat. Add up to 1.5ml/¼ tsp garam masala (depending on the quantity of food), and allow to bubble gently for 10–15 seconds. Add the thawed food to the pan and increase the heat to high. Let the food bubble or sizzle in the pan until it is heated through, stirring from time to time to make sure the heat is well distributed. Add a little water if the food looks particularly dry. Stir in 15ml/1 tbsp chopped fresh coriander (cilantro). Remove from the heat, transfer to a warmed platter and serve immediately.

A certain amount of water separation is to be expected as a defrosted dish thaws out. The dish will return to its normal consistency when it is reheated, as the water will be reabsorbed by the meat or vegetables.

Thawed food can be reheated in the microwave or in a covered casserole on the stove top. If using a microwave, cover the food with microwave cling film (plastic wrap). Stir the food from time to time as it is heated, to ensure the heat passes right the way through. You may need to add a small amount of water when reheating, to ensure that the dish does not dry out.

AROMATICS, SPICES and HERBS

Spices are integral to both the flavour and aroma of a dish. Some spices are used principally for the taste they impart, while other spices, known as aromatics, are used mainly for their aroma. One individual spice can completely alter the taste of a dish and a combination of several spices will also affect its colour and texture.

The quantities of spices and salt specified in recipes are measured to achieve a balance of flavours, although you may prefer to increase or decrease the quantities according to taste. This is particularly true of fresh chillies and chilli powder: experiment with quantities, adding less or more than specified.

Fresh and dried herbs also play an important part in the combinations of colour, flavour, aroma and texture that make up a curry. Because herbs require only a minimal amount of cooking, they retain a marvellous intensity of flavour and fragrance.

PULPING GARLIC

Fresh garlic is used so often in Indian cooking that you may find it more practical to prepare garlic in bulk and store in the refrigerator or freezer until needed.

Separate the garlic bulb into cloves and peel off the papery skin. Process the whole cloves in a food processor until smooth. Freeze the garlic pulp in ice-cube trays used specially for the purpose. Put 5ml/ 1 tsp in each compartment, freeze, remove from the tray and store in the freezer in a sealed plastic bag. Alternatively, store the pulp in an airtight container in the refrigerator for 3–4 weeks.

Garlic

Widely available fresh and dried, garlic is used for its strong, aromatic flavour, and is a standard ingredient, along with ginger, in most curries. Fresh garlic can be pulped, crushed or chopped, or the cloves can be used whole. Garlic powder is mainly used in spice mixtures.

Ginger

One of the most popular spices in India and also one of the oldest, fresh root ginger is an important ingredient in many Indian curries. Its refreshing scent is reminiscent of citrus and it has a pleasant, sharp flavour. The root should be plump with a fairly smooth skin, which is peeled off before use. Young root ginger is tender and mild, whereas older roots are quite fibrous, with a more pungent flavour. Dried powdered ginger is a useful standby, but the flavour is not quite the same. It is often blended with other spices to make curry powder.

Below: *Fresh root ginger*

Below: *Ground ginger*

PREPARING FRESH ROOT GINGER

Fresh root ginger has a delightfully clean and pungent taste, and is easy to prepare. It is widely available from supermarkets and markets.

To grate ginger, carefully remove the skin using a sharp knife or vegetable peeler. Grate the peeled ginger using the fine side of a metal cheese grater. To chop, slice the ginger into fine strips, then chop as required.

PULPING FRESH ROOT GINGER

Pulped fresh root ginger is time-consuming to prepare for each individual recipe. Instead, prepare a large quantity and store in the freezer until needed.

Peel off the tough outer skin using a sharp knife or a vegetable peeler. Roughly chop, then process in a food processor, adding a little water to get a smooth consistency. Store the pulp in the refrigerator for 3–4 weeks or freeze in ice-cube trays used for the purpose.

Left: Green and red Bird's eye chillies

Chillies

These hot peppers belong to the genus capsicum, along with sweet (bell) peppers. Some varieties are extremely fiery and all chillies should be used with caution. Much of the severe heat of fresh chillies is contained in the seeds, and the heat can be toned down by removing these before use. Like other spicy foods, chillies are perfect for hot climates as they cause blood to rush to the surface of the skin, promoting instant cooling.

Chillies vary in size and colour, but as a rule, dark green chillies tend to be hotter than light green ones. Red chillies are usually hotter still, and some will darken to brown or black when fully ripe. Shape and colour give no sure indication of the hotness, and it is wise to be wary of any unfamiliar variety. Dried chillies can be used whole or coarsely crushed.

Chilli powder is a fiery ground spice that should be used with great caution. The heat varies from brand to brand, so adjust quantities to suit your taste buds. Some brands include other spices and herbs, as well as ground chillies, and these may not be appropriate to the dish you are cooking. Always check the label carefully.

PREPARING DRIED CHILLIES

Dried chillies are available from good supermarkets and Indian food stores.

To prepare the chillies, remove the stems and seeds, then break each chilli into two or three pieces. Put the pieces in a small bowl and cover with hot water. Leave to stand for 30 minutes, then drain (using the soaking water in the recipe, if appropriate). Use the chilli pieces as they are, or chop them finely.

WATCHPOINT

All chillies contain capsaicin, an oily substance, that can cause intense irritation to sensitive skin. If you get capsaicin on your hands and transfer it to your eyes by rubbing, you will experience considerable pain. Wash hands with soapy water after handling. Dry your hands and rub a little oil into the skin to remove any stinging juices. Many cooks prefer to wear rubber (latex) gloves.

Above: The colour of chillies gives no sure indication of hotness, although red chillies are usually hotter.

PREPARING FRESH CHILLIES

Using two or more fresh chillies will make a dish quite hot. If you prefer a milder flavour, reduce the amount of chilli used, and remove the seeds and pithy membrane. If you have sensitive skin, you may prefer to wear rubber (latex) gloves to protect your hands when preparing chillies.

1 Cut the chillies in half lengthways. Remove the membranes and seeds.

2 Cut the chilli flesh lengthways into long, thin strips.

3 If required, cut the strips of chilli crossways into tiny dice.

Below: *From left, cloves, ground cinnamon, and cinnamon sticks*

Aniseed

These liquorice-flavoured seeds are used in many fried and deep-fried Indian dishes as an aid to digestion.

Cinnamon

One of the earliest known spices, cinnamon has a highly aromatic, sweet, warm flavour. It is sold ready-ground and as sticks, which are quill-like shapes rolled from the bark of the cinnamon tree. Use cinnamon sticks whole or broken, as directed in individual recipes, and remove them from the food before serving. Ground cinnamon is a useful pantry staple.

Above: *From left, cumin seeds, fenugreek and ground cumin*

Cloves

Originally found in the Spice Islands of Indonesia, cloves were taken to the Seychelles and Mauritius early in the 18th century. Cloves are the unopened flower buds of a tree that belongs to the myrtle family. They have an aromatic and sometimes fiery flavour and an intense fragrance, and are used to flavour many sweet and savoury dishes. Cloves are usually added whole to recipes. Their warm flavour complements all rich meats, and they need no preparation. Ground cloves are one of the ingredients added to spice mixtures.

Left: *Ground and fresh turmeric*

Cumin

White cumin seeds are oval, ridged and greenish brown in colour. They have a strong aroma and flavour and can be used whole or ground. Ready-ground cumin powder is widely available, but it should be bought in small quantities as it loses its flavour rapidly. Black cumin seeds are dark and aromatic. They are one of the ingredients used to make garam masala, and can be used to flavour curries and rice.

Turmeric

A member of the ginger family but without ginger's characteristic heat, turmeric is a rhizome that is indigenous to Asia. Turmeric is sometimes referred to as Indian saffron, as it shares saffron's ability to colour food yellow, although it lacks that spice's subtlety. Fresh turmeric adds a warm and slightly musky flavour to food, but it has a strong, bitter flavour and should be used sparingly. Turmeric has a natural affinity with fish, and is also used in rice, *dhal* and vegetable dishes.

Dhana jeera powder

This spice mixture is made from ground roasted coriander and cumin seeds. The proportions are generally two parts coriander to one part cumin.

Fennel seeds

Similar in appearance to cumin, fennel seeds have a sweet taste and are used to flavour curries. They can be chewed as a mouth-freshener after a spicy meal.

Mustard seeds

Whole black and brown mustard seeds are indigenous to India and appear often in Indian cooking. The seeds have no aroma in their raw state, but when roasted or fried in ghee or hot oil they release a rich, nutty flavour and aroma. Mustard seeds are commonly used with vegetables and dhal dishes.

DRY-FRYING MUSTARD SEEDS

Mustard seeds release their aroma when heated so should be dry-fried before they are added to a dish.

Heat a little ghee or vegetable oil in a wok, karahi or large pan, and add the mustard seeds. Shake the pan over the heat until the seeds start to change colour. Stir the seeds from time to time. Use the pan lid to stop the seeds jumping out of the pan when they start to splutter and pop.

Left: Small green cardamom pods and the larger bown variety

Nigella seeds

This aromatic spice has a sharp and tingling taste, and is frequently used in Indian vegetarian dishes.

Onion seeds

Black, triangular shaped and aromatic, onion seeds are used in pickles and to flavour vegetable curries and lentil dishes.

Garam masala

This is a mixture of spices that can be made at home from freshly ground spices, or purchased ready-made. There is no set recipe, but a typical mixture might include black cumin seeds, peppercorns, cloves, cinnamon and black cardamom pods. Many variations on garam masala are sold commercially, as pastes ready-made in jars. These can be subtituted for garam masala, and will make useful pantry standbys.

Asafoetida

This seasoning is a resin with an acrid and very bitter taste and a strong odour. It is used primarily as an anti-flatulent, and only minute quantities are used in recipes. Store in a glass jar with a strong airtight seal to prevent the smell dispersing into other ingredients in the pantry.

Cardamom pods

This spice is native to India, where it is considered the most prized spice after saffron. The pods can be used whole or the husks can be removed to release the seeds; whole pods should be always removed from the dish before serving. They have a slightly pungent, but very aromatic taste. They come in three varieties: green, white and black or brown. The green and white pods can be used for both sweet and savoury dishes or to flavour rice. Black or brown pods are used only for savoury dishes.

Nutmeg

Whole nutmeg should be grated to release its sweet, nutty flavour. Grated nutmeg imparts a similar, though less intense, flavour, and makes a very useful pantry standby.

Below: From left, paprika, whole nutmeg and grated nutmeg

Above: From left, white, black and pink peppercorns

Peppercorns

Black peppercorns are native to India, and are an essential ingredient in garam masala. White peppercorns are less aromatic, and the pink variety is mildly toxic and should only be used in small amounts. Peppercorns can be used whole or ground.

Paprika

A mild, sweet red powder, paprika is often used in place of or alongside chillies in westernized Indian cooking to add colour to a dish.

Saffron

The dried stigmas of the saffron crocus, which is native to Asia Minor, is the world's most expensive spice. To produce 450g/1lb of saffron requires 60,000 stigmas. Fortunately, only a small quantity of saffron is needed to flavour and colour a dish. Saffron is sold as threads and as a powder. It has a beautiful flavour and aroma.

Below: From left, saffron powder and threads

Curry leaves

Bright green and shiny, curry leaves are similar in appearance to bay leaves, but they have a different flavour. The leaves of a hardwood tree that is indigenous to India, they are widely used in Indian cooking, particularly in southern and western India (although not in Goa) and in Sri Lanka. Curry leaves have a warm fragrance with a subtle hint of sweet, green pepper or tangerine. They release their full flavour when bruised, and impart a highly distinctive flavour to curries. Curry leaves are sold dried and occasionally fresh in Indian food stores. Fresh leaves freeze well, but the dried leaves make a poor substitute, as they rapidly lose their fragrance.

Bay leaves

Indian bay leaves come from the cassia tree, which is similar to the tree from which cinnamon is taken. Bay leaves sold in the West are taken from the laurel tree. When used fresh, bay leaves have a deliciously sweet flavour, but they keep well in dried form, if stored in a cool, dark place in an airtight jar. Bay leaves are used in meat and rice dishes.

Left: Dried curry leaves

Below: Bay leaves

Freezing fresh coriander

Fresh coriander (cilantro) is widely used in Indian cooking. Its flavour and aroma make it an important ingredient, and the fresh leaves make a attractive garnish. Buy bunches of coriander and freeze what is not required immediately.

1 Cut off the roots and any thick stalks, retaining the fine stalks.

2 Wash the leaves in cold water and leave in a strainer to drain.

3 When the leaves are dry, chop them finely and store them in small quantities in plastic bags or airtight containers in the freezer.

Below: Fresh coriander

Coriander

There is no substitute for fresh coriander (cilantro), and the more that is used in Indian cooking the better. Coriander imparts a wonderful aroma and flavour, and is used both as an ingredient in cooking, and sprinkled over dishes as a garnish. Chopped coriander can be frozen successfully; the frozen coriander does not need to be defrosted before use. Coriander seeds and ground coriander powder are used for flavouring. The seeds have a pungent, slightly lemony flavour, and are used coarsely ground in meat, fish and poultry dishes. Ground coriander, a brownish powder, is an important constituent of any curry spice mixture.

Mint

There are many varieties of mint available, and the stronger-flavoured types tend to be used in Indian cooking. These taste slightly sweet and have a cool aftertaste. Mint has a fresh, stimulating aroma and is traditionally used with lamb, as well as for flavouring some vegetables, and for making chutneys and refreshing raitas. Mint is added at the end of cooking time, in order to retain the flavour.

Fenugreek

Fresh fenugreek is generally sold in bunches. It has very small leaves and is used to flavour meat and vegetarian dishes. Always discard the stalks, which will impart an unpleasant bitterness to a dish if used. Fenugreek seeds are flat, extremely pungent and slightly bitter. They only appear in a few recipes, where they are added whole, mainly for taste; these should be used cautiously. Dried fenugreek leaves are sold in Indian food stores. Store them in an airtight jar, in a cool, dark place; they will keep for about 12 months. Fenugreek seeds are small and pungent, and are widely used in spice mixtures.

Below: Aromatic fresh fenugreek leaves are widely used in savoury Indian dishes.

CURRY POWDERS and PASTES

Powders and pastes are blends of spices, chillies and herbs that are used as the basis of a curry. Traditional Indian households would blend individual spices as needed, but for convenience you may prefer to prepare a quantity in advance.

Curry powder

This is a basic recipe for a dry spice blend for use in any curry dish. It is a mild recipe, but you could increase the quantity of dried chilli for a hotter taste.

MAKES ABOUT 115G/4OZ/½ CUP

50g/2oz/½ cup coriander seeds
60ml/4 tbsp cumin seeds
30ml/2 tbsp fennel seeds
30ml/2 tbsp fenugreek seeds
4 dried red chillies
5 curry leaves
15ml/1 tbsp chilli powder
15ml/1 tbsp ground turmeric
2.5ml/½ tsp salt

1 Dry-roast the whole spices in a wok, karahi or large pan for 8–10 minutes, shaking the pan until the spices darken and release a rich aroma. Allow to cool.

2 Put the dry-roasted whole spices in a spice mill and grind to a fine powder.

3 Add the ground, roasted spices to the chilli powder, turmeric and salt in a large glass bowl and mix well. Store the curry powder in an airtight container.

Garam masala

Garam means hot and masala means spices, and this mixture uses spices that are known to heat the body, such as black peppercorns and cloves. Garam masala is used mainly for meat, although it can be used in poultry and rice dishes. The aroma is generally considered too strong for fish or vegetable dishes.

MAKES ABOUT 50G/2OZ/¼ CUP

10 dried red chillies
3 × 2.5cm/1in pieces cinnamon stick
2 curry leaves
30ml/2 tbsp coriander seeds
30ml/2 tbsp cumin seeds
5ml/1 tsp black peppercorns
5ml/1 tsp cloves
5ml/1 tsp fenugreek seeds
5ml/1 tsp black mustard seeds
1.5ml/¼ tsp chilli powder

1 Dry-roast the whole dried red chillies, cinnamon sticks and curry leaves in a wok, karahi or large pan over a low heat for about 2 minutes.

2 Add the coriander and cumin seeds, black peppercorns, cloves, fenugreek and mustard seeds, and dry-roast for 8–10 minutes, shaking the pan from side to side until the spices begin to darken in colour and release a rich aroma. Allow the mixture to cool.

3 Using either a spice mill or a stainless steel mortar and pestle, grind the roasted spices to a fine powder.

4 Transfer the powder to a glass bowl and mix in the chilli powder. Store in an airtight container.

COOK'S TIP

Both the curry powder and the garam masala will keep for 2–4 months in an airtight container in a cool, dark place. Once opened, store in the refrigerator.

VARIATIONS

For convenience, you can buy garam masala ready-made, or try any of the following pastes in alternative flavours:

- Tandoori masala
- Kashmiri masala
- Madras masala
- Sambhar masala
- Dhansak masala
- Green masala

Curry paste

A curry paste is a wet blend of spices, herbs and chillies cooked with oil and vinegar, which help to preserve the spices during storage. It is a quick and convenient way of adding a spice mixture to a curry, and different blends will produce different flavours. As only a small amount of paste is added at a time, a little will last a long time. Store in the refrigerator and use as required.

MAKES ABOUT 600ML/1 PINT/2½ CUPS

50g/2oz/½ cup coriander seeds
60ml/4 tbsp cumin seeds
30ml/2 tbsp fennel seeds
30ml/2 tbsp fenugreek seeds
4 dried red chillies
5 curry leaves
15ml/1 tbsp chilli powder
15ml/1 tbsp ground turmeric
150ml/¼ pint/⅔ cup wine vinegar
250ml/8fl oz/1 cup vegetable oil

1 Grind the whole spices to a powder in a spice mill. Transfer to a bowl and add the remaining ground spices.

2 Mix the spices until well blended. Add the wine vinegar and stir. Add 75ml/5 tbsp water and stir to form a paste.

3 Heat the oil in a wok, karahi or large pan and stir-fry the spice paste for about 10 minutes, or until all the water has been absorbed. When the oil rises to the surface the paste is cooked. Allow to cool slightly before spooning the paste into airtight jars.

COOK'S TIP

Once the paste has been cooked, heat a little more oil and pour on top of the paste in an airtight jar. This will help to preserve the paste and, as the oil stays on top as the paste is used, it will stop any mould from forming during storage. Store in the refrigerator.

Tikka paste

This is a delicious, versatile paste. It has a slightly sour flavour, and can be used in a variety of Indian dishes, including chicken tikka, tandoori chicken and tikka masala. Use sparingly as a little bit goes a long way. Store the paste in airtight glass jars in the refrigerator until required.

MAKES ABOUT 475ML/16FL OZ/2 CUPS

30ml/2 tbsp coriander seeds
30ml/2 tbsp cumin seeds
25ml/1½ tbsp garlic powder
30ml/2 tbsp paprika
15ml/1 tbsp garam masala
15ml/1 tbsp ground ginger
10ml/2 tsp chilli powder
2.5ml/½ tsp ground turmeric
15ml/1 tbsp dried mint
1.5ml/¼ tsp salt
5ml/1 tsp lemon juice
a few drops of red food colouring
a few drops of yellow food colouring
150ml/¼ pint/⅔ cup wine vinegar
150ml/¼ pint/⅔ cup vegetable oil

1 Grind the coriander and cumin seeds to a fine powder using a spice mill or mortar and pestle. Spoon the mixture into a bowl and add the remaining spices, the mint and salt, stirring well.

2 Mix the spice powder with the lemon juice, food colourings and wine vinegar and add 30ml/2 tbsp water to form a thin paste.

3 Heat the oil in a large pan, wok or karahi, and stir-fry the paste for 10 minutes, until all the water has been absorbed. When the oil rises to the surface, the paste is cooked. Allow to cool before spooning into airtight jars.

COOK'S TIP

Curry pastes will keep for 3–4 weeks after opening, if stored in the refrigerator.

ADDITIONAL INGREDIENTS

Besides the essential spices, aromatics and herbs, there are several other ingredients that are central to Indian cooking. Among the additional ingredients listed here are popular thickening and souring agents, flavourings and Indian cheese.

Above: Cashew nuts

Almonds

In the West, almonds are readily available whole, sliced, ground, and as thin slivers. The whole kernels should be soaked in boiling water before use to remove the thin red skin; once blanched, they can be eaten raw. Almonds have a uniqe aroma and they impart a sumptuous richness to curries. They make an effective thickener for sauces, and are also used for garnishing. Almonds are considered a delicacy in India and, because they are not indigenous, they are very expensive to buy.

Left: Whole almond kernels

Cashew nuts

These full-flavoured nuts can be used raw and roasted in Indian cooking. Cashews are ground and used in korma dishes to enrich and thicken the sauce, or they can also be toasted and sprinkled over pulaos and biryanis, as a garnish. In India, cashews are often used in vegetable and rice dishes as a substitute for the more expensive almonds.

Pistachio nuts

These small, greenish purple nuts are not indigenous to India, but they are frequently used as a thickening agent and to add their characteristic rich and creamy flavour. Raw or toasted pistachio nuts also make an attractive garnish.

Poppy seeds

These seeds are usually toasted to bring out their full, nutty flavour. They can be sprinkled over dry meat and vegetable dishes, or ground and added to curries to thicken sauces.

Sesame seeds

These small, flat, pear-shaped seeds probably originated in Africa but have been cultivated in India since ancient times. They are usually white but can be cream to brown, red or black. Raw sesame seeds have very little aroma and taste until they have been roasted or dry-fried, when they take on a slightly nutty taste. They can be ground with a mortar and pestle, or in a spice mill, and used to enrich curries. They are also added to chutneys. The high fat content of sesame seeds means that they do not keep well: buy them in small quantities and store in a cool, dark place.

Pomegranate seeds

These can be extracted from fresh pomegranates or, for convenience, they can be bought in jars from Asian food stores. Pomegranate seeds impart a delicious tangy flavour.

Dry mango powder

Mangoes are indigenous to India, and they have many uses in Indian cooking. The fruit is used in curries at different stages of ripeness, but the unripe fruit is also sun-dried and ground into a dry powder called *amchur*. The powder has a sour taste, and is sprinkled over dishes as a garnish; it is not used in cooking.

Above: White and black poppy seeds

Right: Black sesame seeds and white sesame seeds

Above: Fresh coconut

Coconut

Used in both sweet and savoury Indian dishes, fresh coconut is available from Indian food stores and supermarkets. Desiccated (dry, unsweetened, shredded) coconut, and coconut cream and creamed coconut, which are made from grated coconut, will all make acceptable substitutes in most recipes if fresh coconut is out of season. Coconut milk is used in Indian curries to thicken and enrich sauces. In Western supermarkets, it is sold in cans and in powdered form, as a convenient alternative to the fresh fruit; the powdered milk has to be blended with hot water before use. Coconut milk can be made at home from desiccated coconut. Coconut cream is used to add fragrance and aroma to dishes, while creamed coconut adds richness.

Below: Clockwise from left, coconut cream, coconut milk and desiccated coconut

MAKING COCONUT MILK

You can make as much of the milk as you like from this recipe by adapting the quantities accordingly, although the method is more practical for larger quantities.

Tip 225g/8oz/2⅔ cups desiccated (dry, unsweetened, shredded) coconut into a food processor and pour over 450ml/¾ pint/scant 2 cups boiling water. Process for 20–30 seconds, then cool. Place a sieve lined with muslin (cheesecloth) over a bowl in the sink. Ladle some of the softened coconut into the muslin. Bring up the ends of the cloth and twist it over the sieve to extract the liquid. Use the milk as directed in recipes. Coconut milk will keep for 1–2 days in the refrigerator, or it can be frozen for use on a later occasion.

Yogurt

In India, yogurt is known as curd. It can be added to sauces to give a thick and creamy texture, although it is most often used as a souring agent, particularly in the dairy-dominated north. Yogurt will curdle quickly when heated, and it should be used with care in recipes: add only a spoonful at a time, stir well and allow the sauce to simmer for five minutes before adding the next spoonful. In India, yogurt would be made at home on a daily basis, although ready-made natural (plain) yogurt is an acceptable substitute. Always choose live yogurt because of its beneficial effect on the digestive system.

Below: *Fresh paneer*

Paneer

This traditional North Indian cheese is made from rich dairy milk. Paneer is white in colour and smooth-textured. It is usually available from Indian food stores and large supermarkets, but tofu and beancurd are adequate substitutes.

MAKING PANEER

Paneer is very easy to make, and adventurous cooks may prefer to make their own at home.

Bring 1 litre/1¾ pints/4 cups milk to the boil over a low heat. Add 30ml/2 tbsp lemon juice, and stir gently until the milk thickens and begins to curdle. Strain the curdled milk through a sieve lined with muslin (cheesecloth). Set the curd aside for 1½–2 hours, under a heavy weight to press it into a flat shape, about 1cm/½in thick. Cut into wedges and use as required. Paneer will keep for up to 1 week in the refrigerator.

Tamarind

The brown fruit pods of the tamarind tree are 15–20cm/6–8in long. Inside, the seeds are surrounded by a sticky brown pulp. Tamarind is cultivated in India, as well as in other parts of South-east Asia, East Africa and the West Indies, and it is undoubtably one of the natural treasures of the East. The high tartaric acid content makes tamarind an excellent souring agent, and for this purpose it has no substitute. It doesn't have a strong aroma but the flavour is wonderful: tart without being bitter, fruity and refreshing. Tamarind is sold compressed in blocks, and dried in slices. Fresh tamarind and concentrate and paste are also available.

PREPARING COMPRESSED TAMARIND

Asian food stores and supermarkets sell compressed tamarind in a solid block, and in this form it looks rather like a packet of dried dates.

To prepare compressed tamarind, tear off a piece that is roughly equivalent to 15ml/1 tbsp. Put the tamarind in a jug (pitcher) and add 150ml/ ¼ pint/⅔ cup warm water. Leave to soak for 10 minutes. Swirl the tamarind around with your fingers so that the pulp is released from the seeds. Using a nylon sieve, strain the juice into a bowl. Discard the contents of the sieve, and use the liquid as required. Store any leftover liquid in the refrigerator for use in another recipe.

Below: *Tamarind, compressed into a block*

FRUITS

Indians love fruit and, as well as eating fresh fruits raw as a dessert at the end of a meal, they will also cook them with spices, chilli and coconut milk in savoury dishes. The exotic fruits listed here are all native to India, and they are as diverse in colour and shape as they are in flavour.

Mangoes

Ripe, fresh mangoes grow in India throughout the summer months, and are used in sweet dishes. Unripe green mangoes, sold in the springtime, are used to make tangy pickles and chutneys, and are added to curries as a souring agent for seasoning.

Papayas

Also known as pawpaw, these pear-shaped fruits are native to tropical America, and were not introduced to Asia until the 17th century. When ripe, the green skin turns a speckled yellow and the pulp is a vibrant orange-pink. The edible small black seeds taste peppery when dried. Peel off the skin using a sharp knife and eat the creamy flesh of the ripe fruit raw. The unripe green fruit is used in cooking: one of the unique properties of papaya is that it will help to tenderize meat.

Pineapples

These distinctive-looking fruits have a sweet, golden and exceedingly juicy flesh. Unlike most other fruits, pineapples do not ripen after picking, although leaving a slightly unripe fruit at room temperature will help to reduce its acidity. Pineapples are cultivated in India, mainly in the South, and are gently cooked with spices to make palate-cleansing side dishes.

Bananas

The soft and creamy flesh of bananas is high in starch, and is an excellent source of energy. Indians use several varieties of banana in vegetarian curries, including plantains, green bananas, and the sweet red-skinned variety.

Lemons and limes

These citrus fruits are indigenous to India, although limes, which in India are confusingly called lemons, are the most commonly available of the two. Both fruits are used as souring agents and are added to curries at the end of the cooking process; adding them any sooner would prevent any meat in the dish from becoming tender while it cooks.

Above: Lemons (top) and limes are used as souring agents in Indian curries.

Above: A whole papaya, with the cut fruit showing the small black, edible seeds.

Right: Sweet, red-skinned bananas and the more familiar large and small yellow-skinned varieties.

VEGETABLES

Indian cooking specializes in a huge range of excellent vegetable dishes, using everything from cauliflower, potatoes and peas to the more exotic and unusual varieties, such as okra, bottle gourds and aubergines (eggplant). When it comes to Indian cooking, vegetables are simply indispensable.

Left: Small and large onions

Aubergines

Available in different varieties, the shiny deep purple aubergine is the most common and widely used variety in Indian cooking. Aubergines have a strong flavour and some have a slightly bitter taste. The cut flesh may be sprinkled with salt to extract these bitter juices.

Left: Various sizes of purple aubergines

Bottle gourds

One of the many bitter vegetables used in Indian cooking, this long, knobbly green vegetable comes from Kenya and has a strong, bitter taste. It is known to have properties that purify the blood. To prepare a gourd, peel the ridged skin with a sharp knife, scrape away and discard the seeds and chop the flesh.

Okra

Also known as ladies' fingers, okra are one of the most popular vegetables in Indian cooking. These small green five-sided pods are indigenous to India. They have a very distinctive flavour and a sticky, pulpy texture when they are cooked.

Onions

A versatile vegetable belonging to the allium family, onions have a strong pungent flavour and aroma. Globe onions are the most commonly used variety for Indian cooking. Spring onions (scallions) are also used in some dishes to add colour and for their mild taste.

Peppers

Large, hollow pods belonging to the capsicum family, (bell) peppers are available in a variety of colours. Red peppers are sweeter than green peppers. They are used in a wide variety of dishes, adding both colour and flavour.

Above: Peppers

Spinach

Available all year round, this leafy green vegetable has a mild, delicate flavour. The leaves vary in size and only the large thick leaves need to be trimmed of their stalks. Spinach is a favourite vegetable in Indian cooking, and it is cooked in many ways, with meat, other vegetables, and with beans, peas and lentils.

Corn

Although it originated in South America, corn is now grown worldwide, and is grown extensively in North India. It has a delicious sweet, juicy flavour, which is at its best just after picking.

Tomatoes

These are an essential ingredient, and are used to make sauces for curries, chutneys and relishes. Salad tomatoes are quite adequate but are usually peeled. Use canned tomatoes in sauces and curries for their rich colour.

BEANS, PEAS and LENTILS

These play an important role in Indian cooking and are an excellent source of protein and fibre. Some are cooked whole, some are puréed and made into soups or dhals, and some are combined with vegetables or meat. Beans and chickpeas should be soaked before cooking. Lentils do not need to be soaked. Red and green split lentils cook to a soft consistency, and whole lentils hold their shape when cooked.

Left: From left, haricot (navy) beans, red kidney beans and pinto beans

Black-eyed beans

These are small and cream-coloured, with a black spot or "eye". When cooked, black-eyed beans (peas) have a tender, creamy texture and a mild, smoky flavour. They are used widely in Indian cooking.

PREPARING AND COOKING BEANS AND PEAS

Beans and chickpeas should be boiled for at least 10 minutes before cooking to destroy the potentially harmful toxins that they contain.

Wash the beans or chickpeas under cold running water, then place in a large bowl of fresh cold water and leave to soak overnight. Discard any pulses that float to the surface, drain and rinse again. Put in a large pan and cover with plenty of fresh cold water. Bring to the boil and boil rapidly for 10–15 minutes. Reduce the heat and simmer until tender. Drain and use as required.

Above: Chickpeas

Chana dhal

This round, yellow split lentil is similar in appearance to the yellow split pea, which will make a good substitute. It is cooked in a variety of vegetable dishes and can be deep-fried and mixed with spices for the Indian snack Bombay mix. Chana dhal is often used as a binding agent in Indian curries.

Chickpeas

These round, beige-coloured pulses have a strong, nutty flavour when cooked. As well as being used for curries, they are also ground into a flour that is widely used in many Indian dishes, such as pakoras and bhajiyas, and are also added to Indian snacks.

Flageolet beans

These white or pale green oval beans have a very mild, refreshing flavour.

Green lentils

Also known as continental lentils, these have a strong flavour and they retain their shape during cooking.

Haricot beans

These small, white oval beans come in different varieties. Known as navy in the United States, these beans are ideal for Indian cooking because they retain their shape and absorb flavours.

Kidney beans

These red-brown kidney-shaped beans have a distinctive flavour. They belong to the same family as the pinto bean.

Mung beans

These small, round green beans have a sweet flavour and creamy texture. When sprouted, mung beans produce beansprouts. Split mung beans are also used, and are often cooked with rice.

Red split lentils

Another lentil that can be used for making dhal. Use instead of tuvar dhal.

Tuvar dhal

A dull orange-coloured split pea with a distinctive earthy flavour. Tuvar dhal is available plain and in an oily variety.

Urid dhal

This lentil is available split, either with the blackish hull retained or removed. It has quite a dry texture when cooked.

Above: Red lentils

RICE

This staple grain is served with almost every meal in some parts of India, so it is no surprise that the Indians have created a variety of ways of cooking it, each quite distinctive. Plain boiled rice is an everyday accompaniment; for special occasions and entertaining, it is often combined with other ingredients.

There is no definitive way to cook plain rice, but whatever the recipe, the aim is to produce dry, separate-grained rice that is cooked through yet still retains some bite. The secret is the amount of water added: the rice must be able to absorb it all.

Basmati rice

Known as the prince of rices, basmati is the recommended rice for Indian curries – not only because it is easy to cook and produces an excellent finished result, but because it has a cooling effect on hot and spicy curries. Basmati is a slender, long grain, milled rice grown in northern India, the Punjab, parts of Pakistan and in the foothills of the Himalayas. Its name means fragrant, and it has a distinctive and appealing aroma. After harvesting it is aged for a year, which gives it the characteristic flavour and a light, fluffy texture. Basmati can be used in almost any savoury dish, particularly curries or pilaus, and is the essential ingredient in biryanis. White and brown basmati rices are widely available from supermarkets and Indian food stores.

COOKING PLAIN BOILED RICE

Always make sure you use a tight-fitting lid for your rice pan. If you do not have a lid that fits tightly, you can either wrap a dishtowel around the lid or put some foil between the lid and the pan to make a snug fit. Try not to remove the lid until the rice is cooked. (The advantage of using just a lid is that you can tell when the rice is ready because steam begins to escape, visibly and rapidly.)

As a rough guide, allow 75g/3oz/ scant ½ cup rice per person.

1 Put the dry rice in a colander and rinse it under cold running water until the water runs clear.

2 Place the rice in a large, deep pan and pour in enough cold water to come 2cm/¾in above the surface of the rice. Add a pinch of salt and, if you like, 5ml/1 tsp vegetable oil, stir once and bring to the boil.

3 Stir once more, reduce the heat to the lowest possible setting and cover the pan with a tight-fitting lid.

4 Cook the rice for 12–15 minutes, then turn off the heat and leave the rice to stand, still tightly covered, for about 10 minutes.

5 Before serving, gently fluff up the rice with a fork or slotted rice spoon – the slotted spoon will prevent you from breaking up the grains, which would make the rice mushy.

Above: White basmati, probably the most commonly eaten rice in India.

Below: Patna rice, a long grain rice native to eastern India.

Patna rice

This rice takes its name from Patna in eastern India. At one time, most of the long grain rice sold in Europe came from Patna, and the term was used loosely to mean any long grain rice, whatever its origin. The custom still persists in parts of the United States, but elsewhere Patna is used to describe the specific variety of rice grown in the eastern state of Bihar. Patna rice is used in the same way as other long grain rices, and is suitable for use wherever plain boiled rice is called for.

BREADS

Above: *Chapatis and parathas*

Breads are an integral part of any Indian meal. Most traditional Indian breads are unleavened, that is, made without any raising agent, and are made with wholemeal (whole-wheat) flour, known as chapati flour or atta.

Throughout India, breads vary from region to region, depending on local ingredients. Some breads are cooked dry on a hot griddle, while some are fried with a little oil, and others are deep-fried to make small savoury puffs. To enjoy Indian breads at their best they should be made just before you are ready to serve the meal, so that they can be eaten hot.

Naan

Probably the most well-known Indian bread outside India is naan, from the north of the country. Naan is made with plain (all-purpose) flour, yogurt and yeast; some contemporary recipes favour the use of a chemical raising agent such as bicarbonate of soda (baking soda) or self-raising (self-rising) flour as a leaven in place of yeast. The yogurt is important for the fermentation of the dough, and some naan are made entirely using a yogurt fermentation. Fermentation gives the bread its characteristic light, puffy texture and soft crust. The flavour comes partly from the soured yogurt and partly from the *tandoor*, which is the the clay oven, sunk into the ground, in which the bread is traditionally cooked. The bread is flattened against the blisteringly hot walls of the oven and the pull of gravity produces the characteristic teardrop shape. As the dough scorches and puffs up, it produces a bread that is soft and crisp. Naan can be eaten with almost any meat or vegetable dish. There are many types of flavoured naan sold commercially, including plain, coriander (cilantro) and garlic, and masala naan.

Chapatis

The favourite bread of central and southern India is the chapati, a thin, flat, unleavened bread made from ground wholemeal flour. Chapatis are cooked on a hot *tava*, a concave-shaped Indian griddle. Chapatis have a light texture and fairly bland flavour, which makes them an ideal accompaniment for highly spiced curry dishes. Spices can be added to the flour to give more flavour.

Below: *Poppadums*

Rotis

There are many variations of chapatis, including *rotis* and *dana rotis*. These are unleavened breads, made using chapati flour to which ghee, oil, celery seeds and/or fresh coriander are added. They are rolled out thinly and cooked like chapatis.

Parathas

A paratha is similar to a chapati except that it contains ghee (clarified butter), which gives the bread a richer flavour and flakier texture. Parathas are much thicker than chapatis and are shallow-fried.

Plain parathas are often eaten for lunch, and they go well with most vegetable dishes. They can be stuffed with various fillings, the most popular being spiced potato. Stuffed parathas are served as a snack.

Pooris

Another popular variation on the chapati is the poori, which is a small, deep-fried puffy bread made from chapati flour. Pooris are best eaten sizzling hot and are traditionally served for breakfast. They can be plain or flavoured with spices, such as cumin, turmeric and chilli powder, which are mixed into the dough. Pooris are often served with fish or vegetable curries.

Poppadums

These are now widely available outside of India. These are large, thin crisp disks, which can be bought ready cooked or ready-to-cook. In India they are served with vegetarian meals. They are sold in markets and by street vendors, and are available plain or flavoured with spices or seasoned with ground red or black pepper. The dough is generally made from dried beans, but can also be made from potatoes or sago. It is thinly rolled and left to dry in the sun. Poppadums are cooked either by deep-frying or placing under a hot grill (broiler).

Above: *Naan*

EQUIPMENT and UTENSILS

While a reasonably stocked kitchen will provide most of the equipment needed for cooking Indian curries, it may still be necessary to invest in one or two more specialist items to ensure perfect results.

Chapati griddle

Known in India as a *tava*, the chapati griddle allows chapatis and other breads to be cooked without burning. The heavy wrought-iron frying pan can also be used to dry-roast spices. Traditionally, the griddle would be set over an open fire but it will work equally well on a gas flame or electric hob.

Chapati rolling board

This round wooden board on short stubby legs is used to mould breads into shape; the extra height provided by the legs helps to disperse excess dry flour. A wooden pastry board makes an appropriate substitute.

Chapati rolling pin

The traditional chapati rolling pin is thinner in shape than Western rolling pins, and comes in many different sizes. Use whichever size feels the most comfortable in your hands.

Heat diffuser

Many curries are left to simmer slowly over a low heat, and a heat diffuser will help to prevent burning on the base of the karahi or wok.

Grinding stone and pin

The traditional oblong grinding stone is the Indian equivalent of the Western food processor. Fresh and dry ingredients are placed on the heavy slate stone, which is marked with notches to hold ingredients in place. The ingredients are then pulverized against the stone, using the heavy rolling pin.

Table sizzler

This heated appliance allows food that is still cooking to be brought to the dinner table ready for serving. It is very useful for entertaining.

Slotted spoon

Stirring cooked, drained rice with a slotted spoon will make the rice soft, fluffy by allowing air in between the grains; the slots in the spoon prevent the grains from breaking as the rice is moved around the pan. The spoon also used to remove foods from hot oil or other cooking liquids.

Above: Chapati griddle and chapati rolling pin

Left: Grinding stone and rolling pin, tongs and stainless steel mortar and pestle

Below right: Heat diffuser

Chapati spoon

The square, flat-headed chapati spoon is used for turning roasting breads on the hot chapati griddle. A fish slice (spatula) may also be used.

Spice mill

An electric spice mill is useful for grinding small quantities of

ingredients such as spices. A coffee grinder – used solely for this purpose, as it will retain the strong smell of the spices – would make a good substitute.

Stainless steel mortar and pestle

These are ideal for grinding small amounts of wet ingredients, such as fresh root ginger, chillies and garlic. Stainless steel is everlasting and will not retain the strong flavours of the spices.

Stone mortar and pestle

A heavy granite mortar and pestle is traditionally used to grind small amounts of ingredients, both wet and dry.

Pastry brush

Use for brushing and basting meats and vegetables lightly with oil before and during grilling (broiling).

Balloon whisk

A metal whisk is useful for beating yogurt and dairy or coconut cream before adding to recipes.

Knives

Kitchen knives in a range of sizes are essential. Keep knives sharp to make it easier to chop ingredients and to ensure neat edges when cutting.

Below: A traditional cast-iron karahi

Karahi

Basically an Indian frying pan, the karahi, is similar to a wok but is more rounded in shape and is made of heavier metal: originally, the karahi would be made of cast iron, although a variety of metals are now used. Karahis are available in various sizes, including small ones for cooking single portions. Serving food from a karahi at the table adds an authentic touch to the meal.

Wok

This is a good substitute for a karahi for cooking most types of Indian dish. Buy the appropriate wok for your cooker. Round-bottomed woks can be used on gas hobs only; flat-bottomed woks are for use on electric hobs.

Stainless steel pans

Quality kitchen pans in various sizes are essential for cooking rice, vegetables and other ingredients. A heavy-based non-stick frying pan can be used in place of a karahi or wok.

Above: Stainless steel pans

Colander and sieve

Use for draining boiled rice and vegetables, and for straining ingredients. Choose a long-handled, sturdy colander and sieve made from stainless steel, as these allow you to stand back to pour steaming rice out of a pan, and will not discolour like plastic ones.

Food processor

This is essential for blending the ingredients. Smaller quantities can be ground in a mortar and pestle.

Right: From left, stainless steel colander and sieve

NORTH INDIA

The cuisine of northern India has been heavily influenced by a great many foreign settlers, traders and pilgrims. The most notable of these were the Moguls, who added Mughlai food and a selection of exotic fruit and nuts to the established traditions of Kashmir and Punjab.

KASHMIRI CHICKEN CURRY

Surrounded by the snow-capped Himalayas, Kashmir is popularly known as the "Switzerland of the East". The state is also renowned for its rich culinary heritage, and this aromatic dish is one of the simplest among the region's rich repertoire.

SERVES 4–6

20ml/4 tsp Kashmiri masala paste
60ml/4 tbsp tomato ketchup
5ml/1 tsp Worcestershire sauce
5ml/1 tsp five-spice powder
5ml/1 tsp granulated sugar
8 chicken joints, skinned
45ml/3 tbsp vegetable oil
5cm/2in piece fresh root ginger, finely shredded
4 garlic cloves, crushed
juice of 1 lemon
15ml/1 tbsp coriander (cilantro) leaves, finely chopped
salt

1 To make the marinade, mix the masala paste, tomato ketchup, Worcestershire sauce, five-spice powder, salt and sugar. Allow the mixture to rest in a warm place until the sugar has dissolved.

2 Rub the chicken pieces with the marinade and allow to rest in a cool place for a further 2 hours, or in the refrigerator overnight. Bring to room temperature before cooking.

3 Heat the oil in a wok, karahi or large pan and fry half the ginger and all the garlic until golden. Add the chicken and fry until both sides are sealed. Cover and cook until the chicken is tender, and the oil has separated from the sauce.

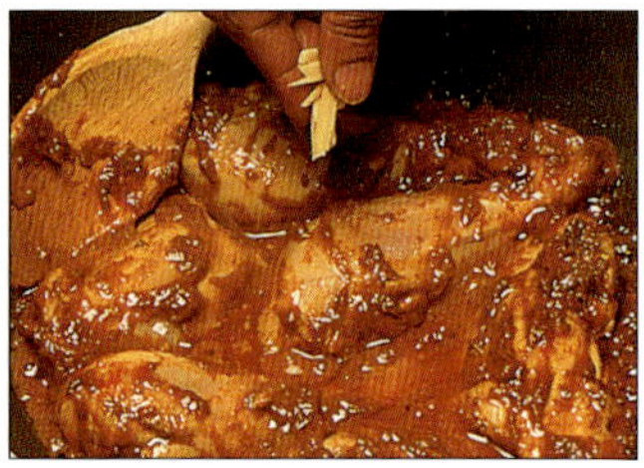

4 Sprinkle the chicken with the lemon juice, remaining ginger and chopped coriander leaves, and mix in well. Serve hot. Plain boiled rice would make a good accompaniment.

TANDOORI CHICKEN

Punjab, in northern India, is the home of tandoori food. The tandoor, or clay oven, originated in Egypt and found its way into India with the Moguls. It is probably the most versatile oven in the world, capable of roasting, grilling and baking all at the same time.

SERVES 4–6

1.3kg/3lb oven-ready chicken
250ml/8fl oz/1 cup natural (plain) yogurt, beaten
60ml/4 tbsp tandoori masala paste
75g/3oz/2 tbsp ghee or vegetable oil
salt
lemon slice and onion rings, to garnish
lettuce, to serve

1 Using a small, sharp knife or scissors, remove the skin from the chicken and trim off any excess fat. Using a fork, prick the flesh at random.

2 Cut the chicken in half down the centre and through the breast. Cut each piece in half again. Make a few deep gashes diagonally into the flesh.

3 Mix the yogurt with the masala paste and season with salt. Spread the chicken with the yogurt mixture, spreading some into the gashes. Leave to marinate in a cool place for at least 2 hours, or in the refrigerator overnight.

4 Preheat the oven to 240°C/475°F/Gas 9. Place the chicken quarters on a wire rack in a deep baking tray. Spread the chicken with any excess marinade, reserving a little for basting halfway through the cooking time.

5 Melt the ghee and pour over the chicken pieces to seal the surface. This helps to keep the centre moist during roasting. Roast the chicken for about 10 minutes, then remove from the oven, leaving the oven on.

6 Baste the chicken with the remaining marinade. Return to the oven and switch off the heat. Leave the chicken in the oven for 15–20 minutes without opening the door. Serve on a bed of lettuce and garnish with the lemon and onion rings.

COOK'S TIP

If the chicken is left overnight in the refrigerator, remove it a hour or two before you want to start cooking to allow it to return to room temperature.

KARAHI CHICKEN with MINT

A karahi is similar to a Chinese wok, and its use is most widespread in northern India, which is closest to the Chinese border. It is made of heavy cast iron, which is excellent for heat distribution and retention, and it is used extensively for cooking all types of meat, poultry and vegetable dishes. Because of its shape, it is also ideal for deep-frying and is used for this purpose all over India.

SERVES 4

450g/1lb chicken breast fillets, skinned and cut into strips
300ml/½ pint/1¼ cups water
30ml/2 tbsp vegetable oil
2 small bunches spring onions (scallions), roughly chopped
5ml/1 tsp grated fresh root ginger
5ml/1 tsp crushed dried red chilli
30ml/2 tbsp lemon juice
30ml/2 tbsp chopped fresh coriander (cilantro), plus extra sprigs to garnish
30ml/2 tbsp chopped fresh mint, plus extra sprigs to garnish
3 tomatoes, seeded and roughly chopped
5ml/1 tsp salt

1 Put the chicken and water into a large pan, bring to the boil and lower the heat to medium. Cook for about 10 minutes or until the water has evaporated and the chicken is cooked. Remove the pan from the heat and set aside.

2 Heat the oil in a large pan, add the chopped spring onions and stir-fry for about 2 minutes until soft.

3 Add the boiled chicken strips to the pan and stir-fry briskly over a medium heat for about 3 minutes, or until the chicken is browned.

4 Add the grated fresh root ginger, chilli, lemon juice, chopped coriander and mint, tomatoes and salt, and stir gently to blend the flavours.

5 Transfer the curry to a warmed serving platter and garnish with fresh coriander and mint sprigs before serving. Plain boiled rice would make a good accompaniment to this dish.

VARIATION

Use strips of turkey breast meat or pork tenderloin instead of chicken. If using, pork tenderloin, flatten the meat with a steak mallet first to tenderize it, then cut into strips and use as directed.

KARAHI CHICKEN with FRESH FENUGREEK

This karahi chicken was the dish that inspired a style of cooking known as karahi cuisine in northern India, where fenugreek is a typical flavouring agent. In the West, dried fenugreek leaves can be used for convenience, as fresh fenugreek is generally more difficult to find. The dried leaves are sold in Indian and Pakistani food stores throughout the year, and will keep well in an airtight jar.

SERVES 4

225g/8oz chicken thigh meat, skinned and cut into strips
225g/8oz chicken breast fillets, skinned and cut into strips
2.5ml/½ tsp crushed garlic
5ml/1 tsp chilli powder
2.5ml/½ tsp salt
10ml/2 tsp tomato purée (paste)
30ml/2 tbsp vegetable oil
1 bunch fresh fenugreek leaves or 15ml/1 tbsp dried
15ml/1 tbsp chopped fresh coriander (cilantro)

1 Bring a large pan of water to the boil, add the chicken strips and cook for 5–7 minutes. Drain and set aside.

2 In a bowl, combine the garlic, chilli powder and salt with the tomato purée.

COOK'S TIP

Discard the stems of fresh fenugreek, as they will impart a bitter flavour to the dish.

3 Heat the oil in a wok, karahi or large pan. Lower the heat and add the tomato purée and spice mixture.

4 Add the chicken pieces and stir-fry for 5–7 minutes. Lower the heat further.

5 Add the fenugreek leaves and the chopped fresh coriander to the pan. Continue to stir-fry for 5–7 minutes, then pour in 300ml/½ pint/1¼ cups water, cover and cook for a further 5 minutes. Serve hot.

CHICKEN TIKKA MASALA

Though chicken tikka is a traditional dish from northern India, masala is pure invention. The word refers to the sauce in which the cooked tikka is simmered and which is a western adaptation. However, it is not dissimilar to another traditional Indian dish known as butter chicken, in which cooked tandoori chicken is simmered in a creamy sauce.

SERVES 4

675g/1½lb chicken breast fillets, skinned
90ml/6 tbsp Tikka Paste
60ml/4 tbsp natural (plain) yogurt
30ml/2 tbsp vegetable oil
1 onion, chopped
1 garlic clove, crushed
1 fresh green chilli, seeded and chopped
2.5cm/1in piece fresh root ginger, grated
15ml/1 tbsp tomato purée (paste)
15ml/1 tbsp ground almonds
250ml/8fl oz/1 cup water
45ml/3 tbsp ghee or butter, melted
50ml/2fl oz/¼ cup double (heavy) cream
15ml/1 tbsp lemon juice
fresh coriander (cilantro) sprigs, natural (plain) yogurt and toasted cumin seeds to garnish
naan bread, to serve

1 Cut the chicken into 2.5cm/1in cubes. Put half of the tikka paste and the yogurt into a bowl, then stir in the chicken. Leave to marinate for 20 minutes.

COOK'S TIP

Soak wooden kebab skewers in water before use to prevent them from burning while under the grill (broiler).

2 For the tikka sauce, heat the oil and fry the onion, garlic, chilli and ginger for 5 minutes. Add the remaining tikka paste and fry for 2 minutes. Add the tomato purée, almonds and water, and simmer for 15 minutes.

3 Thread the chicken on to wooden kebab skewers. Preheat the grill (broiler).

4 Brush the chicken pieces with the melted butter and grill (broil) under a medium heat for about 15 minutes. Occasionally, turn and brush the chicken pieces with more butter.

5 Put the tikka sauce in a blender or food processor and process until smooth. Return the sauce to the pan and stir in the cream and lemon juice.

6 Remove the chicken from the grill, slide the cubes off the wooden skewers and add them to the pan. Simmer gently for 5 minutes more. Garnish with fresh coriander, yogurt and cumin seeds, and serve with warm naan bread.

CHICKEN TIKKA

The word tikka refers to the use of boneless, skinless cubes of chicken breast. Strictly speaking, the term cannot be applied to other types of meat, even if they are prepared and cooked in a similar way. Traditionally cooked in the tandoor (Indian clay oven), chicken tikka is enduringly popular in the West as well as in India.

SERVES 6

450g/1lb chicken breast fillets, skinned, and cubed
5ml/1 tsp grated fresh root ginger
5ml/1 tsp crushed garlic
5ml/1 tsp chilli powder
1.5ml/¼ tsp ground turmeric
5ml/1 tsp salt
150ml/¼ pint/⅔ cup natural (plain) yogurt
60ml/4 tbsp lemon juice
15ml/1 tbsp chopped fresh coriander (cilantro)
15ml/1 tbsp vegetable oil

To serve (optional)
lettuce
1 small onion, cut into rings
lime wedges
fresh coriander (cilantro)

1 In a large bowl, mix the chicken cubes, ginger, garlic, chilli powder, turmeric, salt, yogurt, lemon juice and coriander. Leave to marinate in a cool place for at least 2 hours, or in the refrigerator overnight.

COOK'S TIP
Thread the meat on to oiled skewers, and turn and baste it during cooking.

2 Place the chicken on a grill (broiler) tray, or in a flameproof dish lined with foil, and baste with the oil.

3 Preheat the grill to medium. Grill (broil) the chicken for 15–20 minutes until cooked, turning and basting two or three times. Serve with lettuce, onion rings, lime wedges and fresh coriander.

CHICKEN SAAG

The word saag means greens and, traditionally, spinach is the usual choice for adding to meat and poultry, although other greens also work well. Chicken saag is one of the best-known dishes to have originated in the state of Punjab.

SERVES 4

225g/8oz fresh spinach leaves, washed
2.5cm/1in piece fresh root ginger, grated
2 garlic cloves, crushed
1 fresh green chilli, roughly chopped
200ml/7fl oz/scant 1 cup water
30ml/2 tbsp vegetable oil
2 bay leaves
1.5ml/¼ tsp black peppercorns
1 onion, finely chopped
4 tomatoes, skinned and finely chopped
10ml/2 tsp curry powder
5ml/1 tsp salt
5ml/1 tsp chilli powder
45ml/3 tbsp natural (plain) yogurt, plus extra to serve
8 chicken thighs, skinned
naan bread, to serve

1 Cook the spinach, without water, in a tightly covered pan for 5 minutes. Put the spinach, ginger, garlic and chilli with 50ml/2fl oz/¼ cup of the water into a food processor and process to a purée.

2 Heat the oil, add the bay leaves and peppercorns and fry for 2 minutes. Add the onion and fry for 6–8 minutes more.

3 Add the chopped tomatoes to the pan and simmer for a further 5 minutes. Add the curry powder, salt and chilli powder and stir well to mix. Allow to cook for 2 minutes.

4 Add the spinach purée and the remaining water to the pan, and leave to simmer for 5 minutes.

5 Stir in the yogurt, about 15ml/1 tbsp at a time, and simmer for 5 minutes.

6 Add the chicken. Cover and cook for 25–30 minutes or until the chicken is tender. Serve with warm naan, drizzle over some natural yogurt and dust lightly with the chilli powder.

CHICKEN in GREEN MASALA SAUCE

The use of green spice mixes is popular all over India. Although in southern India the mixes are generally used to cook vegetables and fish, in the north, where most people are meat-eaters, they are more often used to prepare meat and poultry dishes.

SERVES 4

1 crisp green eating apple, peeled, cored and cubed
60ml/4 tbsp fresh coriander (cilantro) leaves
30ml/2 tbsp fresh mint leaves
150ml/¼ pint/⅔ cup natural (plain) yogurt
45ml/3 tbsp fromage frais or ricotta cheese
2 fresh green chillies, seeded and chopped
1 bunch spring onions (scallions), chopped
5ml/1 tsp salt
5ml/1 tsp granulated sugar
5ml/1 tsp crushed garlic
5ml/1 tsp grated fresh root ginger
15ml/1 tbsp vegetable oil
225g/8oz chicken breast fillets, skinned and cubed
25g/1oz sultanas (golden raisins)

1 Place the apple, 45ml/3 tbsp of the coriander, the mint, yogurt, fromage frais or ricotta, chillies, spring onions, salt, sugar, garlic and ginger in a food processor and process for 1 minute. Scrape around the outside of the bowl and process for a few seconds more.

2 Heat the oil in a wok, karahi or large pan, pour in the yogurt mixture and cook gently over a low heat for about 2 minutes.

3 Add the chicken pieces and stir well to blend everything together. Cook over a medium-low heat for 12–15 minutes or until the chicken is fully cooked.

4 Sprinkle the sultanas and the remaining coriander over the chicken (do not mix in, but leave as a garnish). Serve with Nut Pulao, if you like.

COOK'S TIP

This dish makes a good dinner-party main course. Nut Pulao would make a good accompaniment.

SPICY GRILLED CHICKEN

This dish is inspired by the tandoori style of cooking, in which the meat and poultry are marinated before being grilled or roasted in a clay oven. Serve it with rice and a salad, or, for a real treat, with a mushroom curry.

SERVES 6

12 chicken thighs
90ml/6 tbsp lemon juice
5ml/1 tsp grated fresh root ginger
5ml/1 tsp crushed garlic
5ml/1 tsp crushed dried red chillies
5ml/1 tsp salt
5ml/1 tsp soft light brown sugar
30ml/2 tbsp clear honey
30ml/2 tbsp chopped fresh coriander (cilantro), plus extra sprigs to garnish
1 fresh green chilli, finely chopped
30ml/2 tbsp vegetable oil
Saffron Rice and a mixed salad, to serve (optional)

1 Prick the chicken thighs with a fork, rinse under running water, pat dry with kitchen paper and set aside.

2 In a bowl, mix the lemon juice, ginger, garlic, red chillies, salt, sugar and honey.

3 Transfer the chicken thighs to the spice mixture in the bowl and coat well. Leave to marinate for 45 minutes.

4 Preheat the grill (broiler) to medium. Add the fresh coriander and chopped green chilli to the chicken and mix well, then transfer the marinated chicken thighs to a flameproof dish.

5 Pour any remaining marinade over the chicken and baste with the oil, using a pastry brush.

6 Grill (broil) the chicken thighs for 15–20 minutes, turning and basting the meat occasionally, until cooked through and browned.

7 Transfer the chicken to a warmed serving dish and garnish with the fresh coriander sprigs. Serve with Saffron Rice and a salad, if you like.

COOK'S TIP

If you prefer, you can cook the chicken on a barbecue for a wonderful smoky flavour. Baste with the oil only when the chicken is almost cooked.

CHICKEN in a CASHEW NUT SAUCE

Nut pastes were introduced into north Indian cooking by the Moguls, the travellers who provided what was probably the most important outside influence on Indian cuisine. Mughlai food, as this style of cooking is known, is famed for its rich yet delicate flavours.

SERVES 4

2 onions
30ml/2 tbsp tomato purée (paste)
50g/2oz/⅓ cup cashew nuts
7.5ml/1½ tsp garam masala
5ml/1 tsp crushed garlic
5ml/1 tsp chilli powder
15ml/1 tbsp lemon juice
1.5ml/¼ tsp ground turmeric
5ml/1 tsp salt
15ml/1 tbsp natural (plain) yogurt
30ml/2 tbsp vegetable oil
15ml/1 tbsp chopped fresh coriander (cilantro), plus extra to garnish
15ml/1 tbsp sultanas (golden raisins)
450g/1lb chicken breast fillets, skinned and cubed
175g/6oz button (white) mushrooms
300ml/½ pint/1¼ cups water

1 Cut the onions into quarters, then place in a food processor or blender. Process for 1 minute.

2 Add the tomato purée, cashew nuts, garam masala, crushed garlic, chilli powder, lemon juice, turmeric, salt and yogurt to the onions and process for a further 1–1½ minutes.

3 In a wok, karahi or large pan, heat the oil, lower the heat to medium and pour in the onion and spice mixture from the food processor or blender. Fry gently, stirring frequently, for about 2 minutes, lowering the heat if necessary.

4 Add the fresh coriander, sultanas and cubed chicken to the pan and continue to stir-fry for a further minute.

5 Add the mushrooms, pour in the measured water and bring to a simmer. Cover the pan and cook over a low heat for about 10 minutes.

6 After this time, check that the chicken is cooked all the way through and the sauce is thick. Continue to cook for a little longer if necessary.

7 Transfer to a warmed serving dish and garnish with chopped fresh coriander. Plain boiled rice and a fruit chutney would go well with this dish.

CHICKEN DOPIAZA

With lashings of onions, dopiaza's popularity is timeless. The origin of the word is rather unclear. In the Hindi language Do means two and piaz is onion. Hence the popular belief that the word refers to the use of twice the amount or two different types of onions. However, dopiaza is essentially a Mogul dish and history has it that it was named after Emperor Akbar's courtier, Mullah Dopiaza.

SERVES 4

45ml/3 tbsp vegetable oil
8 small onions, halved
2 bay leaves
8 green cardamom pods
4 cloves
3 dried red chillies
8 black peppercorns
2 onions, finely chopped
2 garlic cloves, crushed
2.5cm/1in piece fresh root ginger, finely chopped
5ml/1 tsp ground coriander
5ml/1 tsp ground cumin
2.5ml/½ tsp ground turmeric
5ml/1 tsp chilli powder
2.5ml/½ tsp salt
4 tomatoes, skinned and finely chopped
120ml/4fl oz/½ cup water
8 chicken pieces, skinned
plain boiled rice or chapatis, to serve

1 Heat 30ml/2 tbsp oil in a wok, karahi or large pan and fry the halved small onions until soft. Remove and set aside.

2 Add the remaining oil and fry the bay leaves, cardamoms, cloves, chillies and peppercorns for 2 minutes. Add the chopped onions, garlic and ginger and fry for 5 minutes. Add the spices and salt and cook for 2 minutes.

COOK'S TIP

Soak the onions in boiling water for 2 minutes to make them easier to peel.

3 Add the tomatoes and water to the pan and simmer for 5 minutes until the sauce begins to thicken. Add the chicken pieces and cook for 15 minutes more.

4 Add the reserved small onions, then cover and cook for a further 10 minutes, or until the chicken is tender. Serve with plain boiled rice or chapatis.

CHICKEN KORMA

Korma is not really a dish but a technique employed in Indian cooking; it simply means braising. It is a misconception to think that kormas are always rich and creamy as there are several different types. They can be light and aromatic or rich and creamy, and some are fiery looking, with a taste to match. All depends on where the recipe originated. This recipe comes from Delhi, the centre of Mogul cuisine.

SERVES 4

25g/1oz blanched almonds
2 garlic cloves, crushed
2.5cm/1in piece fresh root ginger, chopped
30ml/2 tbsp vegetable oil
675g/1½lb chicken breast fillets, skinned and cubed
3 green cardamom pods
1 onion, finely chopped
10ml/2 tsp ground cumin
1.5ml/¼ tsp salt
150ml/¼ pint/⅔ cup natural (plain) yogurt
175ml/6fl oz/¾ cup single (light) cream
toasted flaked (sliced) almonds and fresh coriander (cilantro) sprigs, to garnish
plain boiled rice, to serve

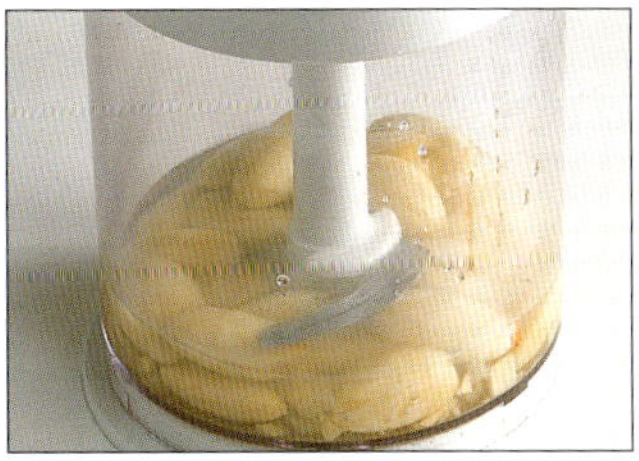

1 Process the almonds, garlic and ginger in a food processor with 30ml/2 tbsp water.

2 Heat the oil in a wok, karahi or large pan, and cook the chicken for 10 minutes. Remove the chicken and set aside. Add the cardamom pods and fry for 2 minutes. Add the onion and fry for 5 minutes.

3 Stir the almond, garlic and ginger paste into the cardamom and onions in the pan. Add the cumin and season to taste with salt. Cook for 5 minutes more, stirring frequently.

4 Whisk the yogurt and add it to the onion mixture a tablespoonful at a time. Cook over a low heat, until the yogurt has all been absorbed. Return the chicken to the pan. Cover and simmer over a low heat for 5–6 minutes, or until the chicken is tender.

5 Stir in the cream and simmer for a further 5 minutes. Garnish with toasted flaked almonds and coriander, and serve with plain boiled rice.

COOK'S TIP

For a true Mogul flavour, replace the cumin with 15ml/1 tbsp ground coriander.

LAHORE-STYLE LAMB

Named after the city of Lahore, which has been in Pakistan since the Independence, this hearty dish has a wonderfully aromatic flavour imparted by the winter spices such as cloves, black peppercorns and cinnamon. Serve with a hot puffy naan in true north Indian style.

SERVES 4

60ml/4 tbsp vegetable oil
1 bay leaf
2 cloves
4 black peppercorns
1 onion, sliced
450g/1lb lean lamb, boned and cubed
1.5ml/¼ tsp ground turmeric
7.5ml/1½ tsp chilli powder
5ml/1 tsp crushed coriander seeds
2.5cm/1in piece cinnamon stick
5ml/1 tsp crushed garlic
7.5ml/1½ tsp salt
1.5 litres/2½ pints/6¼ cups water
50g/2oz/⅓ cup chana dhal or yellow split peas
2 tomatoes, quartered
2 fresh green chillies, chopped
15ml/1 tbsp chopped fresh coriander (cilantro)

1 Heat the oil in a wok, karahi or large pan. Lower the heat slightly and add the bay leaf, cloves, peppercorns and onion. Fry for about 5 minutes, or until the onion is golden brown.

2 Add the cubed lamb, turmeric, chilli powder, coriander seeds, cinnamon stick, garlic and most of the salt, and stir-fry for about 5 minutes over a medium heat.

3 Pour in 900ml/1½ pints/3¾ cups of the water and cover the pan with a lid or foil, making sure the foil does not come into contact with the food. Simmer for 35–40 minutes or until the lamb is tender.

4 Put the chana dhal or split peas into a large pan with the remaining measured water and a good pinch of salt and boil for 12–15 minutes, or until the water has almost evaporated and the lentils or peas are soft enough to be mashed. If they are too thick, add up to 150ml/¼ pint/⅔ cup water.

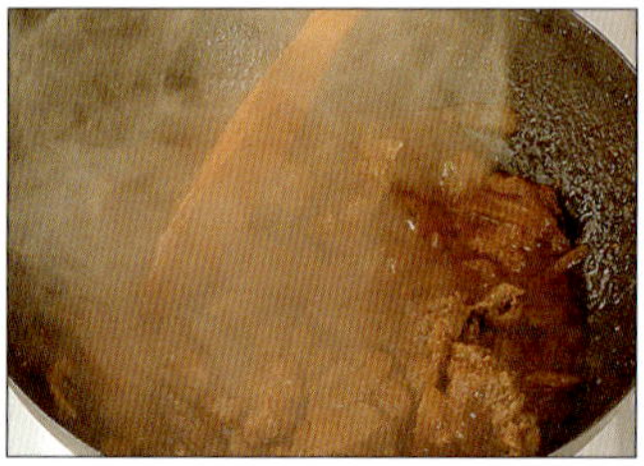

5 When the lamb is tender, remove the lid or foil and stir-fry the mixture using a wooden spoon, until some free oil begins to appear on the sides of the pan.

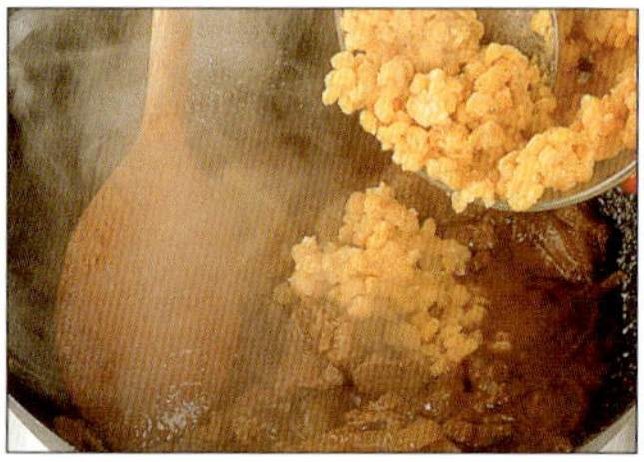

6 Add the cooked lentils to the lamb and mix together well. Stir in the tomatoes, chillies and chopped fresh coriander and serve.

COOK'S TIP

Boned and cubed chicken can be used in place of the lamb. At step 3, reduce the amount of water to about 300ml/½ pint/1¼ cups and cook uncovered, stirring occasionally, for 10–15 minutes, or until the water has evaporated and the chicken is cooked through.

MUGHLAI-STYLE LEG of LAMB

In India, there are different names for this style of cooking a leg of lamb, two of which are shahi raan *and* peshawari raan. *Roasting a whole leg of lamb was first popularized by the Mongolian warrior Genghis Khan (1162–1227) and is known as Chengezi Raan.*

SERVES 4–6

4 large onions, chopped
4 garlic cloves
5cm/2in piece fresh root ginger, chopped
45ml/3 tbsp ground almonds
10ml/2 tsp ground cumin
10ml/2 tsp ground coriander
10ml/2 tsp ground turmeric
10ml/2 tsp garam masala
4–6 fresh green chillies
juice of 1 lemon
300ml/½ pint/1¼ cups natural (plain) yogurt, beaten
1.8kg/4lb leg of lamb
8–10 cloves
salt
15ml/1 tbsp blanched almond flakes, to garnish
4 firm tomatoes, halved and grilled (broiled), to serve

1 Place the first ten ingredients in a food processor or blender, with salt to taste, and process to a smooth paste. Gradually add the yogurt and blend. Grease a large, deep roasting pan and preheat the oven to 190°C/375°F/Gas 5.

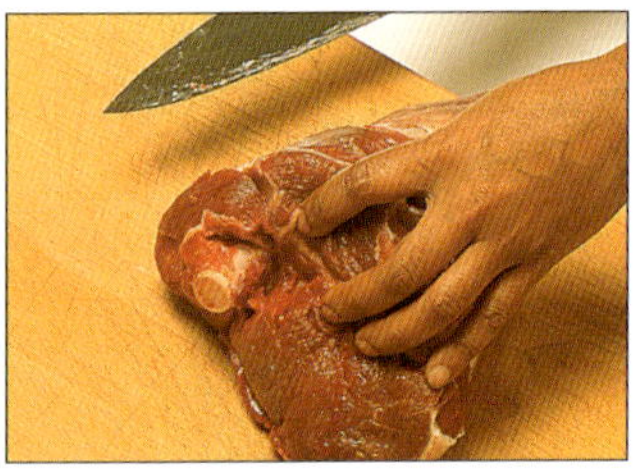

2 Remove most of the fat and skin from the lamb. Using a sharp knife, make deep pockets above the bone at each side of the thick end. Make deep diagonal gashes on both sides of the lamb.

COOK'S TIP

If time permits, allow the joint to stand at room temperature for a couple of hours before putting it in the oven.

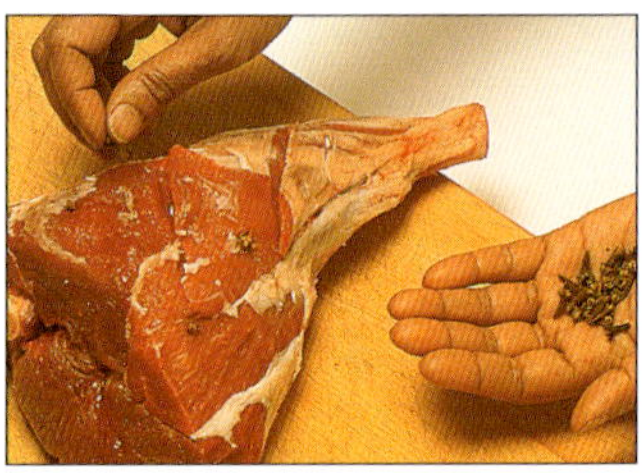

3 Push the cloves firmly into the meat, spaced evenly on all sides.

4 Push some of the spice mixture into the pockets and gashes and spread the remainder evenly all over the meat. Place the meat on the roasting pan and loosely cover the whole pan with foil. Roast for 2–2½ hours, or until the meat is cooked, removing the foil for the last 10 minutes of cooking time.

5 Remove from the oven and allow to rest for about 10 minutes before carving. Garnish the joint with almond flakes, and serve with grilled tomatoes.

SHAMMI KABAB

Kababs came to India from the Middle East, where the word is spelt kebab and refers to a skewered meat. There is a delectable range of kababs in Indian cuisine, most of which can be served either as appetizers or side dishes with an accompanying raita or chutney.

SERVES 5–6

2 onions, finely chopped
250g/9oz lean lamb, boned and cubed
50g/2oz chana dhal or yellow split peas
5ml/1 tsp cumin seeds
5ml/1 tsp garam masala
4–6 fresh green chillies
5cm/2in piece fresh root ginger, grated
175ml/6fl oz/¾ cup water
a few fresh coriander (cilantro) and mint leaves, chopped, plus extra coriander (cilantro) sprigs to garnish
juice of 1 lemon
15ml/1 tbsp gram flour (besan)
2 eggs, beaten
vegetable oil, for shallow frying
salt

1 Put the first seven ingredients and the water into a large pan with salt, and bring to the boil. Simmer, covered, until the meat and dhal are cooked. Remove the lid and continue to cook for a few more minutes, to reduce the excess liquid. Set aside to cool.

2 Transfer the cooled meat and dhal mixture to a food processor or blender and process to a rough paste.

3 Put the paste into a large mixing bowl and add the chopped coriander and mint leaves, lemon juice and gram flour. Knead well with your hands to make sure the ingredients are evenly distributed through the mixture.

4 Divide the mixture into 10–12 even-size portions and use your hands to roll each into a ball, then flatten slightly. Chill for 1 hour. Dip the kababs in the beaten egg and shallow fry each side until golden brown. Pat dry on kitchen paper and serve hot.

ROGAN JOSH

This is one of the most popular lamb dishes to have originated in Kashmir. Traditionally, fatty meat on the bone is slow cooked until most of the fat is separated from the meat. The fat that escapes from the meat in this way is known as rogan and josh refers to the rich red colour. The Kashmiris achieve this colour by using a combination of mild and bright Kashmiri chillies and the juice extracted from a brightly coloured local flower.

SERVES 4–6

45ml/3 tbsp lemon juice
250ml/8fl oz/1 cup natural (plain) yogurt
5ml/1 tsp salt
2 garlic cloves, crushed
2.5cm/1in piece fresh root ginger, finely grated
900g/2lb lean lamb fillet, cubed
60ml/4 tbsp vegetable oil
2.5ml/½ tsp cumin seeds
2 bay leaves
4 green cardamom pods
1 onion, finely chopped
10ml/2 tsp ground coriander
10ml/2 tsp ground cumin
5ml/1 tsp chilli powder
400g/14oz can chopped tomatoes
30ml/2 tbsp tomato purée (paste)
150ml/¼ pint/⅔ cup water
toasted cumin seeds and bay leaves, to garnish
plain boiled rice, to serve

1 In a large bowl, mix together the lemon juice, yogurt, salt, one crushed garlic clove and the ginger. Add the lamb and marinate in the refrigerator overnight.

2 Heat the oil in a wok, karahi or large pan and fry the cumin seeds for 2 minutes until they splutter. Add the bay leaves and cardamom pods and fry for 2 minutes.

3 Add the onion and remaining garlic and fry for 5 minutes. Add the coriander, cumin and chilli powder. Fry for 2 minutes.

4 Add the marinated lamb to the pan and cook for a further 5 minutes, stirring occasionally to prevent the mixture from sticking to the base of the pan.

5 Add the tomatoes, tomato purée and water. Cover and simmer for 1–1½ hours. Garnish with toasted cumin seeds and bay leaves, and serve.

MINCED LAMB with PEAS

This dish, known as kheema mattar, is a favourite all over India, although it originated in the north. Generally, in India minced mutton is used, as lamb is not very easy to obtain. Minced turkey, pork or chicken would all work equally well.

SERVES 4

45ml/3 tbsp vegetable oil
1 onion, finely chopped
2 garlic cloves, crushed
2.5cm/1in piece fresh root ginger, grated
2 fresh green chillies, finely chopped
675g/1½lb minced (ground) lamb
5ml/1 tsp ground cumin
5ml/1 tsp ground coriander
5ml/1 tsp chilli powder
5ml/1 tsp salt
175g/6oz/1½ cups frozen peas, thawed
30ml/2 tbsp lemon juice
naan and natural (plain) yogurt, to serve

1 Heat the oil and fry the onion for about 5 minutes over a medium heat until browned. Add the garlic, ginger and chillies and fry for 2–3 minutes.

2 Add the minced lamb and stir-fry briskly for 5 minutes over a high heat.

3 Stir in the cumin, coriander, chilli powder and salt with 300ml/½ pint/1¼ cups water. Cover the pan and simmer for about 25 minutes.

4 Add the peas and lemon juice. Cook for 10 minutes, uncovered. Garnish with fresh coriander and chilli powder and serve with warm naan and natural yogurt.

COOK'S TIP

To reduce the fat content, dry-fry the lamb in a non-stick frying pan until the natural fat is released. Drain the fat and use the lamb as directed in the recipe.

LAMB with APRICOTS

This recipe comes from the wonderful fruit-laden valley of Kashmir. The cuisine of Kashmir is renowned for the imaginative use of all the exotic fruits and nuts that grow abundantly in that state. Serve with an apricot chutney to complement the fruit in the recipe.

SERVES 4–6

900g/2lb stewing lamb
30ml/2 tbsp vegetable oil
2.5cm/1in piece cinnamon stick
4 green cardamom pods
1 onion, chopped
15ml/1 tbsp curry paste
5ml/1 tsp ground cumin
5ml/1 tsp ground coriander
1.5ml/¼ tsp salt
175g/6oz/¾ cup ready-to-eat dried apricots
350ml/12fl oz/1½ cups lamb stock
fresh coriander (cilantro), to garnish

1 Cut away and discard any visible fat from the lamb, then cut the meat into 2.5cm/1in cubes.

2 Heat the oil in a wok, karahi or large pan and fry the cinnamon stick and cardamoms for 2 minutes. Add the onion and fry for 6–8 minutes until soft.

3 Add the curry paste and fry for about 2 minutes. Stir in the cumin, coriander and salt and fry for 2–3 minutes.

4 Add the cubed lamb, dried apricots and the lamb stock to the pan. Cover with the lid and cook over a medium heat for 1–1½ hours.

5 Transfer to a serving dish and garnish with the fresh coriander. Classic Pulao and Apricot Chutney would make good accompaniments to this dish.

LAMB KOFTA CURRY

Koftas, or meatballs, reveal a Middle Eastern influence on Indian cuisine. The Middle Eastern technique for making the meatballs is still used, combined with the skilful blending of Indian spices. Koftas make an inexpensive but delicious main course.

SERVES 4

675g/1½lb minced (ground) lamb
1 fresh green chilli, roughly chopped
1 garlic clove, chopped
2.5cm/1in piece fresh root ginger, chopped
1.5ml/¼ tsp garam masala
1.5ml/¼ tsp salt
45ml/3 tbsp chopped fresh coriander (cilantro)

For the sauce

30ml/2 tbsp vegetable oil
2.5ml/½ tsp cumin seeds
1 onion, chopped
1 garlic clove, chopped
2.5cm/1in piece fresh root ginger, grated
5ml/1 tsp ground cumin
5ml/1 tsp ground coriander
2.5ml/½ tsp salt
2.5ml/½ tsp chilli powder
15ml/1 tbsp tomato purée (paste)
400g/14oz can chopped tomatoes
fresh coriander (cilantro) sprigs, to garnish
coriander (cilantro) rice, to serve

1 To make the meatballs, put the lamb, chilli, garlic, ginger, garam masala, salt and coriander into a food processor and process until the mixture binds together.

2 Shape the mixture into 16 balls, using your hands. Cover with clear film (plastic wrap) and chill for 10 minutes.

COOK'S TIP

You can make the meatballs the day before. Store them in the refrigerator until needed.

3 To make the sauce, heat the oil and fry the cumin seeds until they splutter. Add the onion, garlic and ginger and fry for 5 minutes. Stir in the remaining sauce ingredients and simmer for 5 minutes.

4 Add the meatballs. Bring to the boil, cover and simmer for 25–30 minutes, or until the meatballs are cooked through. Garnish with sprigs of fresh coriander and serve with coriander rice.

KARAHI LAMB

Lamb dishes are a speciality in the state of Kashmir, the only region of India where the climate is ideal for rearing lamb. Karahi lamb is widely eaten, and in this version the sautéed dried apricots flavoured with cinnamon and cardamom add an irresistible touch.

SERVES 4

15ml/1 tbsp tomato purée (paste)
175ml/6fl oz/¾ cup natural (plain) yogurt
5ml/1 tsp Garam Masala
1.5ml/¼ tsp cumin seeds
5ml/1 tsp salt
5ml/1 tsp crushed garlic
5ml/1 tsp grated fresh root ginger
5ml/1 tsp chilli powder
450g/1lb lean spring lamb, cut into strips
30ml/2 tbsp vegetable oil
2 onions, finely sliced
25g/1oz ghee, butter or margarine
2.5cm/1in piece cinnamon stick
2 green cardamom pods
5 dried apricots, quartered
15ml/1 tbsp chopped fresh coriander (cilantro)

1 In a bowl, blend the tomato purée, yogurt, Garam Masala, cumin seeds, salt, garlic, ginger and chilli powder. Add the lamb and leave to marinate for 1 hour.

2 Heat 10ml/2 tsp of the oil in a wok, karahi or large pan and fry the onions until crisp and golden brown.

3 Remove the onions using a slotted spoon, allow them to cool and then grind them down by processing briefly in a food processor or blender, or with a pestle in a mortar. Reheat the oil and return the onions to the pan.

4 Add the lamb and stir-fry for about 2 minutes. Cover the pan, lower the heat and cook, stirring occasionally, for 15 minutes, or until the meat is cooked through. If required, add up to 150ml/¼ pint/⅔ cup water during the cooking. Remove from the heat and set aside.

5 Heat the ghee, butter or margarine with the remaining oil and add the cinnamon stick and cardamoms. Stir in the apricots and cook over a low heat for 2 minutes. Pour this sauce over the lamb.

6 Garnish with the chopped coriander leaves and serve immediately.

COOK'S TIP

If you want this curry to be slightly hotter, increase the garam masala and chilli powder to 7.5ml/1½ tsp each.

STIR-FRIED CHILLI-GARLIC PRAWNS

Prawns have a particular affinity with garlic. To enhance the flavour of the garlic, fry it very gently without letting it brown completely. The spice-coated prawns make a mouthwatering appetizer or light lunch, when served with a salad, or they can be transformed into a main meal with the addition of warm naan bread.

SERVES 4

15ml/1 tbsp vegetable oil
3 garlic cloves, roughly halved
3 tomatoes, chopped
2.5ml/½ tsp salt
5ml/1 tsp crushed dried red chillies
5ml/1 tsp lemon juice
Mango Chutney, to taste
1 fresh green chilli, chopped
16–20 peeled, cooked king prawns (jumbo shrimp)
fresh coriander (cilantro) sprigs and chopped spring onions (scallions), to garnish

1 In a wok, karahi or large pan, heat the vegetable oil over a low heat and fry the garlic halves gently until they are tinged with golden brown.

2 Add the chopped tomatoes, salt, crushed red chillies, lemon juice, Mango Chutney and the chopped fresh chilli. Stir the ingredients well.

3 Add the prawns to the pan, then raise the heat and stir-fry briskly, mixing the prawns with the other ingredients until they are thoroughly heated through.

4 Transfer the prawns in the sauce to a warm serving dish and garnish with fresh coriander sprigs and chopped spring onions. Serve immediately.

GRILLED KING PRAWNS with STIR-FRIED SPICES

Traditionally, king prawns are marinated and then grilled in the tandoor to produce the delectable tandoori king prawns. It is possible to achieve similar results by grilling the prawns under a very hot electric or gas grill as in this recipe.

SERVES 4

15ml/3 tbsp natural (plain) yogurt
5ml/1 tsp paprika
5ml/1 tsp grated fresh root ginger
16–20 peeled, cooked king prawns (jumbo shrimp), thawed if frozen
15ml/1 tbsp vegetable oil
3 onions, sliced
2.5ml/½ tsp fennel seeds, crushed
2.5cm/1in piece cinnamon stick
5ml/1 tsp crushed garlic
5ml/1 tsp chilli powder
1 yellow (bell) pepper, seeded and roughly chopped
1 red (bell) pepper, seeded and roughly chopped
salt
15ml/1 tbsp fresh coriander (cilantro) leaves, to garnish

1 Blend together the yogurt, paprika, ginger and add salt to taste. Add to the prawns and leave in a cool place to marinate for 30–45 minutes.

2 Meanwhile, heat the oil in a wok, karahi or large pan and fry the sliced onions with the fennel seeds and the cinnamon stick over a medium heat until the onions soften and turn golden.

3 Lower the heat and stir in the crushed garlic and chilli powder.

4 Add the chopped yellow and red peppers to the pan and stir-fry gently for 3–5 minutes.

5 Remove the pan from the heat and transfer the onion and spice mixture to a warm serving dish, discarding the cinnamon stick. Set the dish aside.

COOK'S TIP

It is important not to overcook the prawns, they only need heating through.

6 Preheat the grill (broiler) to medium. Put the marinated prawns in a grill pan or flameproof dish and place under the grill to darken their tops and achieve a chargrilled effect. Add the prawns to the onion and spice mixture, and garnish with fresh coriander. Serve with plain rice and Creamy Black Lentils, if you like.

CORN on the COB in RICH ONION SAUCE

Corn is grown extensively in the Punjab region, where it is used in many delicacies. Corn bread, makki ki roti, *along with spiced mustard greens,* sarson ka saag, *is a combination that is hard to beat and is what the Punjabis thrive on. Here, corn is cooked in a thick rich onion sauce, in another classic Punjabi dish. It is excellent served with naan bread.*

SERVES 4–6

4 corn cobs, thawed if frozen
vegetable oil, for frying
1 large onion, finely chopped
2 cloves garlic, crushed
5cm/2in piece fresh root ginger, crushed
2.5ml/½ tsp ground turmeric
2.5ml/½ tsp onion seeds
2.5ml/½ tsp cumin seeds
2.5ml/½ tsp five-spice powder
6–8 curry leaves
2.5ml/½ tsp granulated sugar
200ml/7fl oz/scant 1 cup natural (plain) yogurt
chilli powder, to taste

1 Cut each corn cob in half, using a heavy knife or cleaver to make clean cuts. Heat the oil in a wok, karahi or large pan and fry the corn until golden brown. Remove the corn and set aside.

2 Remove any excess oil, leaving 30ml/2 tbsp in the wok. Grind the onion, garlic and ginger to a paste using a pestle and mortar or in a food processor. Transfer the paste to a bowl and mix in the spices, chilli powder, curry leaves and sugar.

3 Heat the oil gently and fry the onion paste mixture for 8–10 minutes until all the spices have blended well and the oil separates from the sauce.

4 Cool the mixture and fold in the yogurt. Mix to a smooth sauce. Add the corn and mix well, so that all the pieces are covered with the sauce. Reheat gently for about 10 minutes. Serve hot.

STIR-FRIED INDIAN CHEESE with MUSHROOMS and PEAS

Indian cheese, known as paneer, *is a very versatile ingredient. It is used in both sweet and savoury dishes. Indian housewives generally make this cheese at home, although in recent years it has become available commercially. It is a useful source of protein for the the people in the north who are vegetarian.*

SERVES 4–6

90ml/6 tbsp ghee or vegetable oil
225g/8oz paneer, cubed
1 onion, finely chopped
a few fresh mint leaves, chopped, plus extra sprigs to garnish
50g/2oz chopped fresh coriander (cilantro)
3 fresh green chillies, chopped
3 garlic cloves
2.5cm/1in piece fresh root ginger, sliced
5ml/1 tsp ground turmeric
5ml/1 tsp chilli powder (optional)
5ml/1 tsp garam masala
225g/8oz/3 cups tiny button (white) mushrooms, washed
225g/8oz/2 cups frozen peas, thawed
175ml/6fl oz/¾ cup natural (plain) yogurt, mixed with 5ml/1 tsp cornflour (cornstarch)
salt

1 Heat the ghee or oil in a wok, karahi or large pan, and fry the paneer cubes until they are golden brown on all sides. Remove, drain on kitchen paper, and keep to one side.

2 Grind the onion, mint, coriander, chillies, garlic and ginger with a pestle and mortar or in a food processor to a fairly smooth paste.

3 Remove to a bowl and mix in the turmeric, chilli powder, if using, and garam masala, and season with salt to taste.

4 Remove excess ghee or oil from the pan, leaving about 15ml/1 tbsp. Heat and fry the paste over a medium heat for 8–10 minutes, or until the raw onion smell disappears and the oil separates.

5 Add the mushrooms, thawed peas and paneer, and mix well. Cool the mixture slightly and gradually fold in the yogurt.

6 Simmer for about 10 minutes, until the vegetables are tender and the flavours well mixed. Remove to a serving dish, garnish with sprigs of fresh mint and serve immediately.

COOK'S TIP

If paneer is not available, you can use grilled goat's cheese instead. Add it just before the garnish.

DRY-SPICED POTATOES with CAULIFLOWER

This dish, known as aloo gobi *in most Indian restaurants, has remained one of the most popular over the years. It is also a healthy dish, as potatoes are 90 per cent fat free and both potatoes and cauliflower are good sources of vitamin C.*

SERVES 4

450g/1lb potatoes
30ml/2 tbsp vegetable oil
5ml/1 tsp cumin seeds
1 fresh green chilli, finely chopped
450g/1lb cauliflower, broken into florets
5ml/1 tsp ground coriander
5ml/1 tsp ground cumin
1.5ml/¼ tsp chilli powder
2.5ml/½ tsp ground turmeric
2.5ml/½ tsp salt
chopped fresh coriander (cilantro), to garnish
Tomato and Onion Salad and a pickle of your choice, to serve

1 Cut the peeled and washed potatoes into 2.5cm/1in cubes, then par-boil them in a large pan of boiling water for about 10 minutes. Drain the potatoes well and set them aside.

2 Heat the oil in a wok, karahi or large pan over a medium heat and fry the cumin seeds for 2 minutes until they begin to splutter. Add the fresh green chilli and fry for a further 1 minute.

3 Add the cauliflower florets to the pan and fry, stirring, for 5 minutes.

4 Add the potatoes, the spices and salt and cook for a further 7–10 minutes, or until both vegetables are tender. Garnish with chopped coriander and serve with Tomato and Onion Salad and a pickle.

VARIATION

Use broccoli instead of some or all of the cauliflower, if you prefer.

KARAHI POTATOES with WHOLE SPICES

All spices work like magic with potatoes. Even just a light touch can bring about a complete transformation. For this recipe choose floury potatoes, as they will absorb the spice flavours better than the waxy variety.

SERVES 4

- 45ml/3 tbsp vegetable oil
- 2.5ml/½ tsp white cumin seeds
- 3 curry leaves
- 5ml/1 tsp crushed dried red chillies
- 2.5ml/½ tsp mixed onion, mustard and fenugreek seeds
- 2.5ml/½ tsp fennel seeds
- 3 garlic cloves, roughly chopped
- 2.5ml/½ tsp grated fresh root ginger
- 2 onions, sliced
- 6 new potatoes, cut into 5mm/¼in slices
- 15ml/1 tbsp chopped fresh coriander (cilantro)
- 1 fresh red chilli, seeded and sliced
- 1 fresh green chilli, seeded and sliced

1 Heat the oil in a wok, karahi or large pan. Lower the heat slightly and add the cumin seeds, curry leaves, dried chillies, mixed onion, mustard and fenugreek seeds, fennel seeds, chopped garlic and grated ginger.

2 Fry for about 1 minute, then add the sliced onions and fry gently for a further 5 minutes, or until the onions are golden brown. Add the sliced potatoes, fresh coriander and red and green chillies. Mix together well. Cover the pan tightly with a lid or foil, making sure the foil does not touch the food. Cook over a very low heat for about 7 minutes, or until the potatoes are tender.

3 Remove the lid or foil from the pan and serve the potatoes hot with parathas and any lentil dish for a vegetarian meal. Serve Shammi Kabab, Tandoori Chicken or Chicken Tikka instead of the lentils for meat eaters.

MUSHROOM CURRY

In India, mushrooms traditionally grow only in the northern state of Kashmir. However, Indians have acquired the taste for them due to frequent travels abroad, and they are now being cultivated in other northern areas where the climate is suitable.

SERVES 4

30ml/2 tbsp vegetable oil
2.5ml/½ tsp cumin seeds
1.5ml/¼ tsp black peppercorns
4 green cardamom pods
1.5ml/¼ tsp ground turmeric
1 onion, finely chopped
5ml/1 tsp ground cumin
5ml/1 tsp ground coriander
2.5ml/½ tsp garam masala
1 fresh green chilli, finely chopped
2 garlic cloves, crushed
2.5cm/1in piece fresh root ginger, grated
400g/4oz can chopped tomatoes
1.5ml/¼ tsp salt
450g/1lb/6 cups button (white) mushrooms
chopped fresh coriander (cilantro), to garnish

1 Heat the vegetable oil in a wok, karahi or large pan and fry the cumin seeds, black peppercorns, cardamom pods and turmeric for 2–3 minutes.

2 Add the onion and fry for 5 minutes or until golden. Stir in the ground cumin, coriander and garam masala and fry for a further 2 minutes.

3 Add the chilli, garlic and ginger and fry for 2–3 minutes, stirring constantly. Add the tomatoes and salt. Bring to the boil and simmer for 5 minutes.

4 Halve the mushrooms, then add them to the pan. Cover and simmer over a low heat for 10 minutes. Transfer to a warm serving platter and garnish with chopped coriander. Serve with an Indian bread, such as naan, parathas or chapatis, and any dry meat or poultry dish, such as Shammi Kabab or Tandoori Chicken.

COOK'S TIP

For authentic Kashmiri style, use ground or crushed fennel in place of the cumin.

COURGETTES in SPICED TOMATO SAUCE

In India, tender marrow would be used for this recipe as courgettes are not grown there. Do try this recipe with a young marrow in the summer. It will also work well with winter squashes, such as butternut and acorn.

SERVES 4

675g/1½lb courgettes (zucchini)
45ml/3 tbsp vegetable oil
2.5ml/½ tsp cumin seeds
2.5ml/½ tsp mustard seeds
1 onion, thinly sliced
2 garlic cloves, crushed
1.5ml/¼ tsp ground turmeric
1.5ml/¼ tsp chilli powder
5ml/1 tsp ground coriander
5ml/1 tsp ground cumin
2.5ml/½ tsp salt
15ml/1 tbsp tomato purée (paste)
400g/14oz can chopped tomatoes
150ml/¼ pint/⅔ cup water
15ml/1 tbsp chopped fresh coriander (cilantro)
5ml/1 tsp garam masala

1 Trim the ends from the courgettes then cut them into 1cm/½in thick slices.

2 Heat the oil in a wok, karahi or large pan. Fry the cumin and mustard seeds for 2 minutes until they begin to splutter.

3 Add the onion and garlic and fry for about 5–6 minutes.

4 Add the ground turmeric, chilli powder, coriander, cumin and salt and fry for about 2–3 minutes.

5 Add the sliced courgettes, and cook for 5 minutes. Add the tomato purée and chopped tomatoes to the pan.

6 Add the water, then cover the pan and simmer for 10 minutes until the sauce thickens. Stir in the fresh coriander and garam masala, then cook for about 5 minutes, or until the courgettes are tender. Serve as an accompaniment to any meat, poultry or fish dish.

CUMIN-SCENTED VEGETABLES with TOASTED ALMONDS

Cabbage is a traditional vegetable in India, although neither baby corn cobs nor mangetouts are used in Indian cooking. Nonetheless, combining new and traditional ideas can create exciting and original dishes, as this recipe shows.

SERVES 4

15ml/1 tbsp vegetable oil
50g/2oz/4 tbsp butter
2.5ml/½ tsp crushed coriander seeds
2.5ml/½ tsp white cumin seeds
6 dried red chillies
1 small savoy cabbage, shredded
12 mangetouts (snow peas)
3 fresh red chillies, seeded and sliced
12 baby corn cobs, halved
salt
25g/1oz/¼ cup flaked (sliced) almonds, toasted and 15ml/1 tbsp chopped fresh coriander (cilantro), to garnish

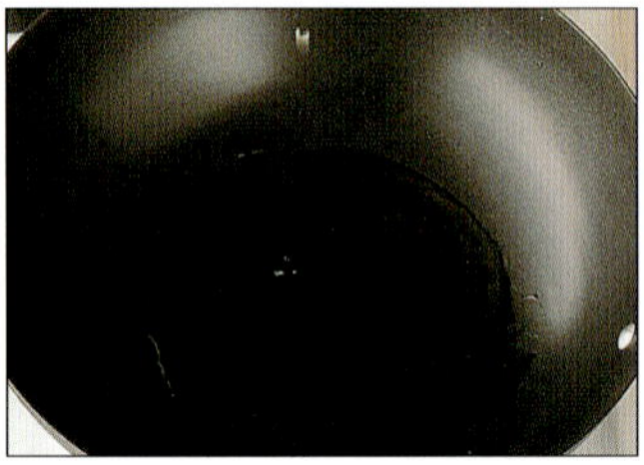

1 Heat the oil and butter in a wok, karahi or large pan and add the crushed coriander seeds, white cumin seeds and dried red chillies.

2 Add the shredded cabbage and mangetouts to the spices in the pan and stir-fry briskly for about 5 minutes, until the cabbage starts to turn crisp.

3 Add the fresh red chillies, and baby corn cobs to the pan and season with salt to taste. Stir-fry for 3 minutes more.

4 Garnish with the toasted almonds and fresh coriander, and serve hot. This dish would go well with any meat curry and with Classic Pulao.

COOK'S TIP

Julienne strips of other vegetables will make this dish visually more appealing, and will add superb taste at the same time. Try julienne carrots and leeks instead of mangetouts and baby corn. Add the cabbage and carrots together, and add the leeks in step 3.

ROASTED AUBERGINES with SPRING ONIONS

This classic dish, made of roasted and mashed aubergines cooked with spring onions, is known as bharta *in the Punjab region. The term* bharta *means to mash. Traditionally, the aubergine is roasted over charcoal, but a hot electric or gas oven will produce similar results, although the smoky flavour will be missing.*

SERVES 4

2 large aubergines (eggplant)
45ml/3 tbsp vegetable oil
2.5ml/½ tsp black mustard seeds
1 bunch spring onions (scallions), finely chopped
115g/4oz/1½ cups button (white) mushrooms, halved
2 garlic cloves, crushed
1 fresh red chilli, finely chopped
2.5ml/½ tsp chilli powder
5ml/1 tsp ground cumin
5ml/1 tsp ground coriander
1.5ml/¼ tsp ground turmeric
5ml/1 tsp salt
400g/14oz can chopped tomatoes
15ml/1 tbsp chopped fresh coriander (cilantro), plus a few extra sprigs to garnish

1 Preheat the oven to 200°C/400°F/Gas 6. Brush both of the aubergines with 15ml/1 tbsp of oil and prick with a fork. Bake for 30–35 minutes until soft.

2 Meanwhile, heat the remaining oil and fry the black mustard seeds for about 2 minutes until they splutter. Add the onions, mushrooms, garlic and chilli, and fry for 5 minutes more. Stir in the chilli powder, cumin, coriander, turmeric and salt and fry for 3–4 minutes. Add the tomatoes and simmer for 5 minutes.

COOK'S TIP

Roast the aubergines (eggplant) over a barbecue for an authentic smoky flavour.

3 Cut the aubergines in half lengthwise and scoop out the soft flesh into a large mixing bowl. Mash the flesh to a course texture, using a fork.

4 Add the aubergines to the pan with the coriander. Bring to the boil and simmer for 5 minutes until the sauce thickens. Serve garnished with coriander.

KIDNEY BEAN CURRY

This dish, known as rajma *in Punjabi, is a fine example of the area's hearty, robust cuisine. It is widely eaten dish all over the state, and is even sold by street vendors. Plain boiled rice makes the perfect accompaniment for this dish.*

SERVES 4

225g/8oz/1¼ cups dried red kidney beans
30ml/2 tbsp vegetable oil
2.5ml/½ tsp cumin seeds
1 onion, thinly sliced
1 fresh green chilli, finely chopped
2 garlic cloves, crushed
2.5cm/1in piece fresh root ginger, grated
30ml/2 tbsp curry paste
5ml/1 tsp ground cumin
5ml/1 tsp ground coriander
2.5ml/½ tsp chilli powder
2.5ml/½ tsp salt
400g/14oz can chopped tomatoes
30ml/2 tbsp chopped fresh coriander (cilantro)

1 Place the kidney beans in a large bowl of cold water and then leave them to soak overnight.

2 Drain the beans and place in a large pan with double the volume of water. Boil vigorously for 10 minutes. Drain, rinse and return the beans to the pan. Add double the volume of water and bring to the boil. Reduce the heat, then cover and cook for 1–1½ hours, or until the beans are soft. This process is essential in order to remove the toxins that are present in dried kidney beans.

3 Meanwhile, heat the oil in a wok, karahi or large pan and fry the cumin seeds for 2 minutes until they begin to splutter. Add the onion, chilli, garlic and ginger and fry for 5 minutes. Stir in the curry paste, cumin, coriander, chilli powder and salt, and cook for 5 minutes.

4 Add the tomatoes and simmer for 5 minutes. Add the beans and fresh coriander, reserving a little for the garnish. Cover and cook for 15 minutes adding a little water if necessary. Serve garnished with the reserved coriander.

COOK'S TIP

Drained and well-rinsed canned beans work very well as an alternative.

CREAMY BLACK LENTILS

Black lentils or urad dhal are available whole, split, and skinned and split. Generally, both split, and skinned and split versions are used in west and south Indian cooking, whereas whole black lentils are a typical ingredient in the north.

SERVES 4–6

175g/6oz/¾ cup black lentils, soaked
50g/2oz/¼ cup red split lentils
120ml/4fl oz/½ cup double (heavy) cream
120ml/4fl oz/½ cup natural (plain) yogurt
5ml/1 tsp cornflour (cornstarch)
45ml/3 tbsp ghee or vegetable oil
1 onion, finely chopped
5cm/2in piece fresh root ginger, crushed
4 fresh green chillies, chopped
1 tomato, chopped
2.5ml/½ tsp chilli powder
2.5ml/½ tsp ground turmeric
2.5ml/½ tsp ground cumin
2 garlic cloves, sliced
salt
coriander (cilantro) sprigs and sliced red chilli, to garnish

1 Drain the black lentils and place in a large pan with the red lentils. Cover with water and bring to the boil. Reduce the heat, cover the pan and simmer until tender. Mash with a spoon, and cool.

2 In a bowl, mix together the cream, yogurt and cornflour, and stir into the lentils in the pan.

3 Heat 15ml/1 tbsp of the ghee or oil in a wok, karahi or large pan, and fry the onion, ginger, two green chillies and the tomato until the onion is soft. Add the ground spices and salt and fry for a further 2 minutes. Stir into the lentil mixture and mix well. Reheat, transfer to a heatproof serving dish and keep warm.

4 Heat the remaining ghee or oil in a frying pan over a low heat and fry the garlic slices and remaining chillies until the garlic slices are golden brown. Pour over the lentils and fold the garlic and chilli into the lentils just before serving. Place extra cream on the table for the diners to add more if they wish.

EAST INDIA

The state of Bengal has developed a strong culinary identity, which makes use of local produce such as mustard, coconut, vegetables, lentils and rice. Fish from the Bay of Bengal is eaten throughout eastern India, and in areas close to the sea, fish is eaten daily, in place of meat.

CHICKEN JHALFRAZI

Jhalfrazi was created by Indian chefs during the British Raj. Leftover cold meat, generally from the Sunday roast, was stir-fried with spices. The dish originated in Calcutta, where the East India Company was established as an important trading post by the British.

SERVES 4

675g/1½lb chicken breast fillets, skinned
30ml/2 tbsp vegetable oil
5ml/1 tsp cumin seeds
1 onion, finely chopped
1 green (bell) pepper, finely chopped
1 red (bell) pepper, finely chopped
1 garlic clove, crushed
2cm/¾in piece fresh root ginger, chopped
15ml/1 tbsp curry paste
1.5ml/¼ tsp chilli powder
5ml/1 tsp ground coriander
5ml/1 tsp ground cumin
2.5ml/½ tsp salt
400g/14oz can chopped tomatoes
30ml/2 tbsp chopped fresh coriander (cilantro)
fresh coriander (cilantro) sprig, to garnish
plain boiled rice or naan bread, to serve

1 Remove any visible fat and cut the chicken into 2.5cm/1in cubes.

2 Heat the oil in a wok, karahi or large pan, and fry the cumin seeds for 30–40 seconds until they begin to splutter. Add the onion, peppers, garlic and ginger and fry for 6–8 minutes.

3 Add the curry paste to the other ingredients in the pan and stir-fry for about 2 minutes. Stir in the chilli powder, ground coriander, cumin and salt, and add 15ml/1 tbsp water. Stir-fry for a further 2 minutes.

4 Add the chicken and stir-fry for about 5 minutes. Add the tomatoes and fresh coriander. Cook, covered, for about 15 minutes until the chicken is tender. Garnish with a sprig of fresh coriander. Serve with plain boiled rice or naan.

CUMIN-SCENTED CHICKEN

Cumin is a wonderful spice that is full of pungency, but without any harshness. Its rather warm and assertive nature gives this dish a distinctive flavour and aroma. Cumin is also known to have curative properties.

SERVES 4

45ml/3 tbsp cumin seeds
45ml/3 tbsp vegetable oil
2.5ml/½ tsp black peppercorns
4 green cardamom pods
2 fresh green chillies, finely chopped
2 garlic cloves, crushed
2.5cm/1in piece fresh root ginger, grated
5ml/1 tsp ground coriander
10ml/2 tsp ground cumin
2.5ml/½ tsp salt
8 chicken pieces, such as thighs and drumsticks, skinned
5ml/1 tsp garam masala
Cucumber Raita, garnished with fresh coriander (cilantro) and chilli powder, to serve (optional)

1 Preheat a wok or round-based frying pan over a medium heat and dry-roast 15ml/1 tbsp of the cumin seeds for 1–2 minutes until they release their aroma. Set aside.

2 Heat the oil in a wok or large pan and fry the remaining cumin seeds, black peppercorns and cardamoms for about 2 minutes.

3 Add the green chillies, garlic and grated fresh root ginger to the spices in the pan and fry for 2 minutes.

4 Add the ground coriander and cumin to the pan with the salt, and cook over a medium heat, stirring, for a further 1–2 minutes.

5 Add the chicken pieces, stir and mix thoroughly with the spices. Cover and allow to simmer for 20–25 minutes.

6 Add the garam masala and reserved dry-roasted cumin seeds, and cook for a further 5 minutes. Serve with Cucumber Raita, if you like.

CHICKEN in COCONUT MILK

In Bengal, this dish is known as murgi malai, *and in the Bengali language, the word* murgi *means chicken and* malai *is cream, either dairy or coconut. Coconut is a favourite ingredient of the region, and it grows in adundant supply in Bengal, Orissa and Assam.*

SERVES 4

15ml/1 tbsp ground almonds
15ml/1 tbsp desiccated (dry, unsweetened, shredded) coconut
85ml/3fl oz/⅔ cup coconut milk
175g/6oz/⅔ cup fromage frais or ricotta cheese
7.5ml/1½ tsp ground coriander
5ml/1 tsp chilli powder
5ml/1 tsp crushed garlic
7.5ml/1½ tsp grated fresh root ginger
5ml/1 tsp salt
30ml/2 tbsp vegetable oil
450g/1lb chicken breast fillets, skinned and cubed
3 green cardamom pods
1 bay leaf
1 dried red chilli, crushed
30ml/2 tbsp chopped fresh coriander (cilantro)

1 Dry-roast the almonds and coconut in a wok, karahi or large pan, until they turn a shade darker. Transfer the mixture to a large glass bowl.

COOK'S TIP

Fromage frais and ricotta cheese are used here in order to reduce the fat content. For a more authentic taste and aroma, use extra coconut milk.

2 Add the coconut milk, fromage frais or ricotta cheese, ground coriander, chilli powder, garlic, ginger and salt to the bowl. Mix together well.

3 Heat the vegetable oil in the pan, and add the chicken cubes, cardamom pods and bay leaf. Stir-fry for about 2 minutes to seal the chicken.

4 Pour in the coconut mixture and stir well. Lower the heat, add the chilli and coriander, then cover and cook for 10–12 minutes, stirring occasionally to prevent the contents from sticking to the pan. Uncover the pan, then stir and cook for 2 minutes more. Classic Pulao would make a good accompaniment.

FISH JHALFRAZI

In Bengal, fish curry and rice are eaten together on a daily basis. This is a rather unusual dish, using canned tuna cooked in the style of jhalfrazi, and is ideal for lunch or supper. Served with boiled basmati rice and tarka dhal, it will also make a satisfying family meal.

SERVES 4

I onion
I red (bell) pepper
I green (bell) pepper
45ml/3 tbsp vegetable oil
1.5ml/¼ tsp cumin seeds
2.5ml/½ tsp ground cumin
2.5ml/½ tsp ground coriander
2.5ml/½ tsp chilli powder
1.5ml/¼ tsp salt
2 garlic cloves, crushed
400g/14oz can tuna, drained
I fresh green chilli, finely chopped
2.5cm/1in piece fresh root ginger, grated
1.5ml/¼ tsp garam masala
5ml/1 tsp lemon juice
30ml/2 tbsp chopped fresh coriander (cilantro)
fresh coriander (cilantro) sprig, to garnish
pitta bread and Cucumber Raita, to serve

1 Thinly slice the onion and the red and green peppers. Set aside.

2 Heat the oil in a wok, karahi or large pan over a medium heat and fry the cumin seeds for 30–40 seconds until they begin to splutter.

3 Add the ground cumin and coriander, chilli powder and salt to the pan. Cook for 2 minutes. Add the garlic, onion and peppers and increase the heat a little.

COOK'S TIP
Place the pitta bread on a grill (broiler) rack and grill (broil) until it puffs up. It will then be easy to split with a sharp knife.

4 Stir-fry the vegetables for 5–7 minutes until the onions have browned.

5 Stir in the tuna, fresh chilli and grated ginger and cook for 5 minutes more.

6 Add the garam masala, lemon juice and fresh coriander and continue to cook for a further 3–4 minutes. Serve in warmed pitta bread with the Cucumber Raita, garnished with fresh coriander.

FISH STEW

Cooking fish with vegetables is very much a tradition in eastern regions. This hearty dish with potatoes, peppers and tomatoes is perfect served with breads such as chapatis or parathas. You can try other combinations, such as green beans and spinach, but you do need a starchy vegetable in order to thicken the sauce.

SERVES 4

30ml/2 tbsp vegetable oil
5ml/1 tsp cumin seeds
1 onion, chopped
1 red (bell) pepper, thinly sliced
1 garlic clove, crushed
2 fresh red chillies, finely chopped
2 bay leaves
2.5ml/½ tsp salt
5ml/1 tsp ground cumin
5ml/1 tsp ground coriander
5ml/1 tsp chilli powder
400g/14oz can chopped tomatoes
2 large potatoes, cut into 2.5cm/1in chunks
300ml/½ pint/1¼ cups fish stock
4 cod fillets
chapatis, to serve

1 Heat the oil in a wok, karahi or large pan over a medium heat and fry the cumin seeds for 30–40 seconds until they begin to splutter. Add the onion, red pepper, garlic, chillies and bay leaves and fry for 5–7 minutes more until the onions have browned.

2 Add the salt, ground cumin, ground coriander and chilli powder and cook for 1–2 minutes.

3 Stir in the tomatoes, potatoes and fish stock. Bring to the boil and simmer for a further 10 minutes, or until the potatoes are almost tender.

4 Add the fish fillets, then cover the pan and allow to simmer for 5–6 minutes until the fish is just cooked. Serve hot with chapatis, if you like.

COOK'S TIP

Avoid reheating this dish. Serve it as soon as it is cooked because cod flesh flakes very easily. If preparing in advance, follow the recipe up to the end of step 3, then cover the sauce and store in the refrigerator. Cook step 4 before serving.

FISH in a RICH TOMATO and ONION SAUCE

It is difficult to imagine the cuisine of eastern India without fish. Bengal is as well known for its fish and shellfish dishes as Goa on the west coast. In both regions, coconut is used extensively, and the difference in the taste, as always, lies in the spicing. This onion-rich dish is known as kalia in Bengal, and a firm-fleshed fish is essential.

SERVES 4

675g/1½lb steaks of firm-textured fish such as tuna or monkfish, skinned
30ml/2 tbsp lemon juice
5ml/1 tsp salt
5ml/1 tsp ground turmeric
vegetable oil, for shallow frying
40g/1½ oz/½ cup plain (all-purpose) flour
2.5ml/¼ tsp ground black pepper
60ml/4 tbsp vegetable oil
10ml/2 tsp granulated sugar
1 large onion, finely chopped
15ml/1 tbsp grated fresh root ginger
15ml/1 tbsp crushed garlic
5ml/1 tsp ground coriander
2.5–5ml/½–1 tsp hot chilli powder
175g/6 oz canned chopped tomatoes, including the juice
300ml/½ pint/1¼ cups warm water
30ml/2 tbsp chopped fresh coriander (cilantro) leaves, to garnish
plain boiled rice, to serve

1 Cut the fish into 7.5cm/3in pieces and put into a large bowl. Add the lemon juice and sprinkle with half the salt and half the turmeric. Mix gently with your fingertips and set aside for 15 minutes.

2 Pour enough oil into a 23cm/9in frying pan to cover the base to a depth of 1cm/½in and heat over a medium setting. Mix the flour and pepper and dust the fish in the seasoned flour. Add to the oil in a single layer and fry until browned on both sides and a light crust has formed. Drain on kitchen paper.

3 In a wok, karahi or large pan, heat 60ml/4 tbsp oil. When the oil is hot, but not smoking, add the sugar and let it caramelize. As soon as the sugar is brown, add the onion, ginger and garlic and fry for 7–8 minutes, until just beginning to colour. Stir regularly.

4 Add the ground coriander, chilli powder and the remaining turmeric. Stir-fry for about 30 seconds and add the tomatoes. Cook until the tomatoes are mushy and the oil separates from the spice paste, stirring regularly.

5 Pour the warm water and remaining salt into the pan, and bring to the boil. Carefully add the fried fish, reduce the heat to low and simmer, uncovered, for 5–6 minutes. Transfer to a serving dish and garnish with the coriander leaves. Serve with plain boiled rice.

COOK'S TIP

Like all ground spices, ground turmeric will lose its potency on keeping. Buy only small quantities, and store the powder in an airtight container, in a cupboard away from strong light.

PRAWN CURRY

The Bay of Bengal provides Bengal and Orissa with enormous quantities of fish and shellfish. Eating plenty of fish, greens, lentils and peas is a way of life here. The food is generally cooked in mustard oil, which lends a distinctive, nutty flavour to the final dish.

SERVES 4

675g/1½lb raw tiger prawns (jumbo shrimp)
4 dried red chillies
50g/2oz/1 cup desiccated (dry, unsweetened, shredded) coconut
5ml/1 tsp black mustard seeds
1 large onion, chopped
45ml/3 tbsp vegetable oil
4 bay leaves
2.5cm/1in piece fresh root ginger, chopped
2 garlic cloves, crushed
15ml/1 tbsp ground coriander
5ml/1 tsp chilli powder
5ml/1 tsp salt
4 tomatoes, finely chopped
plain boiled rice, to serve

1 Peel the prawns. Run a sharp knife along the back of each prawn to make a shallow cut and carefully remove the thin black intestinal vein. You might like to leave a few of the prawns unpeeled, setting them aside to use as a garnish for the finished dish.

2 Put the dried red chillies, coconut, mustard seeds and onion in a wok, karahi or large pan and dry-fry over a medium heat for 5–6 minutes, or until the mixture begins to brown. Stir continuously to ensure even browning and to avoid burning the coconut. Put into a food processor or blender and process to a coarse paste.

3 Heat the vegetable oil in the pan and fry the bay leaves for 1 minute. Add the chopped ginger and the garlic, and fry for 2–3 minutes.

4 Add the ground coriander, chilli powder, salt and the paste and fry for about 5 minutes.

5 Stir in the tomatoes and about 175ml/6fl oz/¾ cup water and simmer for 5–6 minutes or until thickened.

6 Add the prawns and cook for about 4–5 minutes, or until they turn pink. Grill (broil) the reserved whole prawns, if using, until pink. Serve the curry on a ring of plain boiled rice and garnish with the whole prawns, if using.

KING PRAWN KORMA

Prawns are the most popular shellfish in Bengal. This dish is cooked in the style of malai chingri, *which means prawns cooked in dairy or coconut cream. Because of the richness of the ingredients, serve plain boiled rice with this korma.*

SERVES 4

10–12 peeled, cooked king prawns (jumbo shrimp), thawed if frozen
45ml/3 tbsp natural (plain) yogurt
5ml/1 tsp paprika
5ml/1 tsp garam masala
15ml/1 tbsp tomato purée (paste)
60ml/4 tbsp coconut milk
5ml/1 tsp chilli powder
150ml/¼ pint/⅔ cup water
15ml/1 tbsp vegetable oil
5ml/1 tsp crushed garlic
5ml/1 tsp grated fresh root ginger
2.5cm/1in piece cinnamon stick, halved
2 green cardamom pods
salt
15ml/1 tbsp chopped fresh coriander (cilantro), to garnish

1 If the prawns had been frozen, drain thoroughly in a sieve (strainer) over a bowl to ensure that all excess liquid is removed before cooking.

2 Place the yogurt, paprika, garam masala, tomato purée, coconut milk, chilli powder and water into a large glass bowl, and season to taste with salt.

3 Blend the ingredients together. Set aside.

4 Heat the oil in a wok, karahi or large pan, add the garlic, ginger, cinnamon, cardamoms and season to taste with salt. Fry over a low heat for 1–2 minutes.

5 Pour in the spice mixture and bring to the boil, stirring occasionally.

6 Add the prawns and cook, stirring constantly, until the sauce starts to thicken. Garnish and serve.

FRAGRANT LAMB CURRY

Essentially a Muslim dish known as rezala*, this delectable recipe comes from Bengal where there is a tradition of Muslim cooking. This is a legacy left by the Muslim rulers during the Mogul era.*

SERVES 4

1 large onion, roughly chopped
10ml/2 tsp grated fresh root ginger
10ml/2 tsp crushed garlic
4–5 garlic cloves
2.5ml/½ tsp black peppercorns
6 green cardamom pods
5cm/2in piece cinnamon stick, halved
8 lamb rib chops
60ml/4 tbsp vegetable oil
1 large onion, finely sliced
175ml/6fl oz/¾ natural (plain) yogurt
50g/2oz/¼ cup butter
2.5ml/1 tsp salt
2.5ml/½ tsp ground cumin
2.5ml/½ tsp hot chilli powder
2.5ml/½ tsp freshly grated nutmeg
2.5ml/½ tsp granulated sugar
15ml/1 tbsp lime juice
pinch of saffron, steeped in 15ml/1 tbsp hot water for 10–15 minutes
15ml/1 tbsp rose water
rose petals, to garnish

1 Process the onion in a blender or food processor. Add a little water if necessary to form a purée.

2 Put the purée in a glass bowl and add the grated ginger, crushed garlic, cloves, peppercorns, cardamom pods, and cinnamon. Mix well.

3 Put the lamb chops in a large shallow glass dish and add the spice mixture. Mix thoroughly, cover the bowl and leave the lamb to marinate for 3–4 hours or overnight in the refrigerator. Bring back to room temperature before cooking.

4 In a wok, karahi or large pan, heat the oil over a medium-high heat and fry the sliced onion for 6–7 minutes, until golden brown. Remove the onion slices with a slotted spoon, squeezing out as much oil as possible on the side of the pan. Drain the onions on kitchen paper.

5 In the remaining oil, fry the marinated lamb chops for 4–5 minutes, stirring frequently. Reduce the heat to low, cover and cook for 5–7 minutes.

6 Meanwhile, mix the yogurt and butter together in a small pan and place over a low heat. Cook for 5–6 minutes, stirring constantly, then stir into the lamb chops along with the salt. Add the cumin and chilli powder and cover the pan. Cook for 45–50 minutes until the chops are tender.

7 Add the nutmeg and sugar, cook for 1–2 minutes and add the lime juice, saffron and rose water. Stir and mix well, simmer for 2–3 minutes and remove from the heat. Garnish with the fried onion and rose petals. Serve with naan bread or boiled basmati rice, if you like.

MASALA CHANNA

This is a typical Calcutta street food known as ghughni. Plates full of ghughni, with the wholesome taste of chickpeas laced with spices and tamarind juice, are enjoyed with flat breads such as chapatis and parathas.

SERVES 4

225g/8oz/1¼ cups dried chickpeas
50g/2oz tamarind pulp
120ml/4fl oz/½ cup boiling water
45ml/3 tbsp vegetable oil
2.5ml/½ tsp cumin seeds
1 onion, finely chopped
2 garlic cloves, crushed
2.5cm/1in piece fresh root ginger, grated
1 fresh green chilli, finely chopped
5ml/1 tsp ground cumin
5ml/1 tsp ground coriander
1.5ml/¼ tsp ground turmeric
2.5ml/½ tsp salt
225g/8oz tomatoes, skinned and finely chopped
2.5ml/½ tsp garam masala
chopped chillies and chopped onion, to garnish

1 Put the chickpeas in a large bowl and cover with plenty of cold water. Leave to soak overnight.

2 Drain the chickpeas and place in a large pan with double the volume of cold water. Bring to the boil and boil vigorously for 10 minutes. Skim off any scum, then cover and simmer for 1½–2 hours or until soft.

3 Meanwhile, break up the tamarind pulp and soak in the boiling water for about 15 minutes. Use the back of a spoon to rub the tamarind through a sieve (strainer) into a bowl, discarding any stones and fibre. (Leave out this step if you are using commercial tamarind paste in place of the fresh pulp.)

4 Heat the vegetable oil in a wok, karahi or large pan and fry the cumin seeds for 2 minutes until they begin to splutter. Add the chopped onion, garlic, ginger and chilli and fry for 5 minutes.

5 Add the cumin, coriander, turmeric and salt and fry for 3–4 minutes. Add the tomatoes and tamarind juice. Bring to the boil and simmer for 5 minutes.

6 Add the chickpeas and garam masala, cover and simmer for about 15 minutes. Garnish with the chillies and onion.

COOK'S TIP

Make double the quantity of tamarind juice and freeze in ice-cube trays. It will keep for up to 12 months. Alternatively, buy tamarind paste sold in Indian stores. It is ready to use and will keep for an indefinite period at room temperature.

MIXED VEGETABLE CURRY

Curries based on a variety of vegetables are cooked throughout India, but they all differ from one another according to the spicing and the method of cooking. This particular version, made with onion seeds, is a typical example from the east and north-east of the country, where the dish is known as chorchori.

SERVES 4–6

350g/12oz mixed vegetables such as green beans, peas, potatoes, cauliflower, carrots, cabbage, mangetouts (snow peas) and button (white) mushrooms
30ml/2 tbsp vegetable oil
2.5ml/½ tsp mustard seeds
5ml/1 tsp cumin seeds, freshly roasted
2.5ml/½ tsp onion seeds
5ml/1 tsp ground turmeric
2 garlic cloves, crushed
6–8 curry leaves
1 dried red chilli
5ml/1 tsp granulated sugar
150ml/¼ pint/⅔ cup natural (plain) yogurt mixed with 5ml/1 tsp cornflour (cornstarch), well beaten
salt
fresh bay leaves, to garnish

1 Prepare all the vegetables you have chosen: string the beans; cube the potatoes; cut the cauliflower into florets; dice the carrots; shred the cabbage; trim the mangetouts; wash the mushrooms and leave them whole.

2 Heat a large, deep-sided pan with enough water to cook all the vegetables and bring to the boil. First add the potatoes and carrots and cook until nearly tender then add all the other vegetables and cook until nearly tender but still firm. All the vegetables should be only just tender except the potatoes, which should be tender. Drain well.

COOK'S TIP

If you have gram flour (besan), mix this with the yogurt instead of cornflour. It prevents the yogurt from curdling and lends a nutty taste.

3 Heat the oil in a large pan and add the mustard and cumin seeds. As they pop, add the remaining spices and fry gently until the garlic is golden and the chilli nearly burnt. Reduce the heat.

4 Fold in the drained vegetables, add the sugar and salt and gradually add the yogurt mixed with the cornflour. Heat through and serve immediately, garnished with fresh bay leaves.

CRISP FRIED AUBERGINE

The vegetarian community in Bengal would happily eat begun bhaja, *fried aubergine, and a lentil dish with rice for a main meal. Choose the large variety of aubergine with an unblemished, glossy skin. There is no need to soak the aubergine in salted water as today's aubergines generally have less bitterness in the skin than they used to.*

SERVES 4

50g/2oz/½ cup gram flour (besan)
15ml/1tbsp semolina or ground rice
2.5ml/½ tsp onion seeds
5ml/1 tsp cumin seeds
2.5ml/½ tsp fennel seeds or aniseeds
2.5–5ml/½–1 tsp hot chilli powder
2.5ml/½ tsp salt, or to taste
1 large aubergine (eggplant)
vegetable oil, for deep-frying

COOK'S TIP

Fennel and aniseeds aid digestion, and most deep-fried Indian recipes use them.

1 Sieve the gram flour into a large mixing bowl and add the remaining ingredients except the aubergine and the vegetable oil.

2 Halve the aubergine lengthwise and cut each half into 5mm/¼in thick slices. Rinse them and shake off the excess water, but do not pat dry. With some of the water still clinging to the slices, add them to the spiced gram flour mixture. Toss them around until they are evenly coated with the flour. Use a spoon if necessary to ensure that all the flour is incorporated.

3 Heat the oil in a deep-fat fryer or other suitable pan over a medium-high heat. If you have a thermometer, check that the oil has reached 190°C/375°F. Alternatively, drop a small piece of day-old bread into the oil. If it floats immediately, then the oil has reached the right temperature.

4 Fry the spice-coated aubergine slices in a single layer. Avoid overcrowding the pan as this will lower the oil temperature, resulting in a soggy texture. Fry until the aubergines are crisp and well browned. Drain on kitchen paper and serve with a chutney.

SWEET-and-SOUR PINEAPPLE

This may sound like a Chinese recipe, but it is a traditional Bengali dish known as tok. The predominant flavour is ginger, and the pieces of golden pineapple, dotted with plump, juicy raisins have plenty of visual appeal with a taste to match. It is equally delicious if made with mangoes instead of the pineapple. Serve as a side dish or digestive.

SERVES 4

800g/1¾lb pineapple rings or chunks in natural juice
15ml/1 tbsp vegetable oil
2.5ml/½ tsp black mustard seeds
2.5ml/½ tsp cumin seeds
2.5ml/½ tsp onion seeds
10ml/2 tsp grated fresh root ginger
5ml/1 tsp crushed dried chillies
50g/2oz/⅓ cup seedless raisins
125g/4oz/⅔ cup granulated sugar
7.5ml/1½ tsp salt

1 Drain the pineapple in a sieve (strainer) and reserve the juice. Chop the pineapple rings or chunks finely (you should have approximately 500g/1¼lb).

2 Heat the vegetable oil in a wok, karahi or large pan over a medium heat and immediately add the mustard seeds. As soon as they pop, add the cumin seeds, then the onion seeds. Add the ginger and chillies and stir-fry the spices briskly for 30 seconds until they release their flavours.

3 Add the pineapple, raisins, sugar and salt. Add 300 ml/½ pint/1¼ cups of the juice (make up with cold water if necessary) and add to the pineapple.

VARIATION

Two or three mangoes can be used for this dish instead of the pineapple, if you prefer. Choose ripe fruits that will be full of flavour. To prepare, cut off both sides of the fruit, keeping close to the stone, then peel off the skin and chop the flesh into chunks. Canned mangoes in natural juice could also be used.

4 Bring the mixture to the boil, reduce the heat to medium and cook, uncovered, for 20–25 minutes.

POTATOES with ROASTED POPPY SEEDS

Poppy seeds are used in Indian cooking as thickening agents, and to lend a nutty taste to sauces. It is the creamy white variety of poppy seed that is used here, rather than the ones with a blue-grey hue that are used for baking.

SERVES 4

45ml/3 tbsp white poppy seeds
45–60ml/3–4 tbsp vegetable oil
675g/1½lb potatoes, peeled and cut into 1cm/½in cubes
2.5ml/½ tsp black mustard seeds
2.5ml/½ tsp onion seeds
2.5ml/½ tsp cumin seeds
2.5ml/½ tsp fennel seeds
1–2 dried red chillies, chopped or broken into small pieces
2.5ml/½ tsp ground turmeric
2.5ml/½ tsp salt
150ml/¼ pint/⅔ cup warm water
fresh coriander (cilantro) sprigs, to garnish
pooris and natural (plain) yogurt, to serve

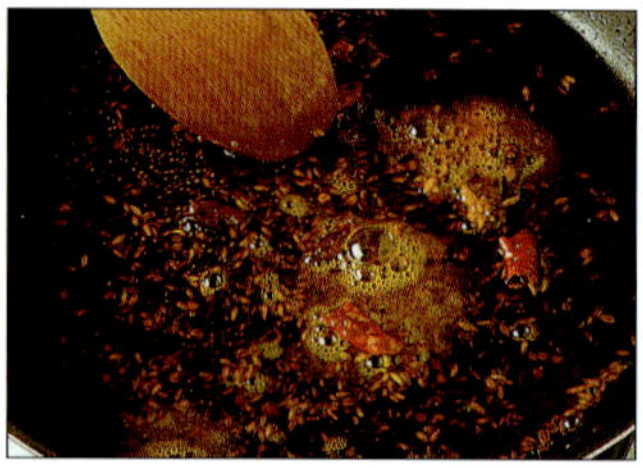

1 Preheat a wok, karahi or large pan over a medium setting. When the pan is hot, reduce the heat slightly and add the poppy seeds. Stir them around in the pan until they are just a shade darker. Remove from the pan and allow to cool.

2 In the pan, heat the vegetable oil over a medium heat and fry the cubes of potatoes until they are light brown. Remove them with a slotted spoon and drain on kitchen paper.

COOK'S TIP

Do not allow the dried chillies to burn or they will become bitter. Remove them from the pan when they have blackened.

3 To the same oil, add the mustard seeds. As soon as they begin to pop, add the onion, cumin and fennel seeds and the chillies. Let the chillies blacken.

4 Stir in the turmeric and follow quickly with the fried potatoes and salt. Stir well and add the warm water. Cover the pan with the lid and reduce the heat to low. Cook for 8–10 minutes, or until the potatoes are tender.

5 Grind the cooled poppy seeds in a pestle and mortar or coffee grinder. Stir the ground seeds into the potatoes. It should form a thick paste which should cling to the potatoes. If there is too much liquid, continue to stir over a medium heat until you have the right consistency. Transfer to a serving dish. Garnish with coriander and serve with pooris and natural yogurt.

COOK'S TIP

As they are ground, poppy seeds release a natural oil, which may prevent the blade of a spice mill or coffee grinder from moving. Scrape away anything that sticks to the blades and start again.

SPINACH with GOLDEN POTATOES

The combination of spinach and potato is generally known as aloo saag *or* saag aloo. *As with most Indian dishes, there are different versions using the same or similar ingredients. This recipe is from Bengal, where it is known as* palong saaker ghonto.

SERVES 4–6

450g/1lb spinach
30ml/2 tbsp vegetable oil
5ml/1 tsp black mustard seeds
1 onion, thinly sliced
2 garlic cloves, crushed
2.5cm/1in piece fresh root ginger, finely chopped
675g/1½lb firm potatoes, cut into 2.5cm/1in chunks
5ml/1 tsp chilli powder
5ml/1 tsp salt
120ml/4fl oz/½ cup water

1 Blanch the spinach in boiling water for 3–4 minutes, then drain in a sieve (strainer) and leave to cool. When it is cool enough to handle, squeeze out any remaining liquid using the back of a wooden spoon or with your hands.

2 Heat the oil in a large pan over a medium heat and fry the mustard seeds until they begin to splutter.

3 Add the sliced onion, crushed garlic and chopped ginger and fry for about 5 minutes, stirring.

4 Stir in the potatoes, chilli powder, salt and water and cook for 8 minutes, stirring occasionally.

VARIATION

For an excellent alternative to spinach, use 450g/1lb spring greens.

5 Add the spinach to the pan. Cover and simmer for 10–15 minutes until the potatoes are tender. Serve.

COOK'S TIP

Enhance the flavour by adding fresh red chillies in step 3. Omit the chilli powder.

CHANA DHAL and BOTTLE GOURD CURRY

Chana dhal, also known as Bengal gram, is a very small type of chickpea grown in India. It has a nutty taste and gives fabulous earthy flavour to the food. Chana dhal is available from good Indian stores. Yellow split peas make a good substitute in terms of appearance and require the same cooking time, but the flavour is not quite the same.

SERVES 4–6

175g/6oz/⅔ cup chana dhal or yellow split peas, washed
450ml/¾ pint/scant 2 cups water
60ml/4 tbsp vegetable oil
2 fresh green chillies, chopped
1 onion, chopped
2 cloves garlic, crushed
5cm/2in piece fresh root ginger, grated
6–8 curry leaves
5ml/1 tsp chilli powder
5ml/1 tsp ground turmeric
450g/1lb bottle gourd or marrow (large zucchini), courgettes (zucchini), squash or pumpkin, peeled, pithed and sliced
60ml/4 tbsp tamarind juice
2 tomatoes, chopped
salt
a handful fresh coriander (cilantro) leaves, chopped

1 In a large pan, cook the chana dhal in the water, seasoned with salt, for about 30 minutes until the chana dhal grains are tender but not mushy. Put aside without draining away any excess water.

2 Heat the oil in a large pan and fry the chillies, onion, garlic, ginger, curry leaves, chilli powder and turmeric and salt until the onions have softened. Add the gourd (or other vegetable) pieces and mix.

3 Add the chana dhal and water and bring to the boil. Add the tamarind juice, tomatoes and coriander. Simmer until the gourd is cooked. Serve hot with a dry meat curry.

COOK'S TIP

If using courgettes (zucchini), add them along with the tamarind juice, tomatoes and coriander in step 3. Courgettes need much less cooking time than the other vegetables in the recipe.

TARKA DHAL

Tarka, also spelt tadka, is a hot oil seasoning that is folded into a dish before serving. In an Indian household, dhal is cooked every day and for most family meals a much simpler version is made. Tarka dhal is commonly found in Bengal, Assam and Bangladesh and it is the combination of spices that gives away its origin.

SERVES 4–6

115g/4oz/½ cup red lentils, washed
50g/2oz/¼ cup chana dhal or yellow split peas, washed
600ml/1 pint/2½ cups water
5ml/1 tsp grated fresh root ginger
5ml/1 tsp crushed garlic
2.5ml/¼ tsp ground turmeric
2 fresh green chillies, chopped
7.5ml/1½ tsp salt

For the tarka
30ml/2 tbsp vegetable oil
1 onion, sliced
2.5ml/¼ tsp mixed mustard and onion seeds
4 dried red chillies
1 tomato, sliced

To garnish
15ml/1 tbsp chopped fresh coriander (cilantro), 1–2 fresh green chillies, seeded and sliced, 15ml/1 tbsp chopped mint

1 Pick over the washed chana dhal or lentils for any stones, then place in a large pan and boil in the water with the ginger, garlic, turmeric and chopped green chillies for 15–20 minutes or until the lentils are until soft.

2 Mash the lentils with the back of a spoon until they are of the same consistency as chicken soup. If the mixture looks too dry, add a little more water.

3 To prepare the tarka, heat the oil in another pan and fry the onion with the mustard and onion seeds, dried red chillies and sliced tomato for 2 minutes.

4 Pour the tarka over the dhal in the frying pan and garnish with the chopped fresh coriander, fresh green chillies and chopped mint. Serve.

SOUTH INDIA

The food in the southern states is light and refreshing, with plenty of fish and shellfish; it is also fiery, with much use being made of the chillies that are grown throughout the region. In south India, coconut milk is used to enrich sauces in place of the dairy cream and nuts used in the north.

MUGHLAI-STYLE CHICKEN

The cuisine of Andhra Pradesh is renowned for its pungency because the hottest variety of chilli is grown there. In sharp contrast, however, the region is also home to the subtle flavours of a style of cooking known as nizami, *which has a distinct Mogul influence. This recipe, with the heady aroma of saffron and the captivating flavour of a silky almond and cream sauce, is a typical example.*

SERVES 4–6

4 chicken breast fillets, rubbed with a little garam masala
2 eggs, beaten with salt and pepper
90ml/6 tbsp ghee or vegetable oil
1 large onion, finely chopped
5cm/2in piece fresh root ginger, finely crushed
4 garlic cloves, finely crushed
4 cloves
4 green cardamom pods
5cm/2in piece cinnamon stick
2 bay leaves
15–20 saffron threads
150ml/¼ pint/⅔ cup natural (plain) yogurt, beaten with 5ml/1 tsp cornflour (cornstarch)
75ml/5 tbsp/⅓ cup double (heavy) cream
50g/2oz ground almonds
salt

1 Brush the chicken fillets with the beaten eggs. In a wok, karahi or large pan, heat the ghee or vegetable oil and fry the chicken until cooked through and browned on both sides. Remove the chicken from the pan and keep warm.

2 In the same pan, fry the chopped onion, ginger, garlic, cloves, cardamom pods, cinnamon and bay leaves. When the onion turns golden, remove the pan from the heat, allow the contents to cool a little and add the saffron and natural yogurt. Mix well to prevent the yogurt from curdling.

3 Return the chicken to the pan, along with any juices, and gently cook until the chicken is tender. Adjust the seasoning if necessary.

4 Just before serving, fold in the double cream and ground almonds. Make sure the curry is piping hot before serving. Tricolour Pulao goes well with this dish.

CHICKEN MADRAS

Madras, one of India's largest cities, is the capital of Tamil Nadu. The city is generally regarded as the heartland of southern Indian cuisine. It is surrounded by long stretches of beautiful beaches, shared between the Bay of Bengal to the east and the Indian Ocean to the south. The food is mainly vegetarian, but the small Muslim and Christian communities have a wonderful range of meat- and poultry-based dishes, such as this one.

SERVES 4

450g/1lb chicken breast fillets, skinned
45ml/3 tbsp tomato purée (paste)
large pinch ground fenugreek
1.5ml/¼ tsp ground fennel seeds
5ml/1 tsp grated fresh root ginger
7.5ml/1½ tsp ground coriander
5ml/1 tsp crushed garlic
5ml/1 tsp chilli powder
1.5ml/¼ tsp ground turmeric
30ml/2 tbsp lemon juice
5ml/1 tsp salt
300ml/½ pint/1¼ cups water
45ml/3 tbsp vegetable oil
2 onions, diced
2–4 curry leaves
2 fresh green chillies, seeded and chopped
15ml/1 tbsp chopped fresh coriander (cilantro), plus extra sprigs to garnish
naan bread, to serve

1 Cut the chicken breast fillets into cubes. Mix the tomato purée in a bowl with the fenugreek, fennel, ginger, ground coriander, garlic, chilli powder, turmeric, lemon juice, salt and water.

2 Heat the oil in a wok, karahi or large pan and fry the onions with the curry leaves until the onions are golden. Add the chicken and stir for 1 minute to seal.

3 Pour the tomato sauce and spice mixture into the pan. Stir for 2 minutes to ensure the ingredients are well mixed.

4 Lower the heat and cook for 8–10 minutes, then add the chillies and fresh coriander. Garnish and serve.

COOK'S TIP

Take care not to use too much ground fenugreek, as it can be quite bitter.

BEEF with GREEN BEANS

Adding vegetables to meat and poultry dishes has been a long-standing practice in Indian cooking. As well as resulting in some interesting combinations, the technique is a practical one, as the final dish makes a nutritious one-pot meal. Although red pepper is not normally used, it does provide visual appeal as well as enhanced flavour. As an alternative, you could use fresh red chillies. Leaving the chillies whole will provide a wonderful flavour without the pungency, but if you like it hot, slit them first to expose the seeds.

SERVES 4

275g/10oz fine green beans, cut into 2.5cm/1in pieces
45–60ml/3–4 tbsp vegetable oil
1 onion, sliced
5ml/1 tsp grated fresh root ginger
5ml/1 tsp crushed garlic
5ml/1 tsp chilli powder
6.5ml/1¼ tsp ground turmeric
2 tomatoes, chopped
450g/1lb beef, cubed
1.2 litres/2 pints/5 cups water
1 red (bell) pepper, sliced (optional)
15ml/1 tbsp chopped fresh coriander (cilantro)
2 fresh green chillies, chopped
salt

1 Boil the green beans in salted water for about 5 minutes, then drain and set them aside.

2 Heat the oil in a large pan over a medium heat and fry the sliced onion until it turns golden brown (this should take about 7–8 minutes).

COOK'S TIP

You could use lamb or turkey thigh meat instead of beef. If using turkey, reduce the quantity of water by half.

3 Mix together the ginger, crushed garlic, chilli powder, salt, turmeric and chopped tomatoes. Spoon this mixture into the onions in the pan and stir-fry for 5–7 minutes.

4 Add the beef and stir-fry for a further 3 minutes. Pour in the water, bring to the boil and lower the heat. Cover and cook for 45 minutes to 1 hour, until most of the water has evaporated and the meat is tender.

5 Add the green beans to the pan and mix everything together well.

6 Finally, add the red pepper, if using, with the chopped fresh coriander and green chillies and cook, stirring, for a further 7–10 minutes. Serve the curry hot. This dish would go very well with Nut Pulao.

MADRAS BEEF CURRY

Although Madras is renowned for the best vegetarian food in the country, meat-based recipes such as this one are also extremely popular. This particular recipe is a contribution by the area's small Muslim community.

SERVES 4–6

60ml/4 tbsp vegetable oil
1 large onion, finely sliced
3–4 cloves
4 green cardamoms
2 whole star anise
4 fresh green chillies, chopped
2 fresh or dried red chillies, chopped
45ml/3 tbsp Madras masala paste
5ml/1 tsp ground turmeric
450g/1lb lean beef, cubed
60ml/4 tbsp tamarind juice
granulated sugar, to taste
salt
a few fresh coriander (cilantro) leaves, chopped, to garnish

1 Heat the vegetable oil in a wok, karahi or large pan over a medium heat and fry the onion slices for 8–9 minutes until they turn golden brown. Lower the heat, add all the spice ingredients, and fry for a further 2–3 minutes.

2 Add the beef and mix well. Cover and cook on low heat until the beef is tender. Cook uncovered on a higher heat for the last few minutes to reduce any excess liquid.

COOK'S TIP

To tenderize the meat, add 60ml/4 tbsp white wine vinegar in step 2, along with the meat, and omit the tamarind juice.

3 Fold in the tamarind juice, sugar and salt. Reheat the dish and garnish with the chopped coriander leaves. Tricolour Pulao and Tomato and Onion Salad would both make excellent accompaniments to this dish.

CHILLI MEAT with CURRY LEAVES

Curry leaves and chillies are two of the hallmark ingredients used in the southern states of India. This recipe is from the state of Andhra Pradesh, where the hottest chillies, known as Guntur after the region where they are produced, are grown in abundance.

SERVES 4–6

30ml/2 tbsp vegetable oil
1 large onion, finely sliced
5cm/2in piece fresh root ginger, grated
4 garlic cloves, crushed
12 curry leaves
45ml/3 tbsp extra hot curry paste, or
60ml/4 tbsp hot curry powder
15ml/1 tbsp chilli powder
5ml/1 tsp five-spice powder
5ml/1 tsp ground turmeric
900g/2lb lean lamb, beef or pork, cubed
175ml/6fl oz/¾ cup thick coconut milk
salt
red onion, finely sliced, to garnish
Indian bread and Fruit Raita, to serve

1 Heat the oil in a wok, karahi or large, pan, and fry the onion, ginger, garlic and curry leaves until the onion is soft. Add the curry paste or powder, chilli and five-spice powder, turmeric and salt.

2 Add the meat and stir well over a medium heat to seal and evenly brown the meat pieces. Keep stirring until the oil separates. Cover the pan and cook for about 20 minutes.

COOK'S TIP

For extra flavour, reserve half the curry leaves and add in step 3, along with the coconut milk.

3 Stir in the coconut milk and simmer, covered, until the meat is cooked. Towards the end of cooking, uncover the pan to reduce the excess liquid. Garnish and serve with any Indian bread, and with Fruit Raita, for a cooling effect.

LAMB KORMA

Although south Indian food is generally free of foreign influences, the city of Hyderabad in Andhra Pradesh has a rich heritage of Mogul cuisine. It was here that the last of the Mogul emperors retired before finally handing over power to the Nizam dynasty.

SERVES 4–6

15ml/1 tbsp white sesame seeds
15ml/1 tbsp white poppy seeds
50g/2oz/½ cup blanched almonds
2 fresh green chillies, seeded
6 garlic cloves, sliced
5cm/2in piece fresh root ginger, sliced
1 onion, finely chopped
45ml/3 tbsp ghee or vegetable oil
6 green cardamom pods
5cm/2in piece cinnamon stick
4 cloves
900g/2lb lean lamb, boned and cubed
5ml/1 tsp ground cumin
5ml/1 tsp ground coriander
300ml/½ pint/1¼ cups double (heavy) cream mixed with 2.5ml/½ tsp cornflour (cornstarch)
salt
roasted sesame seeds, to garnish

1 Preheat a wok, karahi or large pan over a medium heat without any fat, and add the first seven ingredients. Stir until they begin to change colour. They should go just a shade darker.

2 Allow the mixture to cool, then grind to a fine paste using a pestle and mortar or in a food processor. Heat the ghee or oil in the pan over a low heat.

3 Fry the cardamoms, cinnamon and cloves until the cloves swell. Add the lamb, ground cumin and coriander and the prepared paste, and season with salt, to taste. Increase the heat to medium and stir well. Reduce the heat to low, then cover the pan and cook until the lamb is almost done.

4 Remove from the heat, allow to cool a little and gradually fold in the cream, reserving 5ml/1 tsp to garnish. To serve, gently reheat the lamb, uncovered. Garnish with the sesame seeds and the reserved cream. This korma is very good served with Classic Pulao.

COOK'S TIP

If white poppy seeds are not available, use sunflower seeds instead.

CAULIFLOWER in COCONUT SAUCE

Coconut is used for both sweet and savoury dishes in south Indian cooking. This versatile fruit with its many by-products, including coconut oil, which is widely used as a cooking medium, provides the basis for a huge manufacturing industry all over the southern states.

SERVES 4–6

15ml/1 tbsp gram flour (besan)
120ml/4fl oz/½ cup water
5ml/1 tsp chilli powder
15ml/1 tbsp ground coriander
5ml/1 tsp ground cumin
5ml/1 tsp mustard powder
5ml/1 tsp ground turmeric
60ml/4 tbsp vegetable oil
6–8 curry leaves
5ml/1 tsp cumin seeds
1 cauliflower, broken into florets
175ml/6fl oz/¾ cup thick coconut milk
juice of 2 lemons
salt
lime slices, to garnish

1 Mix the gram flour with a little water to make a smooth paste. Add the chilli, coriander, cumin, mustard, turmeric and salt. Add the remaining water and mix to blend the ingredients.

2 Heat the oil in a wok, karahi or large pan, and fry the curry leaves and the cumin seeds. Add the spice paste and simmer for about 5 minutes. If the sauce is too thick, add a little hot water.

COOK'S TIP

Serve this dish southern-style, with plain rice and Spiced Lentils with Spinach. If you prefer, serve a northern-style meal with parathas and Kashmiri Chicken Curry.

3 Add the cauliflower and coconut milk. Bring to the boil, reduce the heat, cover and cook until the cauliflower is tender but crunchy. Cook longer if you prefer. Add the lemon juice, mix throughly and serve hot, garnished with lime slices.

MARINATED FRIED FISH

Fish and shellfish are a strong feature of the cuisine in the coastal region of southern India. Kerala, in the southernmost tip of the country, produces some of the finest fish and shellfish dishes. These are flavoured with local spices, grown in the fabulous spice plantation that is the pride and joy of the state.

SERVES 4–6

1 small onion, coarsely chopped
4 garlic cloves, crushed
5cm/2in piece fresh root ginger, chopped
5ml/1 tsp ground turmeric
10ml/2 tsp chilli powder
4 red mullets or snappers
vegetable oil, for shallow frying
5ml/1 tsp cumin seeds
3 fresh green chillies, finely sliced
salt
lemon or lime wedges, to serve

COOK'S TIP

To enhance the flavour, add 15ml/1 tbsp chopped fresh coriander (cilantro) leaves to the spice paste in step 1.

1 In a food processor, grind the first five ingredients with salt to a smooth paste. Make several slashes on both sides of the fish and rub them with the paste. Leave to rest for 1 hour. Excess fluid will be released as the salt dissolves, so lightly pat the fish dry with kitchen paper without removing the paste.

2 Heat the oil and fry the cumin seeds and sliced chillies for 1 minute. Add the fish, in batches if necessary, and fry on one side. When the first side is sealed, turn them over very gently to ensure they do not break. Fry until golden brown on both sides, drain and serve hot, with lemon or lime wedges.

MIXED VEGETABLES IN COCONUT SAUCE

A vegetable dish is an essential part of an Indian meal, even for a simple occasion, where one or two vegetable dishes may be served with a lentil dhal, a raita, and bread or boiled rice. There are many ways to make a vegetable curry, but this recipe, in which the vegetables are simmered in coconut milk, is typical of South India.

SERVES 4

225g/8oz potatoes, cut into 5cm/2in cubes
125g/4oz/¾ cup French (green) beans
150g/5oz carrots, scraped and cut into 5cm/2in cubes
500ml/17fl oz/2¼ cups hot water
1 small aubergine (eggplant), about 225g/8oz, quartered lengthwise
75g/3oz coconut milk powder
5ml/1 tsp salt
30ml/2 tbsp vegetable oil
6–8 fresh or 8–10 dried curry leaves
1–2 dried red chillies, chopped into small pieces
5ml/1 tsp ground cumin
5ml/1 tsp ground coriander
2.5ml/½ tsp ground turmeric

1 Put the potatoes, beans and carrots in a large pan and add 300ml/½ pint/1¼ cups of the hot water and bring to the boil. Reduce the heat a little, cover the pan and cook for 5 minutes.

2 Cut the aubergine quarters into 5cm/2in pieces. Rinse. Add to the pan.

3 Blend the coconut milk powder with the remaining hot water and add to the vegetables, with the salt. Bring to a slow simmer, cover and cook for 6–7 minutes.

4 In a small pan heat the oil over a medium heat and add the curry leaves and the chillies. Immediately follow with the cumin, coriander and turmeric. Stir-fry the spices for 15–20 seconds and pour the entire contents of the pan over the vegetables. Stir to distribute the spices evenly and remove from the heat. Serve with any Indian bread.

STUFFED AUBERGINES in SEASONED TAMARIND JUICE

The traditional way of cooking with tamarind is in a terracotta dish, which brings out the full fruity tartness of the tamarind. This spicy aubergine dish will add a refreshing tang to any meal.

SERVES 4

12 baby aubergines (eggplant)
30ml/2 tbsp vegetable oil
1 small onion, chopped
10ml/2 tsp grated fresh root ginger
10ml/2 tsp crushed garlic
5ml/1 tsp coriander seeds
5ml/1 tsp cumin seeds
10ml/2 tsp white poppy seeds
10ml/2 tsp sesame seeds
10ml/2 tsp desiccated (dry, unsweetened, shredded) coconut
15ml/1 tbsp dry-roasted skinned peanuts
2.5–5ml/½–1 tsp chilli powder
5ml/1 tsp salt
6–8 curry leaves
1–2 dried red chillies, chopped
2.5ml/½ tsp concentrated tamarind paste

1 Make three deep slits lengthwise on each aubergine, without cutting through, then soak in salted water for 20 minutes.

2 Heat half the oil in a pan and sautée the onion for 3–4 minutes. Add the ginger and garlic and cook for 30 seconds.

3 Add the coriander and cumin seeds and sautée for 30 seconds, then add the poppy seeds, sesame seeds and coconut. Sautée for 1 minute, stirring constantly. Allow to cool slightly, then grind the spices in a food processor, adding 105ml/7 tbsp warm water. The mixture should resemble a thick, slightly coarse paste.

4 Mix the peanuts, chilli powder and salt into the spice paste. Drain the aubergines and dry on kitchen paper. Stuff each of the slits with the spice paste and reserve any remaining paste.

5 Heat the remaining oil in a wok, karahi or large pan over a medium heat and add the curry leaves and chillies. Let the chillies blacken, then add the aubergines and the tamarind blended with 105ml/7 tbsp hot water. Add any remaining spice paste and stir to mix.

6 Cover the pan and simmer gently for 15–20 minutes or until the aubergines are tender. Serve with chapatis and a meat or poultry dish, if you like.

POTATOES in CHILLI TAMARIND SAUCE

In this favourite potato dish from the state of Karnataka, the combination of chilli and tamarind awakens the taste buds immediately. This version adapts the traditional recipe slightly, to reduce the pungency and enhance the dish's fiery appearance.

SERVES 4–6

450g/1lb small new potatoes, washed and dried
25g/1oz whole dried red chillies, preferably Kashmiri
7.5ml/1½ tsp cumin seeds
4 garlic cloves
90ml/6 tbsp vegetable oil
60ml/4 tbsp thick tamarind juice
30ml/2 tbsp tomato purée (paste)
4 curry leaves
5ml/1 tsp granulated sugar
1.5ml/¼ tsp asafoetida
salt
coriander (cilantro) sprigs and lemon wedges, to garnish

1 Boil the potatoes until they are fully cooked, ensuring they do not break. To test, insert a thin sharp knife into the potatoes. It should come out clean when the potatoes are fully cooked. Drain and cool the potatoes in iced water to prevent further cooking.

2 Soak the chillies for 5 minutes in warm water. Drain and grind with the cumin seeds and garlic to a coarse paste either using a pestle and mortar or in a food processor.

COOK'S TIP

Chunks of sweet potatoes can be used as an alternative to new potatoes.

3 Heat the oil and fry the paste, tamarind juice, tomato purée, curry leaves, salt, sugar and asafoetida until the oil separates from the spice paste. Add the potatoes. Reduce the heat, cover and simmer for 5 minutes. Garnish and serve.

MASALA BEANS with FENUGREEK

The term masala refers to the blending of several spices to achieve a distinctive taste, with different spice-combinations being used to complement specific ingredients. Households will traditionally create their own blends, and many are quite unique.

SERVES 4

1 onion
5ml/1 tsp ground cumin
5ml/1 tsp ground coriander
5ml/1 tsp sesame seeds
5ml/1 tsp chilli powder
2.5ml/½ tsp crushed garlic
1.5ml/¼ tsp ground turmeric
5ml/1 tsp salt
30ml/2 tbsp vegetable oil
1 tomato, quartered
225g/8oz/1½ cups French (green) beans, blanched
1 bunch fresh fenugreek leaves, stems discarded
60ml/4 tbsp chopped fresh coriander (cilantro)
15ml/1 tbsp lemon juice

1 Roughly chop the onion. Mix together the cumin and coriander, sesame seeds, chilli powder, garlic, turmeric and salt.

2 Put the chopped onion and spice mixture into a food processor or blender, and process for 30–45 seconds until you have a rough paste.

3 In a wok, karahi or large pan, heat the oil over a medium heat and fry the spice paste for about 5 minutes, stirring the mixture occasionally.

4 Add the tomato quarters, blanched French beans, fresh fenugreek and chopped coriander.

5 Stir-fry the contents of the pan for about 5 minutes, then sprinkle in the lemon juice and serve.

VARIATION

Instead of fresh fenugreek, you can also use 15ml/1 tbsp dried fenugreek for this recipe. Dried fenugreek is readily available from Indian stores and markets. It may be sold by its Indian name, *kasuri methi*.

CHILLI and MUSTARD FLAVOURED PINEAPPLE

Pineapple is cooked with coconut milk and a blend of spices in this South Indian dish, which could be served with any meat, fish or vegetable curry. The chilli adds heat, and the mustard seeds lend a rich, nutty flavour that complements the sharpness of the pineapple, while the coconut milk provides a delectable creamy sweetness.

SERVES 4

1 pineapple
50ml/2fl oz/¼ cup water
150ml/¼ pint/⅔ cup can coconut milk
2.5ml/½ tsp ground turmeric
2.5ml/½ tsp crushed dried chillies
5ml/1 tsp salt
10ml/2 tsp granulated sugar
15ml/1 tbsp groundnut (peanut) oil
2.5ml/½ tsp mustard seeds
2.5ml/½ tsp cumin seeds
1 small onion, finely chopped
1–2 dried red chillies, broken
6–8 curry leaves

1 Halve the pineapple lengthwise and cut each half into two, so that you end up with four boat-shaped pieces. Peel them and remove the eyes and the central core. Cut into bitesize pieces.

2 Put the pineapple in a wok, karahi or large pan and add the measured water, with the coconut milk, turmeric and crushed chillies. Bring to a slow simmer over a low heat, and cook, covered, for 10–12 minutes, or until the pineapple is soft, but not mushy.

3 Add the salt and sugar, and cook, uncovered, until the sauce thickens.

4 Heat the oil in a second pan, and add the mustard seeds. As soon as they begin to pop, add the cumin seeds and the onion. Fry for 6–7 minutes, stirring regularly, until the onion is soft.

5 Add the chillies and curry leaves. Fry for a further 1–2 minutes and pour the entire contents over the pineapple. Stir well, then remove from the heat. Serve hot or cold, but not chilled.

COOK'S TIP

Use canned pineapple in natural juice to save time. You will need approximately 500g/1¼lb drained pineapple.

LENTILS SEASONED with GARLIC-INFUSED OIL

This recipe, known as sambhar, varies considerably within the southern states. Vegetables are added to the lentils, and this can be a single vegetable or a combination of two or more. It is traditionally served with steamed rice dumplings (idlis) or stuffed rice pancakes (dosai). It is also extremely satisfying with plain boiled rice.

SERVES 4–6

120ml/8 tbsp vegetable oil
2.5ml/½ tsp mustard seeds
2.5ml/½ tsp cumin seeds
2 dried red chillies
1.5ml/¼ tsp asafoetida
6–8 curry leaves
2 garlic cloves, crushed, plus 2 garlic cloves, sliced
30ml/2 tbsp desiccated (dry, unsweetened, shredded) coconut
225g/8oz/1 cup red lentils, picked over, washed and drained
10ml/2 tsp sambhar masala
2.5ml/½ tsp ground turmeric
450ml/¾ pint/scant 2 cups water
450g/1lb mixed vegetables, such as okra, courgettes (zucchini), aubergine (eggplant) cauliflower, shallots and (bell) peppers
60ml/4 tbsp tamarind juice
4 firm tomatoes, quartered
a few coriander (cilantro) leaves, chopped

1 Heat half the oil in a wok, karahi or large pan, and stir-fry the next seven ingredients until the coconut begins to brown. Stir in the prepared red lentils, sambhar masala and turmeric. Stir-fry for 2–3 minutes and add the water. Bring it to the boil and reduce the heat to low.

2 Cover the pan and leave to simmer for 25–30 minutes, until the lentils are mushy. Add the mixed vegetables, tamarind juice and tomato quarters. Cook until the vegetables are just tender.

3 Heat the remaining oil in a small pan over a low heat, and fry the garlic slices until golden. Stir in the coriander leaves, then pour over the lentils and vegetables. Mix at the table before serving.

COOK'S TIP

Red lentils are used in this recipe, but the traditional choice would be yellow split lentils, known as toor dhal or tuvar dhal, which are available from Indian stores.

STUFFED BANANAS

Bananas are cooked with spices in many different ways in southern India. Some recipes contain large quantities of chillies, but the taste is skilfully mellowed by adding coconut milk and tamarind juice. Green bananas are available from Indian stores, or you can use plantains or unripe eating bananas that are firm to the touch.

SERVES 4

4 green bananas or plantains
30ml/2 tbsp ground coriander
15ml/1 tbsp ground cumin
5ml/1 tsp chilli powder
2.5ml/½ tsp salt
1.5ml/¼ tsp ground turmeric
5ml/1 tsp granulated sugar
15ml/1 tbsp gram flour (besan)
45ml/3 tbsp chopped fresh coriander (cilantro), plus extra sprigs to garnish
90ml/6 tbsp vegetable oil
1.5ml/¼ tsp cumin seeds
1.5ml/¼ tsp black mustard seeds

1 Trim the bananas or plantains and cut each crossways into three equal pieces, leaving the skin on. Make a lengthwise slit along each piece of banana, without cutting all the way through the flesh.

2 On a plate mix together the ground coriander, cumin, chilli powder, salt, turmeric, sugar, gram flour, chopped fresh coriander and 15ml/1 tbsp of the oil. Use your fingers to combine well.

3 Carefully stuff each piece of banana with the spice mixture, taking care not to break the bananas in half.

4 Heat the remaining oil in a wok, karahi or large pan, and fry the cumin and mustard seeds for 2 minutes or until they begin to splutter. Add the bananas and toss gently in the oil. Cover and simmer over a low heat for 15 minutes, stirring from time to time, until the bananas are soft but not mushy.

5 Garnish with the fresh coriander sprigs, and serve with warm chapatis, if you like. Other good accompaniments include Prawn Biryani and Spiced Yogurt.

COOK'S TIP

Baby courgettes (zucchini) would make a delicious alternative to bananas.

SPICED LENTILS with SPINACH

Spinach cooked with chana dhal *lentils makes a wholesome, healthy dish. It is perfect for a vegetarian diet, as it provides protein, vitamins and minerals in one dish. Serve it with naan bread, chapatis or plain boiled rice to make a satisfying main course. A salad or a chutney will add an extra special zest to the meal.*

SERVES 4

175g/6oz/¾ cup chana dhal or yellow split peas
175ml/6fl oz/¾ cup water
30ml/2 tbsp vegetable oil
1.5ml/¼ tsp black mustard seeds
1 onion, thinly sliced
2 garlic cloves, crushed
2.5cm/1in piece fresh root ginger, grated
1 red chilli, finely chopped
275g/10oz frozen spinach, thawed
1.5ml/¼ tsp chilli powder
2.5ml/½ tsp ground coriander
2.5ml/½ tsp garam masala
2.5ml/½ tsp salt

1 Wash the chana dhal or split peas in several changes of cold water. Put the dhal or peas into a large bowl and cover with plenty of cold water. Leave to soak for about 30 minutes.

2 Drain the chana dhal or split peas and put in a large pan with the water. Bring to the boil, cover, and simmer for about 20–25 minutes until the dhal are soft. Cook, uncovered, until the cooking liquid has evaporated completely.

3 Heat the oil in a wok, karahi or large pan and fry the mustard seeds for about 2 minutes until they begin to splutter. Add the onion, garlic, ginger and chilli and fry for 5–6 minutes, then add the spinach and cook for 10 minutes or until the spinach is dry and the liquid is absorbed. Stir in the remaining spices and salt and cook for 2–3 minutes.

4 Add the chana dhal or split peas to the spinach in the pan and cook, stirring, for about 5 minutes. Serve hot with warm naan bread, or with plain boiled rice, if you like.

COOK'S TIP

Use canned chickpeas in place of chana dhal for a quick alternative. Drain, rinse in water, drain again, and add in step 4.

WEST INDIA

The western states of Gujarat and Maharashtra have developed an excellent repertoire of vegetarian dishes, using fresh vegetables, dairy products and lentils and peas. Goa, to the south of Bombay, shows Portuguese influences; its most famous culinary export is vindaloo.

GOAN CHICKEN CURRY

Lines of swaying palm trees and the raised borders of a vast patchwork of paddy fields are just two of the features that constitute the superb landscape of Goa. Not surprisingly, coconut, in all of its forms, is widely used to enrich Goan cuisine.

SERVES 4

75g/3oz/1½ cups desiccated (dry, unsweetened, shredded) coconut
30ml/2 tbsp vegetable oil
2.5ml/½ tsp cumin seeds
4 black peppercorns
15ml/1 tbsp fennel seeds
15ml/1 tbsp coriander seeds
2 onions, finely chopped
2.5ml/½ tsp salt
8 small chicken pieces, such as thighs and drumsticks, skinned
fresh coriander (cilantro) sprigs and lemon wedges, to garnish

1 Put the desiccated coconut in a bowl with 45ml/3 tbsp water. Leave to soak for 15 minutes.

2 Heat 15ml/1 tbsp of the oil in a wok, karahi or large pan and fry the cumin seeds, peppercorns, fennel and coriander seeds over a low heat for 3–4 minutes until they begin to splutter.

COOK'S TIP

If you prefer, make the spiced coconut mixture the day before and chill it in the refrigerator, then continue from step 6 when required.

3 Add the finely chopped onions and fry for about 5 minutes, stirring occasionally, until the onion has softened and turned opaque.

4 Stir in the coconut, along with the soaking water and salt, and continue to fry for a further 5 minutes, stirring occasionally to prevent the mixture from sticking to the pan.

5 Put the coconut mixture into a food processor or blender and process to form a coarse paste. Spoon into a bowl and set aside until required.

6 Heat the remaining oil and fry the chicken for 10 minutes. Add the coconut paste and cook over a low heat for 15–20 minutes, or until the coconut mixture is golden brown and the chicken is tender.

7 Transfer the curry to a warmed serving plate, and garnish with sprigs of fresh coriander and lemon wedges. Mint and Coconut Chutney, plain boiled rice or a lentil dish would all make good accompaniments to this recipe.

CHICKEN with GREEN MANGO

Green or unripe mango is meant only for cooking purposes. These fruits are smaller than eating mangoes, and they have a sharper taste. They can be bought from Indian stores and markets, but if not available, cooking apples make an easy alternative.

SERVES 4

1 green (unripe) mango or cooking apple
450g/1lb chicken breast fillets, skinned and cubed
1.5ml/¼ tsp onion seeds
5ml/1 tsp grated fresh root ginger
2.5ml/½ tsp crushed garlic
5ml/1 tsp chilli powder
1.5ml/¼ tsp ground turmeric
5ml/1 tsp salt
5ml/1 tsp ground coriander
30ml/2 tbsp vegetable oil
2 onions, sliced
4 curry leaves
300ml/½ pint/1¼ cups water
2 tomatoes, quartered
2 fresh green chillies, chopped
30ml/2 tbsp chopped fresh coriander (cilantro)

1 To prepare the mango, peel the skin and slice the flesh thickly. Discard the stone (pit) from the middle. Place the mango slices in a bowl, cover and set aside. If using apple, coat the slices with lemon juice to prevent discoloration.

2 Put the cubed chicken into a large mixing bowl and add the onion seeds, ginger, garlic, chilli powder, turmeric, salt and ground coriander. Mix the spices with the chicken, then stir in half the mango or apple slices.

3 Heat the oil in a wok, karahi or large pan over a medium heat, and fry the sliced onions until golden brown. Add the curry leaves to the pan, and stir very gently to release their flavour.

4 Gradually add the chicken to the pan, stirring all the time. Stir-fry briskly over a medium heat until the chicken is opaque.

5 Pour in the water, lower the heat and cook for 12–15 minutes, stirring, until the chicken is cooked through and the water has been completely absorbed.

6 Add the remaining mango or apple slices, the tomatoes, green chillies and fresh coriander. Plain boiled rice and Stuffed Okra are good accompaniments to serve with this dish.

VARIATION

Try fillets of rabbit for an unusual treat.

SAMOSAS

The origin of samosas can be attributed to the western states of Maharashtra and Gujarat, which are famous for these fabulous crispy pastries with spiced vegetable fillings. The original samosa is vegetarian, but meat fillings are also used, especially in northern India. In this recipe, ready-made spring roll pastry is used as a quick alternative.

MAKES 30

1 packet spring roll pastry, thawed and wrapped in a damp towel
vegetable oil, for deep-frying
Fresh Coriander Chutney, to serve

For the filling
3 large potatoes, boiled and mashed
75g/3oz/¾ cup frozen peas, thawed and cooked
50g/2oz/⅓ cup canned sweetcorn, drained
5ml/1 tsp ground coriander
5ml/1 tsp ground cumin
5ml/1 tsp amchur (dry mango powder)
1 small red onion, finely chopped
2 fresh green chillies, finely chopped
30ml/2 tbsp each fresh coriander (cilantro) and mint leaves, chopped
juice of 1 lemon
salt

1 Toss all the filling ingredients together in a large mixing bowl until well blended. Adjust the seasoning with salt and lemon juice, if necessary.

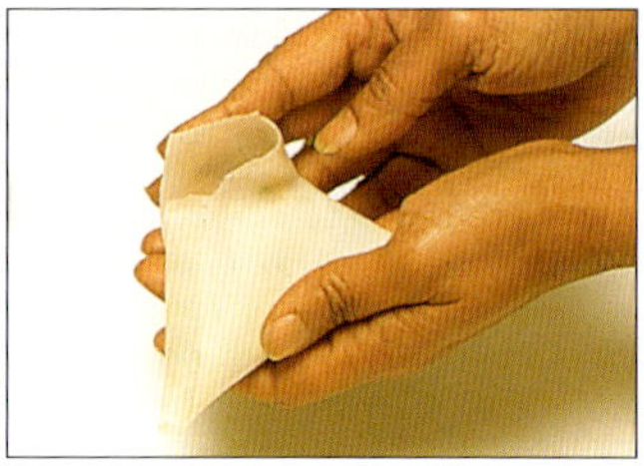

2 Working with one strip of pastry at a time, place 15ml/1 tbsp of the filling mixture at one end of the strip and diagonally fold the pastry to form a triangle. Repeat with the other strips.

3 Heat enough oil for deep-frying and fry the samosas in small batches until they are golden brown. Serve hot. Fresh Coriander Chutney or a chilli sauce are ideal for dipping.

COOK'S TIP
Filo pastry is an excellent alternative. Brush the filo samosas with oil and bake in a preheated hot oven for 25 minutes.

BEEF VINDALOO

Vindaloo is Goa's most famous export, but its origins are in fact Portuguese. In the 16th century, when Portuguese traders embarked on their long voyage to India, they carried pork, preserved in vinegar, garlic and black pepper. The word vin *comes from vinegar and* aloo *is derived from* alho, *the Portuguese word for garlic.*

SERVES 4

15ml/1 tbsp cumin seeds
4 dried red chillies
5ml/1 tsp black peppercorns
5 green cardamom pods, seeds only
5ml/1 tsp fenugreek seeds
5ml/1 tsp black mustard seeds
2.5ml/½ tsp salt
2.5ml/½ tsp demerara (raw) sugar
60ml/4 tbsp white wine vinegar
60ml/4 tbsp vegetable oil
1 large onion, finely chopped
900g/2lb stewing beef, cut into 2.5cm/1in cubes
2.5cm/1in piece fresh root ginger, shredded
1 garlic clove, crushed
10ml/2 tsp ground coriander
2.5ml/½ tsp ground turmeric
plain and yellow rice, to serve

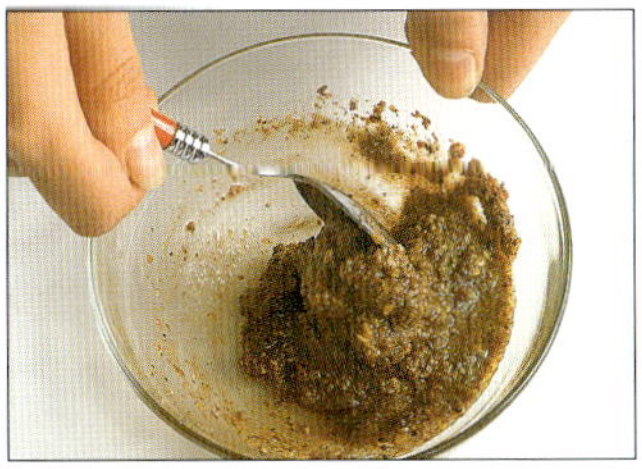

1 Use a pestle and mortar to grind the cumin seeds, chillies, peppercorns, cardamom seeds, fenugreek seeds and mustard seeds to a fine powder. Add the salt, sugar and white wine vinegar and mix to a thin paste.

2 Heat 30ml/2 tbsp of the oil and fry the onion over a medium heat for 8–10 minutes. Put the onion and the spice mixture into a food processor or blender and process to a coarse paste.

VARIATION

Pork tenderloin or leg is the traditional meat for vindaloo. If using leg, remove the crackling and trim off all visible fat.

3 Heat the remaining oil in the pan and fry the meat cubes over a medium heat for 10 minutes or until lightly browned. Remove the beef cubes with a slotted spoon and set aside.

4 Add the shredded ginger and crushed garlic to the pan and fry for 2 minutes. Stir in the coriander and turmeric and fry for 2 minutes more.

COOK'S TIP

To make plain and yellow rice, infuse (steep) a pinch of saffron threads or dissolve a little turmeric in 15ml/1 tbsp hot water in a small bowl. Stir into half the cooked rice until it is uniformly yellow. Carefully mix the yellow rice into the plain rice.

5 Add the spice and onion paste and fry for about 5 minutes.

6 Return the meat to the pan, together with 300ml/½ pint/1¼ cups water. Cover and simmer for 1–1½ hours or until the meat is tender. Serve with plain and yellow rice, and a raita, if you like.

DHANSAK

About 13 centuries ago, a small group of Persians fled their country to avoid religious persecution and landed in the state of Gujarat. They became known as Parsis and they adopted Gujarati as their language; they developed a Parsi version, which is slightly different from the local form. In native Gujarati, dhan *means wealth, but in Parsi Gujarati, it means rice and* sak *is vegetables. A serving of dhansak is not complete without caramelized basmati rice, the traditional accompaniment.*

SERVES 4–6

90ml/6 tbsp vegetable oil
5 fresh green chillies, chopped
2.5cm/1in piece fresh root ginger, grated
3 garlic cloves, crushed, plus 1 garlic clove, sliced
2 bay leaves
5cm/2in piece cinnamon stick
900g/2lb lean lamb, cut into large pieces
600ml/1 pint/2½ cups water
175g/6oz/¾ cup red whole lentils, washed and drained
50g/2oz/¼ cup each chana dhal or yellow split peas, husked moong dhal and red lentils, washed and drained
2 potatoes, cut and soaked in water
1 aubergine (eggplant), cut and soaked in water
4 onions, finely sliced, deep-fried and drained
50g/2oz fresh spinach, trimmed, washed and chopped, or 50g/2oz frozen spinach, thawed
25g/1oz fenugreek leaves, fresh or dried
115g/4oz carrots, or pumpkin if in season
115g/4oz fresh coriander (cilantro), chopped
50g/2oz fresh mint, chopped, or 15ml/1 tbsp mint sauce
30ml/2 tbsp dhansak masala
30ml/2 tbsp sambhar masala
10ml/2 tsp soft brown sugar
60ml/4 tbsp tamarind juice
salt

VARIATION

Pumpkin is the traditional vegetable used for dhansak. It also helps to tenderize the meat, and will add a fabulous rich golden colour to the dish.

COOK'S TIP

All lentils require gentle cooking over a low to medium heat. They will not soften at high temperatures.

1 Heat 45ml/3 tbsp of the oil in a wok, karahi or large pan, and gently fry the fresh chillies, ginger, crushed garlic, bay leaves and cinnamon for 2 minutes. Add the lamb pieces and the measured water. Bring to the boil then simmer, covered, until the lamb is half cooked.

2 Drain the meat stock into another pan and put the lamb aside. Add the lentils to the stock and cook gently for 25–30 minutes until they are tender. Mash the lentils with the back of a spoon.

3 Drain the potatoes and aubergine and add to the lentils. Reserve a little of the deep-fried onions and stir the remainder into the pan, along with the spinach, fenugreek and carrot or pumpkin.

4 Add some hot water to the pan if the mixture seems too thick. Cook until the vegetables are tender, then mash again with a spoon, keeping the vegetables a little coarse.

5 Heat 15ml/1 tbsp of the vegetable oil in a large frying pan. Reserve a few coriander and mint leaves to use as a garnish, and gently fry the remaining leaves with the dhansak and sambhar masala, salt and sugar. Add the lamb pieces and fry gently for 5 minutes.

6 Add the lamb and spices to the lentils and stir. As lentils absorb fluids, adjust the consistency if necessary. Cover, reduce the heat and cook until the lamb is tender. Mix in the tamarind juice.

7 Heat the remaining vegetable oil in a small pan and fry the sliced garlic clove until golden brown.

8 Sprinkle the fried garlic slices over the dhansak. Garnish with the remaining deep-fried onion and the reserved fresh coriander and mint leaves. Serve the dish hot, with Caramelized Basmati Rice if you like.

PORK BALCHAO

Pork and beef dishes are not very common in India, but Goa, on the west coast of the country, has a cuisine that has been influenced by three religions: Hinduism, Islam and Christianity. Goa was colonized by the Portuguese for nearly four centuries and during this time a Jesuit father, Francis Xavier, brought about a calming influence between the religions. The region became known for its religious tolerance, and this is one tradition that has not faded with the passing of time.

SERVES 4

60ml/4 tbsp vegetable oil
15ml/1 tbsp grated fresh root ginger
15ml/1 tbsp crushed garlic
2.5cm/1in piece cinnamon stick, broken up
2–4 dried red chillies, chopped or torn
4 cloves
10ml/2 tsp cumin seeds
10 black peppercorns
675g/1½ lb cubed leg of pork, crackling and visible fat removed
5ml/1 tsp ground turmeric
200ml/7fl oz/scant 1 cup warm water
25ml/1½ tbsp tomato purée (paste)
2.5ml/½ tsp chilli powder (optional)
1 large onion, finely sliced
5ml/1 tsp salt
5ml/1 tsp granulated sugar
10ml/2 tbsp cider vinegar

1 Heat 30ml/2 tbsp of the oil in a wok, karahi or large pan, and add the ginger and garlic. Fry for 30 seconds.

2 Grind the next five ingredients to a fine powder, using a spice mill or coffee grinder. Add the spice mix to the pan and fry for a further 30 seconds, stirring.

3 Add the pork and turmeric and increase the heat slightly. Fry for 5–6 minutes or until the meat starts to release its juices, stirring regularly.

4 Add the water, tomato purée, chilli powder, if using, and bring to the boil. Cover the pan and simmer gently for 35–40 minutes.

5 Heat the remaining oil and fry the onion for 8–9 minutes until browned, stirring regularly.

6 Add the fried onion to the pork along with the salt, sugar and vinegar. Stir, cover and simmer for 30–35 minutes or until the pork is tender. Remove from the heat and serve.

COOKS TIP

Balchao will keep well in the refrigerator for up to 7 days. Before reheating, bring to room temperature. Add a little warm water during reheating, if necessary.

GOAN PRAWN CURRY

The cuisine of Goa is well known for its excellent range of fish and shellfish-based recipes, such as this one for prawns. Numerous varieties of fish and shellfish are found along the extended coastline and the network of inland waterways.

SERVES 4

- 15g/½oz/1 tbsp ghee or butter
- 2 garlic cloves, crushed
- 450g/1lb small raw prawns (shrimp), peeled and deveined
- 15ml/1 tbsp groundnut (peanut) oil
- 4 cardamom pods
- 4 cloves
- 5cm/2in piece cinnamon stick
- 15ml/1 tbsp mustard seeds
- 1 large onion, finely chopped
- ½–1 fresh red chilli, seeded and sliced
- 4 tomatoes, peeled, seeded and chopped
- 175ml/6fl oz/¾ cup fish stock or water
- 350ml/12fl oz/1½ cups coconut milk
- 45ml/3 tbsp Fragrant Spice Mix (see Cook's Tip)
- 10–20ml/2–4 tsp chilli powder
- salt
- turmeric-coloured basmati rice, to serve

1 Melt the ghee or butter in a wok, karahi or large pan, add the garlic and stir over a low heat for a few seconds. Add the prawns and stir-fry briskly to coat. Transfer to a plate and set aside.

VARIATION

For a reduced fat version, use the same quantity of semi-skimmed (low-fat) milk instead of the coconut milk.

2 In the same pan, heat the oil and fry the cardamom, cloves and cinnamon for 2 minutes. Add the mustard seeds and fry for 1 minute. Add the onion and chilli and fry for 7–8 minutes or until softened and lightly browned.

3 Add the remaining ingredients and bring to a slow simmer. Cook gently for 6–8 minutes and add the prawns. Simmer for 5–8 minutes until the prawns are cooked through. Serve the curry with turmeric-coloured basmati rice.

COOK'S TIP

To make a Fragrant Spice Mix, dry-fry 25ml/1½ tbsp coriander seeds, 15ml/1 tbsp mixed peppercorns, 5ml/1 tsp cumin seeds, 1.5ml/¼ tsp fenugreek seeds and 1.5ml/¼ tsp fennel seeds until aromatic, then grind finely in a spice mill.

PARSI PRAWN CURRY

After landing on the west coast of India, the Parsi community migrated to different parts of the country. The majority, however, made Bombay their home. They have cleverly integrated their cooking style into the exotic tastes of Indian cuisine, as this curry shows.

SERVES 4–6

60ml/4 tbsp vegetable oil
1 onion, finely sliced, plus 2 onions, finely chopped
6 garlic cloves, crushed
5ml/1 tsp chilli powder
7.5ml/1½ tsp ground turmeric
50ml/2fl oz/¼ cup tamarind juice
5ml/1 tsp mint sauce
15ml/1 tbsp demerara (raw) sugar
450g/1lb raw king prawns (jumbo shrimp)
75g/3oz coriander (cilantro) leaves, chopped, plus extra leaves to garnish
salt

1 Heat the oil and fry the sliced onion. In a bowl, mix the garlic, chilli powder and turmeric with water to form a paste. Add to the onion and cook.

2 Add the chopped onions to the other ingredients in the pan and fry gently until the chopped onions become translucent, then fold in the tamarind juice, mint sauce, sugar and salt. Simmer for a further 3 minutes.

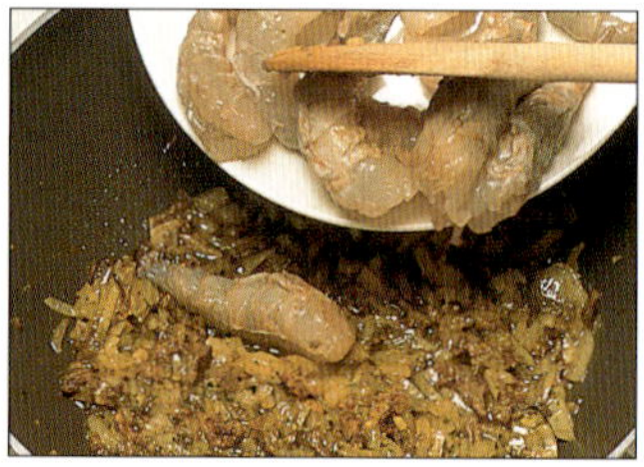

3 Carefully peel and devein the king prawns, then pat them dry with kitchen paper. Add the prawns to the spice mixture with a small amount of water and stir-fry until the prawns turn bright orange/pink.

4 When the prawns are cooked, add the coriander leaves and stir-fry on a high heat to thicken the sauce. Garnish with extra coriander leaves and serve.

FISH CAKES

Goan fish and shellfish are skilfully prepared with spices to make cakes of all shapes and sizes, while the rest of India makes fish kababs. Although haddock is used in this recipe, you can use other less expensive white fish, such as coley or whiting.

MAKES 20

450g/1lb skinned haddock or cod
2 potatoes, peeled, boiled and coarsely mashed
4 spring onions (scallions), finely chopped
4 fresh green chillies, finely chopped
5cm/2in piece fresh root ginger, crushed
a few coriander (cilantro) and mint sprigs, chopped
2 eggs
breadcrumbs, for coating
vegetable oil, for shallow frying
salt and ground black pepper
lemon wedges and chilli sauce, to serve

1 Place the skinned fish in a lightly greased steamer and steam gently until cooked. Remove the steamer from the hob (stovetop) but leave the fish on the steaming tray until cool.

2 When the fish is cool, crumble it coarsely into a large bowl, using a fork. Mix in the mashed potatoes, spring onions, chillies, crushed ginger, chopped coriander and mint, and one of the eggs. Season to taste with salt and pepper.

COOK'S TIP

For a quick version, used canned tuna in brine and omit step 1. Make sure the tuna is thoroughly drained before use.

3 Shape into cakes. Beat the remaining egg and dip the cakes in it, then coat with the breadcrumbs. Heat the oil and fry the cakes until brown on all sides. Serve as an appetizer or as a side dish, with the lemon wedges and chilli sauce.

SPICY OMELETTE

Another popular contribution by the Parsis, this irresistible omelette is known as poro *in their language. Parsi food originated along the shores of the Caspian Sea, and the cuisine offers some unique flavours, which appeal to both Eastern and Western palates.*

SERVES 4–6

30ml/2 tbsp vegetable oil
1 onion, finely chopped
2.5ml/½ tsp ground cumin
1 garlic clove, crushed
1 or 2 fresh green chillies, finely chopped
a few coriander (cilantro) sprigs, chopped, plus extra, to garnish
1 firm tomato, chopped
1 small potato, cubed and boiled
25g/1oz/¼ cup cooked peas
25g/1oz/¼ cup cooked sweetcorn, or canned sweetcorn, drained
2 eggs, beaten
25g/1oz/¼ cup grated cheese
salt and ground black pepper

1 Heat the vegetable oil in a wok, karahi or large pan, and fry the next nine ingredients until they are well blended but the potato and tomato are still firm. Season to taste with salt and ground black pepper.

2 Increase the heat and pour in the beaten eggs. Reduce the heat, cover and cook until the bottom layer is brown. Turn the omelette over and sprinkle with the grated cheese. Place under a hot grill (broiler) and cook until the egg sets and the cheese has melted.

3 Garnish the omelette with sprigs of coriander and serve with salad for a light lunch. If you prefer, serve it for breakfast, in the typical Parsi style.

VARIATION

You can use any vegetable with the potatoes. Try thickly sliced button (white) mushrooms, added in step 1.

EGGS BAKED on CHIPSTICKS

This is an unusual and delicious way of combining eggs with potato sticks, and is known as sali pur eeda *in the Parsi language. The potato sticks are cooked with spices to form a pancake. Eggs are then placed on top of the potato pancake and gently cooked.*

SERVES 4–6

225g/8oz salted chipsticks
2 fresh green chillies, finely chopped
a few coriander (cilantro) sprigs, chopped
1.5ml/¼ tsp ground turmeric
60ml/4 tbsp vegetable oil
75ml/5 tbsp water
6 eggs
3 spring onions (scallions), finely chopped
salt and ground black pepper

1 In a bowl, mix the salted chipsticks, chopped chillies, coriander and turmeric. Heat 30ml/2 tbsp of the oil in a heavy frying pan. Add the chipstick mixture and water. Cook until the chipsticks turn soft, and then crisp.

2 Place a dinner plate over the frying pan, and hold in place as you turn the pan over and carefully transfer the chipstick pancake on to the plate. Heat the remaining oil in the pan and slide the pancake back into the frying pan to brown the other side.

3 Gently break the eggs over the pancake, cover the frying pan and allow the eggs to set over a low heat. Season well and sprinkle with spring onions. Cook until the base is crisp. Serve hot for breakfast in the Parsi style, or with chapatis and a salad for lunch or supper.

STUFFED OKRA

The Gujarati community excels in the art of vegetarian cooking. Although some meat- and poultry-based dishes originated in Gujarat due to the presence of the Parsis, the native Gujaratis are strict vegetarians, who do not even eat eggs. Stuffed okra is easy to make and will happily accompany most meat and poultry dishes.

SERVES 4–6

225g/8oz large okra
15ml/1 tbsp amchur (dry mango powder)
2.5ml/½ tsp ground ginger
2.5ml/½ tsp ground cumin
2.5ml/½ tsp chilli powder (optional)
2.5ml/½ tsp ground turmeric
vegetable oil, for frying and mixing
30ml/2 tbsp cornflour (cornstarch), placed in a plastic bag
salt

1 Wash the okra and trim the tips. Make a slit lengthwise in the centre of each okra; do not cut all the way through.

2 In a bowl, mix the amchur, ginger, cumin, chilli, if using, turmeric and salt with a few drops of vegetable oil. Leave the mixture to rest for 1–2 hours or refrigerate overnight.

3 Using your fingers, part the slit of each okra carefully without opening it all the way and fill each with as much filling as possible. Put all the okra into the plastic bag with the cornflour and shake the bag carefully to cover the okra evenly.

4 Fill a wok, karahi or large pan with enough oil to sit 2.5cm/1in deep. Heat the oil and fry the okra in small batches for 5–8 minutes or until they are brown and slightly crisp. Serve hot with any meat, poultry or fish curry.

COOK'S TIP

When buying okra, choose one without any blemishes. Wash them thoroughly, rubbing each one gently with a soft vegetable brush or your fingertips.

OKRA in YOGURT

This tangy vegetable dish can be served as an accompaniment, but also makes an excellent vegetarian meal served with tarka dhal and chapatis. The secret of cooking okra is not to disturb its glutinous tendencies by overcooking, as the results can be unpleasant. Do follow the temperature and timing carefully.

SERVES 4

450g/1lb okra
30ml/2 tbsp vegetable oil
2.5ml/½ tsp onion seeds
3 fresh red or green chillies, chopped
1 onion, sliced
1.5ml/¼ tsp ground turmeric
10ml/2 tsp desiccated (dry, unsweetened, shredded) coconut
2.5ml/½ tsp salt
15ml/1 tbsp natural (plain) yogurt
2 tomatoes, quartered
15ml/1 tbsp chopped fresh coriander (cilantro)

1 Wash and trim the okra, cut into 1cm/½in pieces and set aside.

2 Heat the oil in a wok, karahi or large pan. Add the onion seeds, green chillies and onion, and fry for 5 minutes.

3 When the onion is golden brown, lower the heat and add the turmeric, desiccated coconut and salt. Fry for about 1 minute, stirring all the time.

4 Add the okra pieces to the pan. Turn the heat to medium-high and stir-fry briskly for a few minutes, until the okra has turned lightly golden.

5 Add the yogurt, tomatoes and fresh coriander. Cook for a further 2 minutes. Transfer to a warmed serving dish and serve immediately, as a side dish.

BOMBAY POTATO

This well-known dish is served in most Indian restaurants in the West, but it does not exist in Bombay. The origin of the name Bombay potato remains a mystery, although one theory is that it resembles a dish sold by street vendors in Bombay.

SERVES 4–6

450g/1lb whole new potatoes
5ml/1 tsp ground turmeric
60ml/4 tbsp vegetable oil
2 dried red chillies
6–8 curry leaves
2 onions, finely chopped
2 fresh green chillies, finely chopped
50g/2oz coarsely chopped fresh coriander (cilantro)
1.5ml/¼ tsp asafoetida
2.5ml/½ tsp each cumin, mustard, onion, fennel and nigella seeds
lemon juice, to taste
salt

1 Scrub the potatoes under running water and cut into small pieces. Boil the potatoes in water with a little salt and 2.5ml/½ tsp of the turmeric until tender. Drain well then coarsely mash. Set aside.

2 Heat the oil and fry the dried chillies and curry leaves until the chillies are nearly burnt. Add the onions, green chillies, coriander, remaining turmeric, asafoetida and spice seeds and cook until the onions are soft.

3 Fold in the potatoes and add a few drops of water. Cook gently over a low heat for 10 minutes, mixing well to ensure even distribution of the spices. Add lemon juice to taste.

4 Serve the potatoes with parathas or, as they would be eaten in Bombay, as a snack with soft white bread rolls.

CHICKPEAS with SPICED POTATO CAKES

This is a typical Bombay street snack; the kind that the Bombayites would happily eat while walking along the beach or watching a cricket match. It is the kind of food that brings together the cosmopolitan population of the city.

MAKES 10–12

30ml/2 tbsp vegetable oil
30ml/2 tbsp ground coriander
30ml/2 tbsp ground cumin
2.5ml/½ tsp ground turmeric
2.5ml/½ tsp salt
2.5ml/½ tsp granulated sugar
30ml/2 tbsp gram flour (besan), mixed with a little water to make a paste
450g/1lb/3 cups boiled chickpeas, drained
2 fresh green chillies, chopped
5cm/2in piece fresh root ginger, crushed
85g/3oz chopped fresh coriander (cilantro)
2 firm tomatoes, chopped
fresh mint sprigs, to garnish

For the potato cakes
450g/1lb potatoes, boiled and mashed
4 fresh green chillies, finely chopped
50g/2oz finely chopped fresh coriander (cilantro)
7.5ml/1½ tsp ground cumin
5ml/1 tsp amchur (dry mango powder)
vegetable oil, for shallow frying
salt

1 To prepare the chickpeas, heat the oil in a wok, karahi or large pan. Fry the coriander, cumin, turmeric, salt, sugar and gram flour paste until the water has evaporated and the oil has separated.

2 Add the chickpeas to the spices in the pan, and stir in the chopped chillies, ginger, fresh coriander and tomatoes. Toss the ingredients well and simmer gently for about 5 minutes. Transfer to a serving dish and keep warm.

3 To make the potato cakes, place the mashed potato in a large bowl and add the green chillies, chopped fresh coriander, cumin and amchur powder and salt. Mix together until all the ingredients are well blended.

4 Using your hands, shape the potato mixture into little cakes. Heat the oil in a shallow frying pan and fry the cakes on both sides until golden brown. Transfer to a serving dish, garnish with mint sprigs and serve with the chickpeas.

POTATOES in a YOGURT SAUCE

The potato was first introduced to India by Dutch traders, and it has since been elevated to gourmet status. In Indian cuisine, the humble potato takes on delicious flavourings of simple whole spices, or of blends of spices ground together.

SERVES 4

12 new potatoes, halved
300ml/½ pint/1¼ cups natural (plain) yogurt, whisked
300ml/½ pint/1¼ cups water
1.5ml/¼ tsp ground turmeric
5ml/1 tsp chilli powder
5ml/1 tsp ground coriander
2.5ml/½ tsp ground cumin
5ml/1 tsp salt
5ml/1 tsp soft brown sugar
30ml/2 tbsp vegetable oil
5ml/1 tsp cumin seeds
15ml/1 tbsp chopped fresh coriander (cilantro), plus extra sprigs to garnish (optional)
2 fresh green chillies, sliced

1 Boil the halved new potatoes with their skins on in a large pan of salted water, until they are just tender. Drain the potatoes and set aside.

2 Mix together the natural yogurt, water, turmeric, chilli powder, ground coriander, ground cumin, salt and sugar in a bowl. Set the mixture aside.

COOK'S TIPS

- If new potatoes are out of season and unavailable, you could use 450g/1lb ordinary potatoes instead. Peel and wash them and cut into large chunks, then cook as described above.
- Add 10ml/2 tsp gram flour (besan) to the yogurt to prevent it curdling.

3 Heat the vegetable oil in a wok, karahi or large pan, and add the cumin seeds. Fry gently until they begin to splutter.

4 Reduce the heat, stir in the yogurt mixture and cook for about 3 minutes over a medium heat.

5 Add the chopped fresh coriander, green chillies and cooked potatoes. Blend everything together and cook for a further 5–7 minutes, stirring the mixture occasionally.

6 Transfer to a warmed serving dish and garnish with the coriander sprig, if you like. This dish goes very well with hot bhaturas or chapatis.

STUFFED VEGETABLES

It is hard to beat the Gujarati community when it comes to the creation of imaginative vegetarian dishes. In this fabulous recipe, two different vegetables are stuffed with an irresistible blend of spices and peanuts.

SERVES 4

12 small potatoes
8 baby aubergines (eggplant)
single (light) cream, to garnish

For the stuffing
15ml/1 tbsp sesame seeds
30ml/2 tbsp ground coriander
30ml/2 tbsp ground cumin
2.5ml/½ tsp salt
1.5ml/¼ tsp chilli powder
2.5ml/½ tsp ground turmeric
10ml/2 tsp granulated sugar
1.5ml/¼ tsp garam masala
15ml/1 tbsp peanuts, roughly crushed
15ml/1 tbsp gram flour (besan)
2 garlic cloves, crushed
15ml/1 tbsp lemon juice
30ml/2 tbsp chopped fresh coriander (cilantro)

For the sauce
30ml/2 tbsp vegetable oil
2.5ml/½ tsp black mustard seeds
400g/14oz can chopped tomatoes
30ml/2 tbsp chopped fresh coriander (cilantro)
150ml/¼ pint/⅔ cup water

1 Preheat the oven to 200°C/400°F/Gas 6. Make slits in the potatoes and baby aubergines, making sure that you do not cut right through.

2 Mix all the ingredients for the stuffing together on a plate.

3 Carefully stuff the potatoes and aubergines with the spice mixture.

4 Place the potatoes and aubergines in a greased ovenproof dish.

5 Heat the oil in a pan and fry the mustard seeds for 2 minutes until they begin to splutter, then add the tomatoes, coriander and any leftover stuffing, together with the water. Simmer for 5 minutes until the sauce thickens.

6 Pour the sauce over the potatoes and aubergines. Cover and bake for 25–30 minutes until the vegetables are soft. Garnish with single cream, if using. Serve with any Indian bread or with a meat or chicken curry of your choice.

RICES AND BREADS

An Indian meal is always served with rice or bread. Basmati rice, with its distinctive aromatic flavour, is the most popular variety. Leavened breads, such as naan, are widely eaten in the north and west, while flat, unleavened chapatis and parathas are the breads of the south.

SAFFRON RICE

The saffron crocus is a perennial bulb that only flowers for two weeks of the year, and each stigma has to be removed by hand and dried with care. Consequently, saffron is said to be worth its weight in gold. Kashmir in the northern region of India and La Manche in Spain are the world's two major producers of saffron. In Indian cooking, saffron is used as a colorant in both sweet and savoury dishes.

SERVES 6

450g/1lb/2⅓ cups basmati rice, soaked for 20–30 minutes
750ml/1¼ pints/3 cups water
3 green cardamom pods
2 cloves
5ml/1 tsp salt
45ml/3 tbsp semi-skimmed (low-fat) milk
2.5ml/½ tsp saffron threads, crushed

COOK'S TIP

The saffron milk can be heated in the microwave. Mix the milk and saffron threads in a suitable container and warm them for 1 minute on Low.

1 Drain the basmati rice and place in a large pan. Pour in the water. Add the cardamoms, cloves and salt. Stir, then bring to the boil. Lower the heat and cover tightly, and simmer for 5 minutes.

2 Meanwhile, place the milk in a small pan. Add the saffron threads and heat through gently.

3 Add the saffron milk to the rice and stir. Cover again and continue cooking over a low heat for 5–6 minutes.

4 Remove the pan from the heat without lifting the lid. Leave the rice to stand for about 5 minutes, then fork through just before serving.

COOK'S TIP

Wash the rice in cold water before soaking for longer, fluffier cooked rice.

CARAMELIZED BASMATI RICE

This is the traditional accompaniment to a dhansak curry. Sugar is caramelized in hot oil before the rice is added, along with a few whole spices.

SERVES 4

225g/8oz/generous 1 cup basmati rice, washed and soaked for 20–30 minutes
45ml/3 tbsp vegetable oil
20ml/4 tsp granulated sugar
4–5 green cardamom pods, bruised
2.5cm/1in piece cinnamon stick
4 cloves
1 bay leaf, crumpled
½ tsp salt
475ml/16fl oz/2 cups hot water

1 Put the basmati rice in a colander and leave to drain.

2 In a large pan, heat the vegetable oil over a medium heat. When the oil is hot, add the granulated sugar and wait until it is caramelized.

3 Reduce the heat to low and add the spices and bay leaf. Let sizzle for about 15–20 seconds, then add the rice and salt. Fry gently, stirring, for 2–3 minutes.

4 Pour in the water and bring to the boil. Let it boil steadily for 2 minutes then reduce the heat to very low. Cover the pan and cook for 8 minutes.

5 Remove the rice from the heat and let it stand for 6–8 minutes. Gently fluff up the rice with a fork and transfer to a warmed dish to serve.

CLASSIC PULAO

The exquisite flavour of basmati rice flavoured with stock and the heady aroma of saffron is the classic character of a traditional pulao. The secret of a perfect pulao is to wash the rice thoroughly, then soak it briefly. Soaking before cooking softens and moistens the grains, enabling the rice to absorb moisture during cooking, and resulting in fluffier rice.

SERVES 4

600ml/1 pint/2½ cups hot chicken stock
generous pinch of saffron threads
50g/2oz/¼ cup butter
1 onion, chopped
1 garlic clove, crushed
2.5cm/1in piece cinnamon stick
6 green cardamom pods
1 bay leaf
250g/9oz/1⅓ cups basmati rice, soaked for 20–30 minutes
50g/2oz/⅓ cup sultanas (golden raisins)
15ml/1 tbsp vegetable oil
50g/2oz/½ cup cashew nuts
naan bread and Tomato and Onion Salad, to serve

1 Pour the hot chicken stock into a jug (pitcher). Stir in the saffron threads and set aside.

2 Heat the butter in a pan and fry the onion and garlic for 5 minutes. Stir in the cinnamon stick, cardamoms and bay leaf and cook for 2 minutes.

3 Drain the rice and add to the pan, then cook, stirring, for 2 minutes more. Pour in the saffron stock and add the sultanas. Bring to the boil, stir, then lower the heat, cover and cook gently for 10 minutes or until the rice is tender and the liquid has all been absorbed.

4 Meanwhile, heat the oil in a wok, karahi or large pan and fry the cashew nuts until browned. Drain on kitchen paper, then sprinkle the cashew nuts over the rice. Serve with naan bread and Tomato and Onion Salad, or with Mughlai-style Leg of Lamb.

NUT PULAO

Known as pilau in Persia, pilaff in Turkey and pulao in India, these rice dishes are always made with the best-quality long grain rice. In India, basmati rice is the natural choice. There are different variations of this recipe, and this one, with walnuts and cashews, makes an ideal dish for vegetarians when served with a raita or natural yogurt.

SERVES 4

15–30ml/1–2 tbsp vegetable oil
1 onion, chopped
1 garlic clove, crushed
1 large carrot, coarsely grated
225g/8oz/generous 1 cup basmati rice, soaked for 20–30 minutes
5ml/1 tsp cumin seeds
10ml/2 tsp ground coriander
10ml/2 tsp black mustard seeds (optional)
4 green cardamom pods
450ml/¾ pint/scant 2 cups vegetable stock
1 bay leaf
75g/3oz/¾ cup unsalted walnuts and cashew nuts
salt and ground black pepper
fresh coriander (cilantro) sprigs, to garnish

1 Heat the oil in a wok, karahi or large pan. Fry the onion, garlic and carrot for 3–4 minutes. Drain the rice and add to the spices. Cook for 2 minutes, stirring to coat the grains in oil.

2 Pour in the vegetable stock, stirring. Add the bay leaf and season well.

3 Bring to the boil, lower the heat, cover and simmer very gently for 10–12 minutes.

4 Remove the pan from the heat without lifting the lid. Leave to stand for 5 minutes, then check the rice. If it is cooked, there will be small steam holes on the surface of the rice. Discard the bay leaf and the cardamom pods.

COOK'S TIP

Use a metal slotted spoon or a fork while stirring in the nuts. Wooden spoons will squash the delicate rice grains.

5 Stir in the walnuts and cashew nuts and check the seasoning. Spoon on to a warmed platter, garnish with the fresh coriander and serve.

PULAO in AROMATIC LAMB STOCK

A typical north Indian dish known as yakhni pulao, *this is rich and highly aromatic. Traditionally, lamb is cooked on the bone, which adds extra flavour to the stock. If you buy a leg of lamb and bone it yourself, do save the bones and add them to the stock at step 1; they can be discarded later in the recipe.*

SERVES 4–6

900g/2lb chicken pieces or lean lamb, cubed
600ml/1 pint/2½ cups water
4 green cardamom pods
2 black cardamom pods
10 whole peppercorns
4 cloves
1 onion, sliced
450g/1lb/2⅓ cups basmati rice, washed and drained
8–10 saffron threads
2 garlic cloves, crushed
5cm/2in piece fresh root ginger, crushed
5cm/2in piece cinnamon stick
salt
175g/6oz/generous 1 cup sultanas (golden raisins) and almonds, sautéed, to garnish

1 Place the chicken pieces or cubed lamb in a large pan with the water, cardamoms, peppercorns, cloves and sliced onion. Add salt to taste, and cook until the meat is tender. Remove the meat with a slotted spoon and keep warm. Strain the stock, if you wish, and return it to the pan.

2 Add the drained rice, saffron, garlic, ginger and cinnamon to the stock in the pan and bring the contents to the boil.

3 Quickly add the meat and stir well. Bring the stock back to the boil, reduce the heat and cover. Cook for about 15–20 minutes.

4 Remove from the heat and stand for 5 minutes. Transfer the contents of the pan to a warmed serving platter and garnish with the sultanas and sautéed almonds before serving.

COOK'S TIP

When washing rice, toss and turn it very gently to avoid damage to the delicate grains of basmati.

CHICKEN PULAO

Like biryanis, pulaos cooked with meat and poultry make a convenient one-pot meal. A vegetable curry makes a good accompaniment, although for a simpler meal, such as supper, you could serve the pulao with a simple raita, combining natural yogurt with any raw vegetable, such as white cabbage, grated carrots, or cauliflower florets.

SERVES 4

400g/14oz/2 cups basmati rice
75g/3oz/6 tbsp ghee or unsalted (sweet) butter
1 onion, sliced
1.5ml/¼ tsp mixed onion and mustard seeds
3 curry leaves
5ml/1 tsp grated fresh root ginger
5ml/1 tsp crushed garlic
5ml/1 tsp ground coriander
5ml/1 tsp chilli powder
7.5ml/1½ tsp salt
2 tomatoes, sliced
1 potato, cubed
50g/2oz/½ cup frozen peas, thawed
175g/6oz chicken breast fillets, skinned and cubed
60ml/4 tbsp chopped fresh coriander (cilantro)
2 fresh green chillies, chopped
700ml/1¼ pints/3 cups water

1 Wash the rice thoroughly under running water, then leave to soak for 30 minutes. Drain and set aside in a sieve (strainer).

2 In a pan, melt the ghee or butter and fry the sliced onion until golden.

3 Add the onion and mustard seeds, the curry leaves, ginger, garlic, ground coriander, chilli powder and salt. Stir-fry for about 2 minutes over a low heat: ground spices require only gentle warmth to release their flavours.

4 Add the sliced tomatoes, cubed potato, peas and chicken and mix everything together well.

5 Add the rice and stir gently to combine with the other ingredients.

6 Add the coriander and chillies. Mix and stir-fry for 1 minute. Pour in the water, bring to the boil and then lower the heat. Cover and cook for 20 minutes. Remove from the heat and leave the pulao to stand for 6–8 minutes. Serve.

TRICOLOUR PULAO

Most Indian restaurants in the West serve this popular vegetable pulao, which has three different vegetables. The effect is easily achieved with canned or frozen vegetables, but for entertaining or a special occasion dinner, you may prefer to use fresh produce.

SERVES 4–6

225g/8oz/1 cup basmati rice, rinsed and soaked for 30 minutes
30ml/2 tbsp vegetable oil
2.5ml/½ tsp cumin seeds
2 dried bay leaves
4 green cardamom pods
4 cloves
1 onion, finely chopped
1 carrot, finely diced
50g/2oz/½ cup frozen peas, thawed
50g/2oz/⅓ cup frozen sweetcorn, thawed
25g/1oz/¼ cup cashew nuts, lightly fried
475ml/16fl oz/2 cups water
1.5ml/¼ tsp ground cumin
salt

1 Heat the oil in a wok, karahi or large pan over a medium heat, and fry the cumin seeds for 2 minutes. Add the bay leaves, cardamoms and cloves, and fry gently for 2 minutes more, stirring the spices from time to time.

2 Add the onion and fry until lightly browned. Stir in the diced carrot and cook, stirring, for 3–4 minutes.

3 Drain the soaked basmati rice and add to the contents in the pan. Stir well to mix. Add the peas, sweetcorn and fried cashew nuts.

4 Add the measured water and the remaining spices, and add salt to taste. Bring to the boil, cover and simmer for 15 minutes over a low heat until all the water is absorbed.

5 Leave to stand, covered, for 10 minutes. Transfer to a warmed dish and serve.

PRAWN BIRYANI

The recipe for biryani originated with mutton, but its popularity has tempted Indian chefs to create versions using other ingredients. As with all biryanis, this one using prawns is a meal in itself. The classic accompaniment to any biryani is a raita.

SERVES 4–6

2 large onions, finely sliced and deep-fried
300ml/½ pint/1¼ cups natural (plain) yogurt
30ml/2 tbsp tomato purée (paste)
60ml/4 tbsp green masala paste
30ml/2 tbsp lemon juice
5ml/1 tsp black cumin seeds
5cm/2in piece cinnamon stick, or 1.5ml/¼ tsp ground cinnamon
4 green cardamom pods
450g/1lb raw king prawns (jumbo shrimp), peeled and deveined
225g/8oz/3 cups small whole button (white) mushrooms
225g/8oz/2 cups frozen peas, thawed
450g/1lb/2⅓ cups basmati rice, soaked for 5 minutes in boiled water and drained
300ml/½ pint/1¼ cups water
1 sachet saffron powder, mixed in 90ml/6 tbsp milk
30ml/2 tbsp ghee or unsalted (sweet) butter
salt

1 In a bowl, mix the onions, yogurt, tomato purée, masala paste, lemon juice, cumin seeds, cinnamon and cardamom, with salt to taste. Fold in the prawns, mushrooms and peas. Leave for 2 hours. Preheat the oven to 190°C/375°F/Gas 5.

2 Grease the base of a heavy pan and add the prawns, vegetables and any marinade juices. Cover with the drained rice and smooth the surface gently until you have an even layer.

3 Pour the water over the surface of the rice. Make holes through the rice with the handle of a spoon and pour into each a little saffron milk. Place knobs (pats) of ghee or butter on the surface.

4 Place a circular piece of foil on top of the rice. Cover and cook in the oven for 45–50 minutes. Allow to stand for 8–10 minutes, then stir the biryani and serve hot.

TOMATO and SPINACH PULAO

A tasty and nourishing dish for vegetarians and meat eaters alike. Serve it with another vegetable curry, or with tandoori chicken, marinated fried fish or shammi kabab. Add a cooling fruit raita for a completely balanced meal.

SERVES 4

30ml/2 tbsp vegetable oil
15ml/1 tbsp ghee or unsalted (sweet) butter
1 onion, chopped
2 garlic cloves, crushed
3 tomatoes, peeled, seeded and chopped
225g/8oz/generous 1 cup brown basmati rice, soaked
10ml/2 tsp dhana jeera powder or 5ml/1 tsp ground coriander and 5ml/1 tsp ground cumin
2 carrots, coarsely grated
900ml/1½ pints/3¾ cups vegetable stock
275g/10oz young spinach leaves
50g/2oz/½ cup unsalted cashew nuts, toasted
salt and ground black pepper
naan bread, to serve

1 Heat the oil and ghee or butter in a wok, karahi or large pan, and fry the onion and garlic for 4–5 minutes until soft. Add the tomatoes and cook for 3–4 minutes, stirring, until thickened.

2 Drain the rice, add it to the pan and cook for a further 1–2 minutes, stirring, until the rice is coated.

3 Stir in the dhana jeera powder or coriander and cumin, then add the carrots. Season with salt and pepper. Pour in the stock and stir well to mix.

4 Bring to the boil, then cover tightly and simmer over a very gentle heat for 20–25 minutes, until the rice is tender. Lay the spinach on the surface of the rice, cover again, and cook for a further 2–3 minutes, until the spinach has wilted. Fold the spinach into the rest of the rice and check the seasoning. Sprinkle with toasted cashews and serve with naan.

COOK'S TIP

Leaving to rest for 6–8 minutes before serving makes the rice dry and fluffy.

CHICKEN BIRYANI

Biryani is a meal in itself and needs no accompaniment, except for a raita and some grilled or fried poppadums. It is a dish that is equally at home on the family dining table or as a dinner-party centrepiece.

SERVES 4

10 whole green cardamom pods
275g/10oz/1½ cups basmati rice, soaked and drained
2.5ml/½ tsp salt
2–3 whole cloves
5cm/2in piece cinnamon stick
45ml/3 tbsp vegetable oil
3 onions, sliced
4 chicken breast fillets, each about 175g/6oz, skinned and cubed
1.5ml/¼ tsp ground cloves
1.5ml/¼ tsp hot chilli powder
5ml/1 tsp ground cumin
5ml/1 tsp ground coriander
2.5ml/½ tsp ground black pepper
3 garlic cloves, chopped
5ml/1 tsp finely chopped fresh root ginger
juice of 1 lemon
4 tomatoes, sliced
30ml/2 tbsp chopped fresh coriander (cilantro)
150ml/¼ pint/⅔ cup natural (plain) yogurt, plus extra to serve
4–5 saffron threads, soaked in 10ml/2 tsp warm milk
150ml/¼ pint/⅔ cup water
toasted flaked (sliced) almonds and fresh coriander (cilantro) sprigs, to garnish

1 Preheat the oven to 190°C/375°F/Gas 5. Remove the seeds from half the cardamom pods and grind them finely, using a pestle and mortar. Set aside the ground seeds.

2 Bring a pan of water to the boil and add the rice, salt, whole cardamom pods, cloves and cinnamon stick. Boil for 2 minutes, then drain, leaving the whole spices in the rice. Keep the rice hot in a covered pan.

3 Heat the oil in a wok, karahi or large pan, and fry the onions for 8 minutes, until softened and browned. Add the chicken and the ground spices, including the ground cardamom seeds. Mix well, then add the garlic, ginger and lemon juice. Stir-fry for about 5 minutes.

4 Transfer the chicken mixture to a casserole and arrange the tomatoes on top. Sprinkle on the fresh coriander, spoon the yogurt evenly on top and cover with the drained rice.

5 Drizzle the saffron milk over the rice and pour over the water. Cover, then bake for 1 hour. Transfer to a serving platter and discard the whole spices. Garnish and serve immediately.

BEEF BIRYANI

This biryani, which uses beef, is a speciality of the Muslim community. The recipe may seem long, but biryani is one of the easiest and most relaxing ways of cooking, especially when you are entertaining. Once the dish is assembled and placed in the oven, it looks after itself and you can happily get on with other things.

SERVES 4

2 large onions
2 garlic cloves, chopped
2.5cm/1in piece of fresh root ginger, peeled and roughly chopped
½–1 fresh green chilli, seeded and chopped
small bunch of fresh coriander (cilantro)
60ml/4 tbsp flaked (sliced) almonds
30–45ml/2–3 tbsp water
15ml/1 tbsp ghee or butter, plus 25g/1oz/2 tbsp butter for the rice
45ml/3 tbsp vegetable oil
30ml/2 tbsp sultanas (golden raisins)
500g/1¼lb braising or stewing steak, cubed
5ml/1 tsp ground coriander
15ml/1 tbsp ground cumin
2.5ml/½ tsp ground turmeric
2.5ml/½ tsp ground fenugreek
good pinch of ground cinnamon
175ml/6fl oz/¾ cup natural (plain) yogurt, whisked
275g/10oz/1½ cups basmati rice
about 1.2 litres/2 pints/5 cups hot chicken stock or water
salt and ground black pepper
2 hard-boiled (hard-cooked) eggs, quartered, to garnish
chapatis, to serve

1 Roughly chop one onion and place it in a food processor or blender. Add the garlic, ginger, chilli, fresh coriander and half the flaked almonds. Pour in the water and process to a smooth paste. Transfer the paste to a small bowl and set aside.

2 Finely slice the remaining onion into rings or half rings. Heat half the ghee or butter with half the oil in a heavy flameproof casserole and fry the onion rings for 10–15 minutes until they are a deep golden brown. Transfer to a plate with a slotted spoon. Fry the remaining flaked almonds briefly until golden and set aside with the onion rings, then quickly fry the sultanas until they swell. Transfer to the plate.

3 Heat the remaining ghee or butter in the casserole with a further 15ml/1 tbsp of the oil. Fry the cubed meat, in batches, until evenly browned on all sides. Transfer the meat to a plate and set aside.

4 Wipe the casserole clean with kitchen paper, heat the remaining oil and pour in the onion, spice and coriander paste made earlier. Cook over a medium heat for 2–3 minutes, stirring all the time, until the mixture begins to brown lightly. Stir in all the additional spices, season with salt and ground black pepper and cook for 1 minute more.

5 Lower the heat, then stir in the yogurt, a little at a time. When all of it has been incorporated into the spice mixture, return the meat to the casserole. Stir to coat, cover tightly and simmer over a gentle heat for 40–45 minutes until the meat is tender. Meanwhile, soak the rice in a bowl of cold water for 15–20 minutes.

6 Preheat the oven to 160°C/325°F/Gas 3. Drain the rice, place in a pan and add the hot chicken stock or water, together with a little salt. Bring back to the boil, cover and cook for 5 minutes.

7 Drain the rice, and pile it in a mound on top of the meat in the casserole. Using the handle of a spoon, make a hole through the rice and meat mixture, to the bottom of the pan. Place the fried onions, almonds and sultanas over the top and dot with butter. Cover the casserole tightly with a double layer of foil and secure with a lid.

8 Cook the biryani in the preheated oven for 30–40 minutes. To serve, spoon the mixture on to a warmed serving platter and garnish with the quartered hard-boiled eggs. Serve with chapatis.

COOK'S TIP

Place a piece of buttered greaseproof (waxed) paper on the rice. This will help to keep the top layer moist in the oven.

CHAPATIS

A chapati is an unleavened bread made from chapati flour, a ground wholemeal flour known as atta, which is finer than the Western equivalent. An equal quantity of standard wholemeal flour and plain flour will also produce satisfactory results, although chapati flour is available from Indian grocers. This is the everyday bread of the Indian home.

MAKES 8–10

225g/8oz/2 cups chapati flour or ground wholemeal (whole-wheat) flour
2.5ml/½ tsp salt
175ml/6fl oz/¾ cup water

1 Place the flour and salt in a mixing bowl. Make a well in the middle and gradually stir in the water, mixing well with your fingers. Form a supple dough and knead for 7–10 minutes. Ideally, cover with clear film and leave on one side for 15–20 minutes to rest.

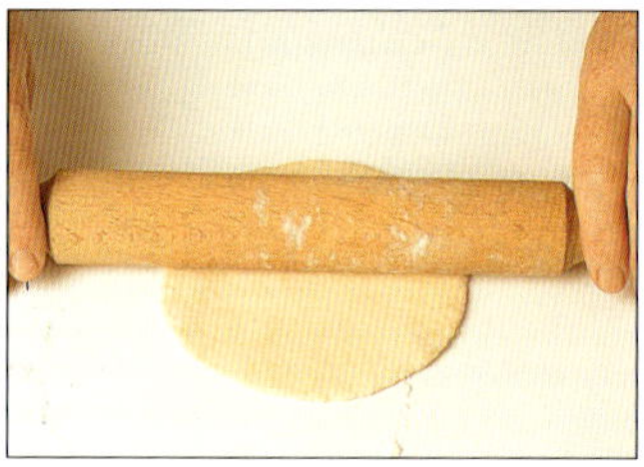

2 Divide the dough into 8–10 equal portions. Roll out each piece in a circle on a well-floured surface.

3 Place a *tava* (chapati griddle) or heavy frying pan over a high heat. When steam rises from it, lower the heat to medium and add the first chapati to the pan.

4 When the chapati begins to bubble, turn it over. Press down with a clean dish towel or a flat spoon and turn once again. Remove the cooked chapati from the pan and keep warm in a piece of foil lined with kitchen paper while you cook the other chapatis. Repeat the process until all the breads are cooked. Serve the chapatis immediately.

NAAN

This bread was introduced to India by the Moguls who originally came from Persia via Afghanistan. In Persian, the word naan *means bread. Traditionally, naan is not rolled, but patted and stretched until the teardrop shape is achieved. You can, of course, roll it out to a circle, then gently pull the lower end, which will give you the traditional shape.*

MAKES ABOUT 6

5ml/1 tsp caster (superfine) sugar
5ml/1 tsp dried yeast
about 150ml/¼ pint/⅔ cup warm water
225g/8oz/2 cups plain (all-purpose) flour, plus extra for dusting
5ml/1 tsp ghee, melted
5ml/1 tsp salt
50g/2oz/¼ cup unsalted (sweet) butter, melted
5ml/1 tsp poppy seeds

1 Put the sugar and yeast into a small bowl and add the water. Mix to dissolve the yeast. Leave on one side for about 10 minutes, or until the mixture froths.

2 Place the flour in a large bowl, make a well in the middle and add the ghee, salt and the yeast mixture. Mix well, using your hands, and adding a little more water if the dough is too dry.

VARIATION
Onion seeds or chopped fresh coriander (cilantro) may also be used as a topping.

3 Turn the dough out on to a lightly floured surface and knead for about 5 minutes, or until smooth.

4 Return the dough to the bowl, cover and leave in a warm place for about 1½ hours, until it has doubled in size.

5 Turn out the dough back on to the floured surface and knead for a further 2 minutes.

6 Break off small pieces of the dough with your hand, and roll into rounds about 13cm/5in in diameter and 1cm/½in thick.

7 Place the naan on a sheet of greased foil under a very hot, preheated grill (broiler) for 7–10 minutes, turning twice to brush with butter and sprinkle with poppy seeds.

8 Serve the naan immediately if possible, or keep them wrapped in foil until required.

RED LENTIL PANCAKES

This is a type of dosa, which is essentially a pancake from southern India, but used in the similar fashion to north Indian bread. North Indian breads are made of wholemeal or refined flour; in the South they are made of ground lentils and rice.

MAKES 6 PANCAKES

150g/5oz/¾ cup long grain rice
50g/2oz/¼ cup red lentils
250ml/8fl oz/1 cup warm water
5ml/1 tsp salt
2.5ml/½ tsp ground turmeric
2.5ml/½ tsp ground black pepper
30ml/2 tbsp chopped fresh coriander (cilantro)
oil, for frying and drizzling

VARIATION

Add 60ml/4 tbsp grated coconut to the batter just before cooking.

1 Place the long grain rice and lentils in a large mixing bowl, cover with the warm water, and set aside to soak for at least 8 hours or overnight.

2 Drain off the water and reserve. Place the rice and lentils in a food processor and blend until smooth. Blend in the reserved water.

3 Scrape into a bowl, cover with clear film (plastic wrap) and leave in a warm place to ferment for about 24 hours.

4 Stir in the salt, turmeric, pepper and coriander. Heat a heavy frying pan over a medium heat for a few minutes until hot. Smear with oil and add about 30–45ml/2–3 tbsp batter.

5 Using the rounded base of a soup spoon, gently spread the batter out, using a circular motion, to make a pancake that is 15cm/6in in diameter.

6 Cook in the pan for 1½–2 minutes, or until set. Drizzle a little oil over the pancake and around the edges. Turn over and cook for about 1 minute, or until golden brown. Keep the cooked pancakes warm in a low oven on a heatproof plate placed over simmering water while cooking the remaining pancakes. Serve warm.

PARATHAS

Making a paratha is somewhat similar to the technique used when making flaky pastry. The difference lies in the handling of the dough; this can be handled freely, unlike that for a flaky pastry. Parathas are rich in saturated fat, so reserve for special occasions.

MAKES 12–15

350g/12oz/3 cups chapati flour or ground wholemeal (whole-wheat), plus 50g/2oz/½ cup for dusting
50g/2oz/½ cup plain (all-purpose) flour
30ml/2 tbsp ghee or unsalted (sweet) butter, plus 10ml/2 tsp, melted
water, to mix
salt

1 Sift the flours and salt into a bowl. Make a well in the centre and add 10ml/2 tsp of unmelted ghee and fold into the flour to make a crumbly texture. Gradually add water to make a soft, pliable dough. Knead until smooth. Cover and leave to rest for 30 minutes.

2 Divide the dough into 12–15 equal portions and keep covered. Take one portion at a time and roll out on a lightly floured surface to about 10cm/4in in diameter. Brush the dough with a little of the melted ghee or sweet butter and sprinkle with chapati flour.

3 With a sharp knife, make a straight cut from the centre to the edge of the dough, then lift a cut edge and roll the dough into a cone shape. Lift it and flatten it again into a ball. Roll the dough again on a lightly floured surface until it is 18cm/7in wide.

4 Heat a griddle and cook one paratha at a time, placing a little of the remaining ghee along the edges. Cook on each side until golden brown. Serve hot.

COOK'S TIP

If you cannot find chapati flour, known as atta, substitute an equal quantity of wholemeal flour and plain flour.

MISSI ROTIS

This is a speciality from Punjab, and is one of a few gluten-free varieties of breads made in India. Gram flour, known as besan, is used instead of the usual chapati flour. In Punjab, missi rotis are very popular with a glass of lassi, a refreshing yogurt drink.

MAKES 4

115g/4oz/1 cup gram flour (besan)
115g/4oz/1 cup wholemeal (whole-wheat) flour
1 fresh green chilli, seeded and chopped
½ onion, finely chopped
15ml/1 tbsp chopped fresh coriander (cilantro)
2.5ml/½ tsp ground turmeric
2.5ml/½ tsp salt
15ml/1 tbsp vegetable oil or melted butter
120–150ml/4–5fl oz/½–⅔ cup lukewarm water
30–45ml/2–3 tbsp melted unsalted (sweet) butter or ghee

1 Mix the two types of flour, chilli, onion, coriander, turmeric and salt together in a large bowl. Stir in the 15ml/1 tbsp oil or melted butter.

2 Mix in sufficient water to make a pliable soft dough. Turn out the dough on to a lightly floured surface and knead until smooth.

3 Place in a lightly oiled bowl, cover with lightly oiled clear film (plastic wrap) and leave to rest for 30 minutes.

4 Turn the dough out on to a lightly floured surface. Divide into four equal pieces and shape into balls in the palms of your hands. Roll out each ball into a thick round about 15–18cm/6–7in in diameter.

5 Heat a griddle or heavy frying pan over a medium heat for a few minutes until hot.

6 Brush both sides of one roti with some melted butter or ghee. Add it to the griddle or frying pan and cook for about 2 minutes, turning after 1 minute. Brush the cooked roti lightly with melted butter or ghee again, slide it on to a plate and keep warm in a low oven while cooking the remaining rotis in the same way. Serve the rotis warm.

TANDOORI ROTIS

Roti means bread and is the most common food eaten in central and northern India. For generations, roti has been made with just wholemeal flour, salt and water, although the art of making rotis is generally more refined these days. Tandoori roti is traditionally baked in a tandoor, or clay oven, but it can also be made successfully in an electric or gas oven at the highest setting.

MAKES 6

350g/12oz/3 cups chapati flour or ground wholemeal (whole-wheat) flour
5ml/1 tsp salt
250ml/8fl oz/1 cup water
30–45ml/2–3 tbsp melted ghee or unsalted (sweet) butter, for brushing

1 Sift the flour and salt into a large mixing bowl. Add the water and mix to a soft, pliable dough.

2 Knead on a lightly floured surface for 3–4 minutes until smooth. Place the dough in a lightly oiled bowl, cover with lightly oiled clear film (plastic wrap) and leave to rest for 1 hour.

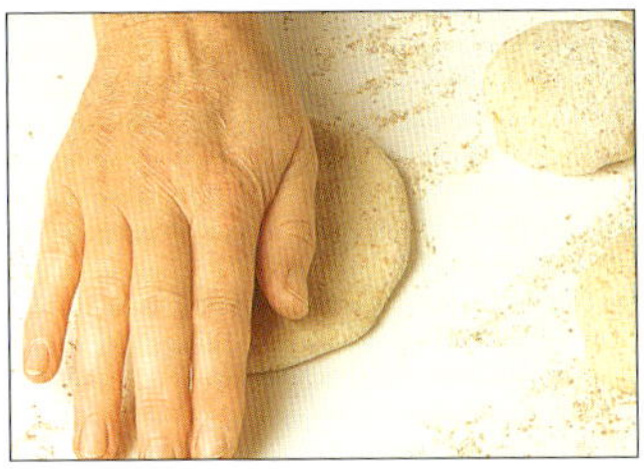

3 Turn out the dough on to a lightly floured surface. Divide the dough into six pieces and shape each into a ball. Press out into a larger round with the palm of your hand, cover with lightly oiled clear film and leave to rest for about 10 minutes.

4 Meanwhile, preheat the oven to 230°C/450°F/Gas 8. Place three baking sheets in the oven to heat. Roll the rotis into 15cm/6in rounds, place two on each baking sheet and bake for 8–10 minutes. Brush with melted ghee or butter and serve warm.

POORIS

These delicious little deep-fried breads, shaped into discs, make it temptingly easy to overindulge. In most areas, they are made of wholemeal flour, but in the east and north-east of India, they are made from plain refined flour, and are known as loochis.

MAKES 12

- 115g/4oz/1 cup unbleached plain (all-purpose) flour
- 115g/4oz/1 cup wholemeal (whole-wheat) flour
- 2.5ml/½ tsp salt
- 2.5ml/½ tsp chilli powder
- 30ml/2 tbsp vegetable oil
- 100–120ml/3½–4fl oz/scant ⅓–½ cup water
- oil, for frying

VARIATION

For spinach-flavoured pooris, thaw 50g/2oz frozen spinach, drain, and add to the dough with a little grated fresh root ginger and 2.5ml/½ tsp ground cumin.

1 Sift the flours, salt and chilli powder, if using, into a large mixing bowl. Add the vegetable oil then add sufficient water to mix to a dough. Turn out on to a lightly floured surface and knead for 8–10 minutes until smooth.

2 Place in an oiled bowl and cover with oiled clear film (plastic wrap). Leave for 30 minutes.

3 Turn out on to the floured surface. Divide the dough into 12 equal pieces. Keeping the rest of the dough covered, roll one piece into a 13cm/5in round. Repeat with the remaining dough. Stack the pooris, layered between clear film, to keep them moist.

4 Pour the oil for frying to a depth of 2.5cm/1in in a deep frying pan and heat it to 180°C/350°F. Using a metal fish slice (spatula), lift one poori and gently slide it into the oil; it will sink but will then return to the surface and begin to sizzle. Gently press the poori into the oil. It will puff up. Turn the poori over after a few seconds and allow it to cook for a further 20–30 seconds.

5 Remove the poori from the pan and pat dry with kitchen paper. Place the cooked poori on a large baking tray, in a single layer, and keep warm in a low oven while you cook the remaining pooris. Serve warm.

BHATURAS

These leavened and deep-fried breads are from Punjab, where the local people enjoy them with a bowl of spicy chickpea curry. The combination has become a classic over the years and is known as choley bhature. *Bhaturas must be eaten hot and cannot be reheated.*

MAKES 10 BHATURAS

15g/½oz fresh yeast
5ml/1 tsp granulated sugar
120ml/4fl oz/½ cup lukewarm water
200g/7oz/1¾ cups plain (all-purpose) flour
50g/2oz/½ cup semolina
2.5ml/½ tsp salt
15g/½oz/1 tbsp ghee or butter
30ml/2 tbsp natural (plain) yogurt
oil, for frying

COOK'S TIP

Ghee is availabe from Indian stores and some supermarkets. However, it is easy to make at home. Melt unsalted (sweet) butter over a low heat. Simmer very gently until the residue becomes light golden, then leave to cool. Strain through muslin (cheesecloth) before using.

1 Mix the yeast with the sugar and water in a jug (pitcher). Sift the flour into a large bowl and stir in the semolina and salt. Rub in the butter or ghee.

2 Add the yeast mixture and yogurt and mix to a dough. Turn out on to a lightly floured surface and knead for 10 minutes until smooth and elastic.

3 Place the dough in an oiled bowl, cover with oiled clear film (plastic wrap) and leave to rise, in a warm place, for about 1 hour, or until doubled in size.

4 Turn out on to a lightly floured surface and knock back (punch down). Divide into ten equal pieces and shape each into a ball. Flatten into discs with the palm of your hand. Roll out on a lightly floured surface into 13cm/5in rounds.

5 Heat oil to a depth of 1cm/½in in a deep frying pan and slide one bhatura into the oil. Fry for about 1 minute, turning over after 30 seconds, then drain well on kitchen paper. Keep each bhatura warm in a low oven while frying the remaining bhaturas. Serve immediately, while hot.

CHUTNEYS, PICKLES AND SALADS

Indians believe that eating sour foods with a meal is good for the health, and they have created a huge range of tart, tangy chutneys and pickles, refreshing yogurt-based raitas, and raw vegetable salads, which all taste good with hot, spicy dishes.

MANGO, CORIANDER and TOMATO CHUTNEYS

Chutneys are always vegetarian, but ingredients vary between regions. Mango and tomato chutneys are made all over India, while herb chutneys are eaten in the North and West.

MANGO CHUTNEY

MAKES 450G/1LB/2 CUPS

3 firm green mangoes, cut into chunks
150ml/¼ pint/⅔ cup cider vinegar
130g/4½oz/⅔ cup light muscovado (brown) sugar
1 small fresh red chilli, split
2.5cm/1in piece resh root ginger, grated
1 garlic clove, crushed
5 cardamom pods, bruised
2.5ml/½ tsp coriander seeds, crushed
1 bay leaf
2.5ml/½ tsp salt

1 Put the mango chunks into a pan, add the cider vinegar and cover. Cook over a low heat for 10 minutes, then stir in the remaining ingredients. Bring to the boil slowly, stirring.

2 Lower the heat and simmer gently for 30 minutes, until the mixture is syrupy. Leave to cool, then ladle into a hot sterilized jar and cover. Leave to rest for 1 week before serving.

CORIANDER CHUTNEY

MAKES 400G/14OZ/1¾ CUPS

30ml/2 tbsp vegetable oil
1 dried red chilli
1.5ml/¼ tsp each cumin, fennel and onion seeds
1.5ml/¼ tsp asafoetida
4 curry leaves
115g/4oz desiccated (dry, unsweetened, shredded) coconut
10ml/2 tsp granulated sugar
3 fresh green chillies, chopped
175–225g/6–8oz coriander (cilantro) leaves
60ml/4 tbsp mint sauce
juice of 3 lemons
salt

1 Heat the oil and fry the next eight ingredients until the coconut turns golden. Season and allow to cool.

2 Use a mortar and pestle to grind the spice mixture with the chillies, coriander and mint sauce. Stir in the lemon juice. Transfer to a sterilized jar, cover and chill.

TOMATO CHUTNEY

MAKES 450–500G/16–18OZ/2–2¼ CUPS

90ml/6 tbsp vegetable oil
5cm/2in piece cinnamon stick
4 cloves
5ml/1 tsp freshly roasted cumin seeds
5ml/1 tsp nigella seeds
4 bay leaves
5ml/1 tsp mustard seeds, crushed
4 cloves garlic, crushed
5cm/2in piece fresh root ginger, grated
5ml/1 tsp chilli powder
5ml/1 tsp ground turmeric
60ml/4 tbsp brown sugar
800g/¾lb canned, chopped tomatoes, drained, juices reserved

1 Heat the oil, then fry the first six spices. Add the garlic and fry until golden.

2 Add the remaining spices, sugar and reserved tomato juices. Simmer until reduced, then add the tomatoes and cook for 15–20 minutes. Leave to cool, then ladle into a sterilized jar and cover.

MINT and COCONUT, APRICOT and TOMATO and FRESH CHILLI CHUTNEYS

Chutneys can be made by grinding fresh ingredients together, or by slow-cooking.

MINT AND COCONUT CHUTNEY

MAKES ABOUT 350ML/12FL OZ/1½ CUPS

50g/2oz fresh mint leaves
90ml/6 tbsp desiccated (dry, unsweetened, shredded) coconut
15ml/1 tbsp sesame seeds
1.5ml/¼ tsp salt
175ml/6fl oz/¾ cup natural (plain) yogurt

1 Finely chop the fresh mint leaves, using a sharp kitchen knife.

2 Put all the ingredients into a food processor or blender and process until smooth. Transfer to a sterilized jar, cover and chill until needed.

COOK'S TIP
This chutney can be stored in the refrigerator for up to 5 days.

APRICOT CHUTNEY

MAKES ABOUT 450G/1LB/2 CUPS

450g/1lb/2 cups dried apricots, finely diced
5ml/1 tsp garam masala
275g/10oz/1¼ cups soft light brown sugar
450ml/¾ pint/scant 2 cups malt vinegar
5ml/1 tsp grated fresh root ginger
5ml/1 tsp salt
75g/3oz/½ cup sultanas (golden raisins)
450ml/¾ pint/scant 2 cups water

1 Put all the ingredients together into a pan and stir well to mix. Bring to the boil, then simmer for 30–35 minutes, stirring occasionally.

2 When the chutney becomes syrupy, remove from the heat. Leave to cool, then ladle into a hot sterilized jar and cover. Chill after opening.

TOMATO AND FRESH CHILLI CHUTNEY

MAKES ABOUT 475ML/16FL OZ/2 CUPS

1 red (bell) pepper
4 tomatoes, chopped
2 fresh green chillies, chopped
1 garlic clove, crushed
1.5ml/¼ tsp salt
2.5ml/½ tsp granulated sugar
5ml/1 tsp chilli powder
45ml/3 tbsp tomato purée (paste)
15ml/1 tbsp chopped fresh coriander (cilantro)

1 Halve the red pepper and remove the core and seeds. Roughly chop the red pepper halves.

2 Process all the ingredients with 30ml/2 tbsp water in a food processor until smooth. Transfer to a sterilized jar, cover and chill until needed.

BOMBAY DUCK PICKLE

Boil is the name of a fish that is found off the west coast of India during the monsoon season. It is salted and dried in the sun and is characterized by a strong smell and distinctive piquancy. How this fish acquired the name Bombay duck in the Western world is still unknown. Bombay duck can be served hot or cold, and is usually eaten with Indian breads as an accompaniment to vegetable dishes.

SERVES 4–6

6–8 pieces boil (Bombay duck), soaked in water for 5 minutes
60ml/4 tbsp vegetable oil
2 fresh red chillies, chopped
15ml/1 tbsp granulated sugar
450g/1lb cherry tomatoes, halved
115g/4oz deep-fried onions
red onion rings, to garnish (optional)

COOK'S TIP

As an alternative to boil, try skinned mackeral fillets, without frying them. You will need only 30ml/2 tbsp vegetable oil to make the sauce.

1 Pat the fish dry with kitchen paper. Heat the oil in a frying pan and fry the fish pieces for about 30–45 seconds on both sides until crisp. Be careful not to burn them as they will taste bitter. Drain well. When cool, break into small pieces.

2 Cook the remaining ingredients until the tomatoes become pulpy and the onions are blended into a sauce. Fold in the Bombay duck and mix well. Leave to cool, then garnish and serve, or ladle into a hot sterilized jar and cover.

HOT LIME PICKLE and GREEN CHILLI PICKLE

Spicy pickles are a perennial favourite with all types of curry. Leaving the pickles to rest for a week after preparation will greatly enhance the flavours.

HOT LIME PICKLE

MAKES 450G/1LB/2 CUPS

25 limes, cut into wedges
225g/8oz/1 cup salt
50g/2oz/¼ cup fenugreek powder
50g/2oz/¼ cup mustard powder
150g/5oz/¾ cup chilli powder
15ml/1 tbsp ground turmeric
600ml/1 pint/2½ cups mustard oil
5ml/1 tsp asafoetida
25g/1oz yellow mustard seeds, crushed

1 Place the limes in a large sterilized jar or glass bowl. Add the salt and toss with the limes. Cover and leave in a warm place for 1–2 weeks, until they become soft and dull brown in colour.

2 Mix the fenugreek, mustard powder, chilli powder and turmeric and add to the limes. Cover and leave to rest in a warm place for a further 2–3 days.

3 Heat the oil and fry the asafoetida and mustard seeds. When the oil reaches smoking point, pour it over the limes. Mix well. Cover and leave in a warm place for 1 week before serving.

GREEN CHILLI PICKLE

MAKES 450–550G/1–1¼LB/2–2½ CUPS

50g/2oz/¼ cup mustard seeds, crushed
50g/2oz/¼ cup freshly ground cumin seeds
25ml/1½ tbsp ground turmeric
50g/2oz/¼ cup crushed garlic
150ml/¼ pint/⅔ cup white vinegar
75g/3oz/scant ½ cup granulated sugar
10ml/2 tsp salt
150ml/¼ pint/⅔ cup mustard oil
20 small garlic cloves
450g/1lb small fresh green chillies, halved

1 Mix the mustard seeds, cumin, turmeric, crushed garlic, vinegar, sugar and salt in a sterilized jar or glass bowl. Cover and allow to rest for 24 hours. This enables the spices to infuse (steep)and the sugar and salt to melt.

2 Heat the mustard oil and gently fry the spice mixture for about 5 minutes. (Keep a window open while cooking with mustard oil as it is pungent and the smoke may irritate the eyes.) Add the whole garlic cloves and fry for a further 5 minutes.

3 Add the halved fresh chillies and cook gently until tender but still green in colour. This will take about 30 minutes on a low heat. Cool thoroughly.

4 Pour into the sterilized jar, ensuring that the oil is evenly distributed if you are using more than one bottle. Leave to rest for 1 week before serving.

SPICED YOGURT and CUCUMBER RAITA

These slightly sour, yogurt-based accompaniments have a cooling effect on the palate when eaten with spicy foods, and they help to balance the flavours of an Indian meal.

SPICED YOGURT

MAKES 450ML/¾ PINT/SCANT 2 CUPS

450ml/¾ pint/scant 2 cups natural (plain) yogurt
2.5ml/½ tsp freshly ground fennel seeds
2.5ml/½ tsp granulated sugar
60ml/4 tbsp vegetable oil
1 dried red chilli
1.5ml/¼ tsp mustard seeds
1.5ml/¼ tsp cumin seeds
4–6 curry leaves
a pinch each of asafoetida and ground turmeric
salt

1 Mix together the yogurt, fennel and sugar, and add salt to taste. Chill.

2 Heat the oil and fry the remaining ingredients. When the chilli turns dark, pour the oil and spices over the yogurt and mix. Cover and chill before serving.

CUCUMBER RAITI

MAKES ABOUT 600ML/1 PINT/2½ CUPS

½ cucumber
1 fresh green chilli, seeded and chopped
300ml/½ pint/1¼ cups natural (plain) yogurt
1.5ml/¼ tsp salt
1.5ml/¼ tsp ground cumin

1 Dice the cucumber finely and place in a large mixing bowl. Add the chilli.

2 Beat the natural yogurt with a fork until smooth, then stir into the cucumber and chilli mixture.

3 Stir in the salt and cumin. Cover the bowl with clear film (plastic wrap) and chill before serving.

VARIATION

Instead of cucumber, use two skinned, seeded and chopped tomatoes and 15ml/1 tbsp chopped fresh coriander (cilantro).

FRUIT RAITA and TOMATO and ONION SALAD

Refreshing yogurt raitas can be made with almost any fruit. Raw vegetable salads, known as cachumbers, are another classic way of adding a tangy touch to a meal.

FRUIT RAITA

SERVES 4

350ml/12fl oz/1½ cups natural (plain) yogurt
75g/3oz seedless grapes, washed and dried
50g/2oz shelled walnuts
2 firm bananas, sliced
5ml/1 tsp granulated sugar
5ml/1 tsp freshly ground cumin seeds
salt
1.5ml/¼ tsp freshly roasted cumin seeds, chilli powder, to garnish

1 Put the yogurt, grapes and walnuts in a bowl. Fold in the bananas.

2 Stir in the sugar, ground cumin and salt. Chill and sprinkle on the roasted cumin seeds and chilli powder before serving.

TOMATO AND ONION SALAD

SERVES 4–6

2 limes
2.5ml/½ tsp granulated sugar
a few fresh coriander (cilantro) sprigs, chopped, plus extra for garnishing
2 onions, finely chopped
4 firm tomatoes, finely chopped
½ cucumber, finely chopped
1 fresh green chilli, finely chopped
salt and ground black pepper
a few fresh mint sprigs, to garnish

1 Extract the juice of the limes into a small bowl. Add the sugar, salt and pepper and allow to rest until the sugar and salt have competely dissolved. Mix together well.

2 Add the remaining ingredients and mix well. Chill, and garnish with fresh coriander and mint sprigs before serving.

VARIATION

For Banana and Coconut Raita, slice 2 bananas and fold into 350ml/12fl oz/1½ cups natural yogurt. Stir in 30ml/2 tbsp desiccated coconut and add a pinch of chilli powder, and salt and lemon juice to taste.

SOUTH-EAST ASIA

Some of the world's most exciting cuisines are found in the south-eastern corner of Asia. Throughout the region, in Burma, Thailand and Vietnam, Malaysia and the islands of Indonesia and the Philippines, each country has its own traditional cooking style, yet all share a passion for fragrant, flavoursome dishes, with an emphasis on using only the freshest of ingredients.

CULTURE and CUISINE

South-east Asian food is a joy to the senses, combining the refreshing aroma of lemon grass and kaffir lime leaves with the pungency of brilliant red chillies and the magical flavours of coconut milk and fresh basil. The curries of the region follow this tradition for flavourings, and they are very different from their Indian counterparts: lemon grass and kaffir lime leaves are rarely used in the Indian subcontinent. Furthermore, Indian curries are traditionally slow-cooked for a rich and creamy taste, while South-east Asian dishes are famously quick and easy to prepare.

The popularity of South-east Asian foods is now firmly established in the West and it continues to grow. Supermarkets and greengrocers have started selling many of the more exotic ingredients from the area: lemon grass, Thai chillies and galangal are all readily available, as are coconut and the milk and cream extracted from it. The appeal of South-east Asian food is obvious: it is full of flavour, always colourful and healthy, with an emphasis on serving the freshest possible foods.

Below: A simple South-east Asian meal might include rice and noodles, eaten with hot relishes and deep-fried onions.

Climate and geography

The area known as South-east Asia starts with Burma near the north-eastern border of India and incorporates Thailand, Cambodia and Vietnam, as well as Malaysia and Singapore in the South China Sea. It includes Indonesia, which, with its 13,000 islands, is the largest archipelago in the world. To the east lies Borneo and, beyond that, the Philippines. The whole area has been referred to as Farther India by European scholars, because of its position at the far side of the Ganges.

For such a vast area, there is surprisingly little temperature variation: a result of the region's location in the tropical belt along the Equator. The countries have long stretches of coastline, and all have their own distinctive geographical and climatic conditions. Irrigated rice fields co-exist with marshlands; majestic snow-capped mountains stand in sharp contrast to lush green rainforests.

Local resources

Such varied conditions have naturally given rise to a wide range of crops, resulting in cuisines that are distinctly different from one country to another. All of the countries enjoy the plentiful fish and shellfish provided by their seas and rivers, and these have become part of the daily diet everywhere. Another common element is rice, the staple food of the whole of Asia. Rice is grown in abundance, as the warm, moist tropical climate provides ideal growing conditions. Noodles also form an important part of the Asian diet, and are usually cooked with other ingredients as part of a dish, rather than served on the side as an accompaniment. Root crops, such as yam and cassava, are cooked in a variety of ways, and are sometimes used as a staple instead of rice and noodles.

Outside influences

The influence of religion on food is pronounced across the whole of Asia, but it is especially apparent in the South-east, where there is a wide variety of beliefs, including Hinduism, Buddhism, Islam and Christianity, along with a range of cultural practices, both indigenous and imposed. Indeed, foreign settlers, traders and invaders have had a significant impact on the cuisine of most countries in the area, one exception being Thailand, which has never been invaded or colonized.

In the 16th century, the Portuguese were among the first European powers to exploit the area, although colonization did not begin until much later. The initial appeal of South-east Asia for Europeans was its spices: the area is noted for the Spice Islands, where Arab traders had long been active. Nutmeg and peppercorns were especially highly prized, and European trading began in these commodities. The Dutch, French, British, Spanish and North Americans colonized the area and had an impact on its cuisine, which is still noticeable today.

REGIONAL DIVERSITY

The food culture of South-east Asia varies widely across the region, with each country following its own long-standing traditions for spice blends, flavourings and cooking styles. However, there are also many similarities, largely because of the trade in ingredients, the influences of climate, geography and religion, and of powerful neighbouring countries, such as China.

Above: A Thai hod market, so named because farmers display their produce in open baskets, which they carry to market on the ends of long poles, known as hods.

Thailand

Between Burma and Vietnam lies Thailand, the only country in South-east Asia that has never been colonized by European powers. The word *thai* means free, and the people of Thailand are proud of their independence. In terms of size, Thailand is roughly equal to Burma, but smaller than both India and China. It is divided into five regions, each with its own distinctive geography and culture.

Bangkok, the capital of Thailand, is popularly known as the Venice of the East, because the city is built around extensive inland waterways, and the majority of the city's population lives along the numerous canals. The floating markets are the workplace of a vast number of people, who sell fruits and vegetables, chillies, fresh fish and a wealth of other exotic ingredients. Thailand is renowned for its excellence in the art of fruit and vegetable carving, and an enjoyable day can be spent watching the various demonstrations on the streets of Bangkok.

Buddhism is the religion of Thailand, although most people seem to have a fairly liberal attitude to Buddhist law, and Thai cuisine includes an extensive range of meat-based recipes. It is fish, shellfish and vegetables, however, that constitute the main part of the Thai diet. Salads are central to a Thai meal, and there are

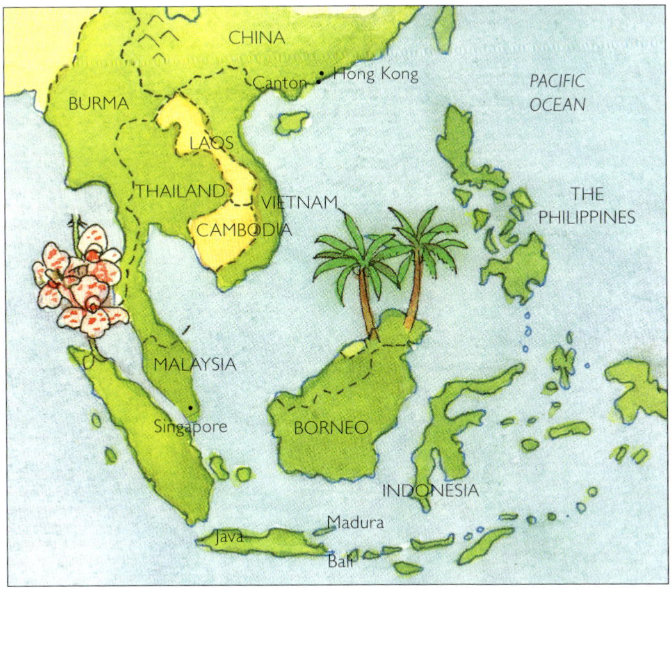

Below: The South-east Asian region covers a multitude of countries, all quite individual.

many varieties made, some of which use exotic fruits such as mangoes, pineapple and papaya, as well as raw vegetables. A small quantity of shredded meat, such as pork, is sometimes added, perhaps with perhaps a few prawns (shrimp). Thai salad dressings are a delicious blend of fish sauce, brown sugar and lime juice.

The particular climate conditions and geographical position of Thailand have given rise to regional variations in the nation's cuisine. In southern Thailand, the Gulf of Thailand and the Andaman Sea provide a wealth of fish and shellfish. Dishes based on these ingredients are popular throughout the country, but are particularly important in the south. In the north, where the climate is slightly cooler, fruits such as lychees are grown in abundance. Chicken, fish and glutinous rice are eaten in the north-east.

Coconut plays a very important role in Thai cooking. Coconut milk, flavoured with ginger, lemon grass, pungent local chillies and basil leaves, forms the basis of most Thai curries. Many desserts are also made using coconut milk and palm sugar. Whatever the dish, there is always a fine balance and complexity of flavour, texture and colour. Thai people regard food as a celebration, and it is considered bad luck to eat alone.

Burma

Colonized by the British in the late 19th century, Burma finally gained its independence in 1948, after a politically turbulent period, one year after the end of British rule in India. The country was officially renamed Myanmar in 1989. The national religion of Burma is Buddhism, which, like Hinduism, forbids the taking of another life for reasons of personal gratification. Although strict followers observe this rule, in practice most people eat a fair amount of meat, and fish is even more popular: Mohingha (Burmese Fish Stew) is flavoured with Indian spices, and is almost the national dish. Burmese food has noticeable Indian and Chinese influences. Spices from India are often sold in the local street markets, although the country's cuisine generally has more subtle flavours than its Indian counterpart. Rice is the staple food, but noodles, a Chinese contribution, are also very popular. The use of groundnut (peanut) oil and coconut suggests an Indian influence, whereas sesame oil, which is also used as a cooking medium, is a distinctly Chinese ingredient.

Below: The lively and colourful floating markets on the waterways of Burma sell supplies of fresh fish, fruits and vegetables.

Vietnam

Lying virtually next door to Thailand, Vietnam has a cuisine that is in a class of its own. The country was ruled by the French for nearly 80 years, and a French culinary influence can still be detected. The most prominent influence, however, is that of the Chinese, who occupied Vietnam for nearly a thousand years.

Vietnamese food is light and delicate, and the use of fat is limited. Generally speaking, the Vietnamese prefer spicy food, with a well-balanced flavour and a clean taste. Rice and noodles are once again the staples, as in other South-east Asian countries. Plenty of fresh fruit and vegetables are consumed, along with small quantities of meat, and fish and shellfish feature high on the menus.

Malaysia

Bordering Thailand in the north and Indonesia in the south, Malaysia is a lush, tropical land, with widely varying landscapes. It has a genuine diversity of races and cultures, and this is reflected in the country's varied cuisine. Navigation is easy throughout this area, and people have long been able to exchange cooking styles and ingredients with neighbouring countries.

The culinary heritage of Malaysia reaches back for at least six centuries, when the country began to attract

traders and travellers from far-flung places. India and Arabia were the first to exploit the country for its precious goods, followed by the Chinese and Portuguese. Trading began in such commodities as raw silk, brocades, fine silver and pearls, which were exchanged for peppercorns (known as black gold in those days), cloves, nutmeg and mace. Chinese princesses were sent by the emperor as gifts for the Malay sultan. Many Chinese men came to Malaysia to find work, married local women and settled in the country. This started a culture of Chinese food in Malaysia, to which the local people added their own touch. A new style of cuisine was thus created, which had Chinese influences, but flavours that were essentially local.

Above: *A street stall in Singapore. One of the strongest influences on Malay cuisine has come from Chinese migrant workers.*

Southern India has also had an impact on Malaysian cooking, as Indian workers from the south were hired to work in the rubber plantations in Malacca. There are striking resemblances evident between southern Indian and Malaysian cooking, with only minor differences, such as the use of lime leaves in Malaysian cooking and curry leaves in south Indian.

The tremendous variety in Malaysian cuisine is also partly a result of the range of religious beliefs within the country. For example, no pork is eaten among the Muslim community, although pork is a particular favourite of the Chinese. The Hindus from India will not eat beef, whereas the local Malay population has excellent beef-based recipes. Dishes such as rendang and sambal, which suggest an Indonesian influence, exist side by side with biryanis and samosas, which are unmistakably Indian. The Malaysian dessert *gula melaka* is a superb local creation, which is made with sago, enriched with thick coconut milk and sweetened with palm sugar with a touch of spices.

Indonesia

Comprising 13,000 islands spread along the Indian Ocean, Indonesia is a lush, green fertile land with steamy tropical heat and snow-capped mountain peaks.

For over two thousand years, waves of foreign traders and merchants entered the islands, and Hindu, Muslim

Right: *A typical Indonesian farmhouse on the island of Java. Green vegetables grow well in this lush tropical climate.*

Above: Local fishermen leave freshly caught mackerel to dry in the hot midday sun on the beaches of Bali, Indonesia.

and Buddhist kingdoms have all been established and destroyed. The Hindus in the 1st century, and the Buddhists in the 8th, established a vegetarian ethos, based on their own strict religious beliefs. Arab traders introduced Islam in the 15th century, and even today the Muslim community in Indonesia does not eat pork. Along with the Arabs, the Indians and Chinese were the first traders to visit Indonesia, lured by its spices, and by nutmeg, mace and cloves, in particular. Arab traders took shiploads of these spices into Europe and sold them at highly inflated prices.

The Europeans soon saw the benefit of eliminating the middle man, and the Portuguese, Dutch, English and Spanish all began sailing to Indonesia themselves, referring to the islands as the Spice Islands of the East. The Portuguese and British set up trading posts, but the Dutch eventually colonized Indonesia, and they stayed for 250 years, until the country gained independence in 1945. Throughout the period of Dutch rule, Chinese migrants, traders and workers continued to add their own distinctive traditions to the already rich tapestry of Indonesian culture.

With such diverse cultural influences, Indonesian cuisine emerged as one of the most varied and interesting in the whole of South-east Asia. Yet, although Indonesia was a Dutch colony, the Dutch themselves have had very little impact on the cuisine of the country. The most significant influences on eating habits undoubtably came from the Hindus and Muslims, and the Chinese.

In no other South-east Asian country does rice play such a major role as in Indonesia. It is eaten twice a day with numerous types of curry. On the island of Bali, Hindus eat rice with fish curries, Muslims eat it with beef and chicken, and the Chinese eat it with almost any meat, including duck. The famous Indonesian style of serving a meal, known as *nasi gerai* (loosely translated as the rice table), was even popular with the Dutch. *Nasi* means rice and *gerar* refers to the endless variety of other dishes served with it. Nasi Goreng (fried rice) is one of the best-known dishes, along with Gado Gado, a cooked vegetable salad with a delicious peanut dressing. Beef Rendang, with the pungency of chillies and ginger, the warmth of cumin and the sweet, mellow flavour of coconut milk, is one of Indonesia's most enduring dishes.

The Philippines

Like that of its neighbours, Filipino cooking is a harmonious blend of the cuisine of many countries and cultures. There are notable similarities with other South-east Asian countries, in terms of the way that ingredients are grown, prepared and cooked.

The original Filipinos are believed to have been of Malayo-Polynesian origin, but the age of discovery and exploitation brought traders from many neighbouring countries, including China, Malaysia, Japan and Indonesia. However, the strongest influence came from the Spanish, who arrived in the 16th century. They ruled the country for nearly 400 years, and during that time they established Christianity, making the Philippines the only Asian country with the Christian faith. Filipinos love both siestas and fiestas, which are both legacies from the Spanish. Dishes such as Bombonese Arroz (rice fritters), Arroz Caldo (rice with chicken) and Puchero (a mixed meat soup) are among the more popular Spanish-influenced dishes still eaten

Above: *Rice is the principal crop grown on the intricately terraced fields in the Luzon region of the Philippines. These terraces will provide employment for all inhabitants of the immediate area.*

today. Before the arrival of the Spanish, the Americans came to the area, and together these two influences helped to make Filipino cuisine a harmonious blend of Eastern and Western styles.

Chinese influence was also strong in the area, and this is clearly evident from the endless variety of noodle-based dishes. Pansit Guisado (Noodles with Chicken, Prawns and Ham) is just one of a number of popular Chinese-inspired dishes. Rice is the staple food of the Philippines, however, and it is eaten daily with almost every meal, even breakfast. The everyday diet of Filipinos is based on a simple dish of rice, stir-fried with meat, fish and vegetables.

Adobo, a Filipino spicy stew made with pork, chicken or even fish and shellfish, is a real speciality of the islands. The sauce in which the ingredeints are cooked is an irresistible blend of flavours, combining the tartness of local palm vinegar with the spiciness of black peppercorns and the unmistakable, pungent flavour of garlic. Although it owes much to Spanish origins, the dish, like so much of Filippino food, has its own distinctive character.

Left: *Fishermen prepare to haul up their nets on the Calamian Islands, in the Philippines. The boat is known as a banca.*

PRINCIPLES of SOUTH-EAST ASIAN COOKING

Food takes centre stage in the daily life of most people in South-east Asian. It is a well-known fact that food brings people together, and nowhere is this more apparent than across the Asian region. Food is one of life's greatest pleasures, and sharing it with family and friends is fundamental to the cultures of these countries. Quite simply, they live to eat.

All over South-east Asia, food is prepared with great attention to detail, using only the freshest ingredients. Dishes are healthy and easy to cook, with enough visual appeal to tempt anyone. Until fairly recently, recipes were not written down, but were handed down from generation to generation. The lack of written recipes has encouraged cooks to use their imagination when creating dishes, to experiment with flavours, while keeping to the principles of their local cooking styles and techniques.

Spices and aromatics

South-east Asian cooks are skilled in the art of combining spices, which they use to add taste, colour and aroma.

The essential spices of South-east Asia are coriander, cumin, turmeric, chilli and peppercorns, and although the same spices are used in India, the curries of South-east Asia are quite different, with a milder heat and more subtle flavours.

As in India, South-east Asian cuisine also makes use of whole spices, which are removed at the end of cooking. These include cinnamon, cloves and cardamom pods, and they are especially popular in Malaysia, where the influence of Indian cuisine is most strongly felt.

Adding flavour

Spice blends are usually combined with coconut milk, the most commonly used ingredient, and other hallmark ingredients, such as lemon grass and kaffir lime leaves. Most South-east Asian curries have a distinctive tangy taste, which comes from tamarind, the souring agent that is characteristic of all Asian cooking. Lime juice and vinegar are also used, and these add a refreshing tartness to curries, while the addition of soy sauce, fish sauce or shrimp paste gives that particular depth and pungent flavour that is so distinctive to South-east Asian cuisine. Among the fresh ingredients used as flavouring agents are shallots, galangal, ginger, garlic and chilli, as well as an array of fresh herbs, especially coriander (cilantro), mint and basil.

Below: Each country in South-east Asia has its own individual cooking style, but the essential approach to eating is the same: food is always fresh, full of flavour and carefully prepared and presented.

PREPARING a SOUTH-EAST ASIAN CURRY

Despite the many regional variations, South-east Asian curries are prepared following the same basic pattern. The differences in the cuisines can be attributed more to culture, lifestyle and local food resources, than to alternative cooking techniques.

Basic ingredients

The first point to consider when making any curry is what cooking medium to use. Coconut and palm oil are widely used throughout South-east Asia, and people in some countries, such as Thailand and the Philippines, use lard. To avoid consuming too much saturated fat, use a lighter cooking oil, such as vegetable oil or sunflower oil.

In South-east Asia, stock is more frequently used than water when making curries. This is probably because meat and poultry are cut into small pieces and are generally cooked off the bone. Stock adds an extra depth of flavour.

For thickening sauces, the common practice is to rely on ingredients such as coconut milk, grated coconut, onions, grated fresh root ginger and crushed garlic. In all curries, colour and pungency are created by the addition of different types of chillies, in varying amounts.

Cooking a curry

The starting point when making a curry is to preheat the oil and fry the onions, which, along with garlic and ginger, are the basic ingredients of all South-east Asian curries. Sometimes the onions are fried until they are crisp before the garlic and ginger are added, while in other dishes they are simply softened. The spices or curry paste are then added and cooked for a short time to eliminate their raw flavour. When the spices are cooked to the right point, the oil begins to separate from the thick spice paste.

By using a wide range of cooking techniques, a variety of flavours can be created from the same basic ingredients: recipes such as Beef Rendang and Thai Mussaman Curry are good examples of this. Although a recipe should initially be used as a guide, it is much more fun to be able to stamp your own personality on to whatever you are cooking. This becomes easier with practice, and, after a while, using spices to prepare delicious South-east Asian curries becomes a work of art. Start to use spices as an artist uses a palette, as you tone and colour the food to your own taste.

Above: Spices and aromatics can be used in many ways, and different flavours can be created from the same ingredients.

Planning and serving

Dishes served at a South-east Asian meal are not categorized into separate courses, but are all brought to the table at the same time. Diners help themselves with many helpings of small quantities.

Rice is the cornerstone of all meals, and is served with one or two vegetable side dishes, relishes (such as different types of sambal), salads and curries. It is customary to serve more than one meat or poultry dish, a vegetable curry and a dry, spiced, stir-fried vegetable dish. A soup is another important part of a South-east Asian meal. Desserts are not generally served, except in Malaysia, where delicious hot and cold rice or sago desserts are cooked in coconut milk, sweetened with palm sugar.

Freezing foods

South-east Asian dishes are prepared very quickly, as meat and vegetables are cut into small pieces so that they can be stir-fried, and they are not marinated before cooking. As time-saving strategies, therefore, chilling and freezing are probably not as important in South-east Asian cuisine as they are to some other types of cooking. However, curries always taste better if they are cooked a day or two in advance. The spices seem to permeate the meat and poultry, and the final flavour is much more mellow.

If you plan to freeze the food you are cooking, the following basic guidelines may be helpful:

- Leave the food slightly underdone.
- Cool the food rapidly. The best way to do this is to tip it into a large tray (a large roasting pan is ideal) and leave it in a cool place.
- Once the food has cooled down, put it into appropriate containers, then label and chill it before finally putting it in the freezer. The food will keep in the freezer for 6–8 months, depending on the star rating of your freezer.
- Food from unplanned freezing, such as leftovers, should not be frozen for longer than 2–3 months.

AROMATICS, SPICES and HERBS

Spices are fresh or dried aromatic parts of plants, including leaves, seeds, bark and roots. Some spices are used for the taste they impart, while others, known as aromatics, are used for aroma. Spices should be added with care: one spice used on its own can completely alter the taste of a dish, and a mixture of spices will affect colour and texture. Fresh and dried herbs also play an important part in the combinations of flavour, colour and aroma and, because herbs require only minimal cooking, they retain an intensity of flavour and fragrance.

The quantities of spices and salt specified in recipes are measured to achieve a balance of flavours. In some cases, however, you may prefer to increase or decrease the quantities according to taste. This is particularly true of fresh chillies and chilli powder: experiment with quantities, adding less than specified, if wished.

MAKING GARLIC OIL

1 Heat 120ml/4fl oz/½ cup vegetable oil in a small pan. Add 30ml/2 tbsp crushed garlic to the pan, and stir it into the oil. Cook gently for about 5 minutes, stirring occasionally.

2 Continue to cook the garlic in the oil until it is pale gold in colour. Do not let it burn or the oil will taste bitter. Allow to cool, then strain into a sterilized jar and use as required.

Garlic

This is a basic ingredient in much of South-east Asian cooking. Vietnamese cooks use a great deal of garlic, and in Thailand a mixture of crushed garlic, coriander (cilantro) root and pepper is the foundation of many dishes. Garlic is an essential ingredient in Thai curry pastes, and it is used throughout South-east Asia, to flavour oil for frying, partly because of the aromatic flavour it imparts, and also because it cuts down on the oiliness of the finished dish. Raw garlic is used in dips, marinades and dressings, and pickled garlic is used as a pickling spice in relishes and sambals.

***Above**: Fresh garlic*

Ginger

Fresh root ginger has a refreshing scent, reminiscent of citrus, and a pleasant, sharp flavour. Young ginger is tender and mild enough to be stir-fried as a vegetable, while older roots are fibrous and more pungent. Root ginger is now widely available in the West. It is also sold dried and as a paste, but these taste quite different to fresh. Both are used mainly as pickling spices and Asian cooks do not consider them an acceptable substitute for the fresh root. Ground ginger tastes different again; in South-east Asia its use is limited to mixing with other spices, such as when making curry powder.

***Above**: Clockwise from top, fresh ginger, ground ginger and ginger paste*

PREPARING FRESH ROOT GINGER

Fresh root ginger is peeled before use. The thin, tough outer skin is easily scraped or cut away, and the flesh is grated, sliced or chopped.

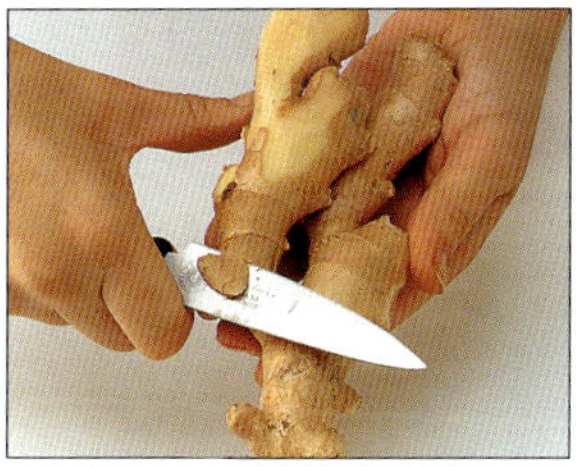

1 Thinly peel the skin using a sharp knife or vegetable peeler.

2 Grate the peeled root finely.

3 Alternatively, cut the ginger into thin batons, then chop the batons coarsely before adding to the dish.

4 Bruise the root with the flat blade of a knife, if it will be removed from the dish and discarded before serving.

***Above**: From left, fresh galangal and dried galangal*

Lengkuas

A member of the ginger family, lengkuas has a creamy coloured root with rings on the skin, and pink nodules. Fresh lengkuas is prepared and used in the same way as fresh root ginger. Ground lengkuas is also available, although the flavour is no match for the fresh root: use 5ml/1 tsp to replace 2.5cm/1in fresh lengkuas. Galangal can be used as a substitute for lengkuas.

Galangal

This is an essential flavouring agent in South-east Asian cooking, particularly in shellfish and meat dishes. It is often pounded with shallots, garlic and chillies to make a spice paste for dips or curries. In Thailand, slices of galangal are added to soups with shreds of lemon grass and lime leaves, while Vietnamese cooks add it to a peanut and lime sauce used as a dressing for meat and vegetable salads.

Greater galangal has a pine-like aroma and a sharp flavour; lesser galangal is more pungent, and a cross between ginger and black pepper. The rhizome is usually used fresh, but it is also avalaible dried and as a powder, known as laos.

Turmeric

Although it comes from the ginger family, turmeric has none of the heat associated with fresh root ginger. Referred to as "Indian saffron", it shares saffron's capacity to tint food yellow, but is not as subtle as the more expensive spice. The bright yellow colour is also used as a dye for silks and cottons, including the robes of Buddhist monks. Fresh turmeric imparts a warm, musky flavour and a rich colour to foods. The dried spice has similar properties. Ground turmeric is used in curry powders, and is responsible for the characteristic yellow colour.

***Right**: Ground turmeric and fresh turmeric*

PREPARING FRESH CHILLIES

The recipes that call for two or more chillies will be quite hot, so feel free to use less, if you prefer. Small, fat chillies are usually milder than long, thin ones.

1 Remove the stalks, then slice the chillies lengthways.

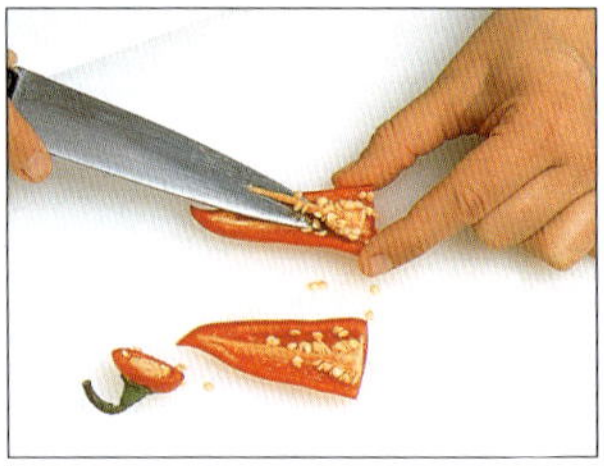

2 Scrape out the pith and seeds from the chillies, then slice, shred or chop the flesh as required. The seeds can be either discarded or added to the dish, depending on the amount of heat that is required.

PREPARING DRIED CHILLIES

Dried chillies are available from Asian food stores and larger supermarkets.

1 Remove the stems and seeds and snap each chilli into two or three pieces. Put these in a bowl, pour over hot water to cover and leave to stand for 30 minutes.

2 Drain, reserving the soaking water if it can usefully be added to the dish. Use the pieces of chilli as they are, or chop them finely.

MAKING CHILLI FLOWERS

Thai cooks are famous for their beautiful presentation, and often garnish platters with chilli flowers, which are quite simple to make.

1 Holding each chilli in turn by the stem, slit it in half lengthways.

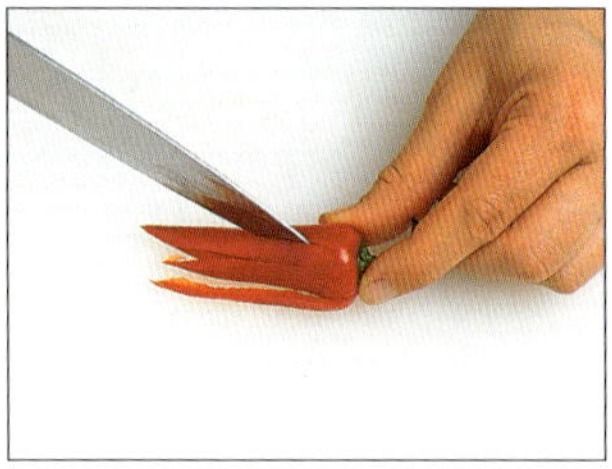

2 Keeping the stem end of the chilli intact, cut it lengthways into strips.

3 Put the chillies in a bowl of iced water, cover and chill for 3–4 hours. The cut chilli strips will curl back to resemble flower petals. Drain well on kitchen paper and use as a garnish. Small chillies may be very hot, so don't be tempted to eat the flowers.

Right: Fresh green chillies

Chillies

Hot chillies and sweet (bell) peppers belong to the same genus, capsicum, and there are scores of varieties. Like sweet peppers, many chillies start out green and ripen to red, while others change from yellow to red and finally to brown or even black, so what might appear to be a basket of assorted chillies could turn out to be the same type of chilli in varying degrees of ripeness. Size also varies. Although South-east Asian cooks tend to use them fresh, chillies are also available dried.

Always treat chillies with caution, as some varieties can be extremely fiery. Much of the severe heat is contained in the seeds, so remove these before use if you prefer a milder flavour. Chillies and other spicy foods are in fact perfect for hot climates because they encourage blood to rush to the surface of the skin, and therefore promote cooling. Chillies

Below: Medium red chillies

CHILLI PASTE

Ready-made chilli paste is sold in jars. However, it is easy to make at home. Simply halve and seed fresh chillies, then place them in a food processor and purée to a smooth paste. A chopped onion can be added to the processor to add bulk to the paste. Store small amounts of the paste in the refrigerator for up to 1 week, or spoon into containers, and freeze for up to 6 months. *Sambal oelek*, an Indonesian chilli sauce, is made in a similar way, but first the chillies are blanched.

are used fresh in South-east Asia in sauces and salads, and are an essential ingredient in Indonesian sambals. They also find their way into a variety of cooked dishes, including stocks, soups, braised dishes, curries and stir-fries, with or without the seeds. Where just a hint of heat is required, chillies are added whole to a dish, then removed just before serving.

Lemon grass

Widely used throughout South-east Asia, lemon grass is an important ingredient in soups, sauces, stir-fries, curries, salads, pickles and marinades. It is a perfect partner for coconut milk, especially in fish, shellfish and chicken dishes. It has a clean, intense lemon flavour with a hint of ginger but none of the acidity associated with lemon or grapefruit. Thai cooks often start a stir-fry by adding a few sliced rings of lemon grass and perhaps a little grated or chopped fresh root ginger or galangal to the oil.

Ground dried lemon grass, also known as serai powder, can be used instead of fresh. As a guide, about 5ml/1 tsp powder is equivalent to 1 fresh stalk. Whole and dried chopped stalks are also available in jars from Asian food stores and larger supermarkets, as are jars of lemon grass paste.

There are two main ways of using lemon grass. The stalk can be bruised, then cooked slowly in a soup or stew until it releases all its flavour and is removed, or the tender portions of the lemon grass can be sliced or finely chopped, then stir-fried or used in a salad or braised dish. Often one stalk will serve both purposes; the tougher top end is used for the background flavouring while the tender lower portion forms the focal point of a dish.

Left: *Fresh lemon grass stalks*

Kaffir limes

These fruits are not true limes, but belong to a subspecies of the citrus family. Native to South-east Asia, kaffir lime leaves are synonymous with Thai cooking, and are also used in Indonesia, Malaysia, Burma and Vietnam. Only the rind and leaves are used, the fruit and juice are not eaten. The scented bouquet is citrus, and the full lemon flavour is released when the leaves are torn or shredded. The leaves are used in soups and curries. The finely grated rind is sometimes added to fish or chicken dishes.

Above: *Kaffir limes and leaves*

Curry leaves

These are the shiny green leaves of a hardwood tree that is indigenous to India. Although they look like bay leaves, their flavour is very different. They are used in Indian cooking, especially in south India and Sri Lanka, and were first introduced to Malaysia by Tamil migrants. The spear-shaped leaves grow on a thin stem. They have an intriguing warm fragrance, with just a hint of sweet, green pepper or tangerine. The full flavour is released when the leaves are bruised. When added to curries or braised dishes, they impart a distinctive flavour. Dried curry leaves come a very poor second to fresh, and they rapidly lose their fragrance.

MAKING A LEMON GRASS BRUSH

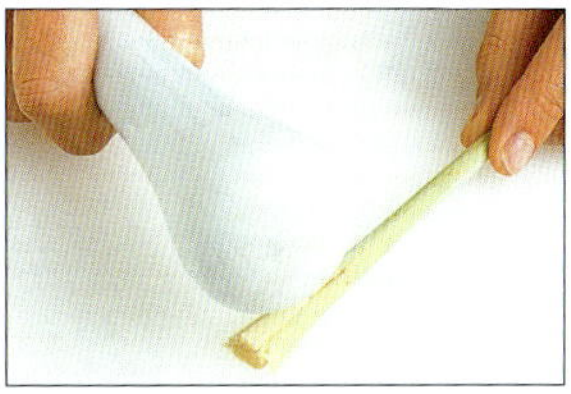

To make a lemon stalk into a basting brush, trim off the bottom 5cm/2in of the stalk to use in a recipe, then flatten the cut end of the remaining stalk using a cleaver or pestle to produce a fibrous brush. Use the brush to baste grilled (broiled) foods.

Mint

The Asian variety of mint is much more strongly flavoured than most European types, and is slightly sweet tasting, imparting a cool aftertaste and a stimulating aroma. Mint is an essential ingredient in Vietnamese cooking, and it was they who introduced it to the Thais. As it has such a dominant flavour, mint is seldom used with other herbs.

Below: *Fresh coriander*

Coriander

This beautifully aromatic herb is widely used in South-east Asian cooking for its wonderful flavour. Fresh coriander (cilantro) also makes an attractive garnish, and it freezes well. Available all over South-east Asia, coriander seeds are more often used than fresh coriander leaves in Indonesia.

Basil

This is one of the oldest herbs known to man, and is thought to have originated in India. However, basil is not used in India as much as it is in the rest of South-east Asia. It is important in Laos, Vietnam and Cambodia, but it is in Thailand that basil is most widely used, and for this reason it is the varieties of basil favoured by the Thais that are most often seen in Asian food stores. If you cannot find Thai basil, any European variety can be used, but the flavour will not be the same, and you should use a little more than the amount recommended. Basil is best used fresh, but freeze-dried leaves are also available from supermarkets. It is added to curries and salads, as an ingredient and as a garnish. Avoid chopping basil leaves, but tear them into pieces or add them to the dish whole.

Below: *Fresh Thai basil*

Star anise

This unusual star-shaped spice comes from an evergreen tree native to South-east China and Vietnam. The points of the star contain amber seeds. Both the seeds and the husk are used for the ground spice. Star anise both smells and tastes like liquorice, and its aromatic flavour complements all rich meats. It is used to flavour beef soups in Vietnam, and is used in light desserts, such as fruit salads.

Star anise can be added whole, and it looks so attractive that it is often left in a dish when serving. When only a small quantity is required, the spice can be broken and just one or two points added. Ground star anise is one of the essential ingredients of five spice powder.

Above: *Star anise*

Cloves

These are unopened flower buds of a tree that is a member of the myrtle family. Cloves originated in the Spice Islands in Indonesia and were taken to the Seychelles and Mauritius in the 18th century. Cloves have an intense fragrance and an aromatic flavour that can be fiery. They also have astringent properties. In South-east Asia, cloves are mainly used in savoury dishes, and their warm, aromatic flavour complements rich meats. Thai cooks use cloves to cut the rich flavour of duck, and also use them with tomatoes, salty vegetables and in ham or pork dishes. Ground cloves are an essential ingredient in many curry spice mixtures.

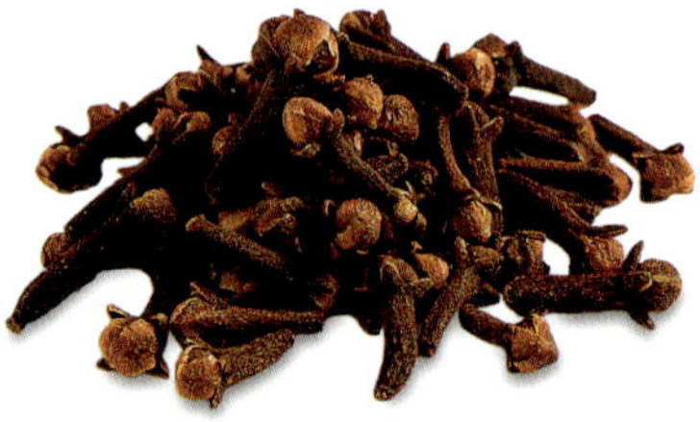

Above: *Cloves*

Above: Ground cinnamon and cinnamon sticks

Cinnamon

The sweet and fragrant bouquet of cinnamon comes from an essential oil, oil of cinnamon, which is used medicinally. The flavour is warm and aromatic, and has universal appeal as a flavouring in sweet and savoury dishes, and cakes and breads. In South-east Asia, the sticks are used in spicy meat dishes, often with star anise, with which cinnamon has an affinity. Add the whole or broken cinnamon stick as directed in the recipe. Pure ground cinnamon is rarely used in Asian cooking.

Cassia

Sometimes known as Chinese cinnamon, cassia smells rather like cinnamon, but is more pungent. Cracked cassia quills and cassia buds (which look like cloves) are used in the East to give a warm aromatic flavour to pickles, curries and meat dishes. Cassia is quite tough. Break the pieces as required with the end of a rolling pin or put them in a mortar and use a pestle to shatter them. Where ground cassia is required, it is best to buy it in that form.

Cumin

This is believed to have originated in the eastern Mediterranean, but is now widely cultivated . The plant is a member of the parsley family, but only the seeds (whole or ground) are used in cooking.

Cumin has a sweet, warm and spicy aroma. The flavour is pungent but not harsh. It is often partnered with whole or ground coriander seeds. Indian cooks are particularly partial to cumin, and it was they who introduced the spice to Singapore, Malaysia and Indonesia.

To bring out the full flavour, the seeds are often dry-fried. They are then used whole, or ground in a spice mill or using a mortar and pestle.

Above: Ground cumin and cumin seeds

Cardamom

Cardamom belongs to the ginger family. It is largely grown for its pods, although Thai cooks sometimes use the leaves for flavouring. The pods are either added whole to spicy dishes, or opened so that the tiny dark seeds can be extracted. The most familiar pods are pale green, and there are also white pods, which are bleached green ones. Black cardamoms, which come from Vietnam and India, are large and coarse. They taste quite different, and are used in red meat dishes. Cardamoms are sweet, pungent and aromatic. They have a warm flavour, with hints of lemon and eucalyptus.

Left: Ground cassia and cassia quills

Above: From left, green and brown cardamom pods

Left: Clockwise from top, brown, black and white mustard seeds

Mustard seeds

These seeds have no aroma in their raw state but when they are roasted they develop a rich, nutty smell. The famous hot taste comes from an enzyme in the seeds, which is only activated when they are crushed and mixed with warm water. Brown mustard seeds, which have largely replaced the black seeds, are not as intensely pungent. White mustard seeds are larger than the other varieties and a little milder.

Throughout Asia, mustard seeds are used for pickling and seasoning, while whole mustard seeds are often used in vegetable and dhal dishes.

Fennel seeds

Sweet, warm and aromatic, fennel seeds have a distinct anise flavour. Fennel seeds are a constituent in many spice mixtures, especially those that are intended to be used with fish or shellfish.

Fennel seeds should be dry-fried before grinding so that the full flavour of the spice is released.

Annatto seeds

The shrub from which the annatto seeds are taken has heart-shaped, glossy leaves and spectacular, pink, rose-like flowers. The plant produces a heart-shaped fruit capsule, which splits itself in half when ripe to reveal fifty or more seeds. The Spanish introduced the seeds to the Philippines, and annatto seeds are widely used in Filipino dishes.

Annatto seeds are brick-red and triangular in shape, with a peppery flavour and bouquet, and just a hint of nutmeg in their aroma. The seeds can be infused in hot water, and will impart a rich red colour to oil when fried for a few minutes. Add the water or oil to rice dishes and use in place of saffron.

Peppercorns

Black peppercorns have an earthy aroma, which is particularly noticeable when they are crushed. The flavour is hot and pungent. White peppercorns are slightly milder.

Pepper can be used before, during and after cooking. Its value is legendary, for it not only has its own flavour, but has the ability to enhance the flavour of other ingredients in a dish.

Below: From left, white and black peppercorns

DRY FRYING MUSTARD SEEDS

Mustard seeds have almost no smell until they are heated so, before adding them to dishes, they should be dry-fried to heighten their aroma.

1 Heat a little sunflower oil in a wok or large pan. Add the seeds and shake the pan over the heat, stirring occasionally, until they start to change colour.

2 Have a pan lid to hand so that you are ready to prevent the mustard seeds from popping out of the pan.

GRINDING SPICES

Spices are often crushed or ground to release their flavour. Only a few, notably mace, dried ginger and turmeric, cinnamon and cassia, are difficult to grind at home and should be bought in powdered form. For the best flavour, grind spices as you need them. Don't grind them more than a day or two in advance.

DRY-FRYING WHOLE SPICES

Many whole spices benefit from being dry-fried before they are ground. This makes sure that no surface moisture remains, and it heightens and develops the flavour. To dry-fry spices, heat a wok or heavy pan for 1 minute, then add the spices. Cook for 2–3 minutes, stirring and shaking the pan constantly to prevent the spices from scorching. When the spices start to give off a warm, rich aroma, remove the pan from the heat and tip the spices into a spice mill or a mortar, and process or grind with a pestle. Purists recommend that each spice is dry-fried separately, but several spices can be cooked together, if watched over closely.

All spices react differently to heat, so follow these basic guidelines for best results:

- Coriander seeds often provide the dominant flavour, especially in powders from Southern India and Singapore. Shake the pan well to keep the seeds on the move, and remove them from the heat when they start to give off a mild, sweet, orangey perfume.
- Dried chillies can be roasted in a cool oven, but it is better to sear them in a heavy pan, where you can keep an eye on them. Place the pan over a medium heat for 2–3 minutes, until the chillies soften and puff up. Do not let them burn, or the flavour will be ruined. Transfer to a plate immediately to stop them overheating or burning.
- Cumin seeds should be dry-fried in a pan, and will be ready for grinding when the seeds release their aroma, usually within 40–50 seconds.
- Black peppercorns need gentle dry-frying, just to heighten the flavour.
- Fenugreek needs to be watched carefully as it will become bitter if it is dry-fried for too long. It is ready when it turns brownish yellow.
- Curry leaves can be dry-fried over a cool to medium heat when fresh. Grind or pound them, using a mortar and pestle, to release their characteristic flavour, then mix them with the other spices. This works well if you are making a curry powder or paste that is to be used immediately, but if it is to be kept for more than 24 hours, make up the powder, then add the whole fresh or frozen leaves just before you are ready to use it. Remove the leaves before serving the curry. Avoid using dried curry leaves if possible, as they will have lost most of their flavour in the dehydration process.

Right: From top, compressed tamarind, compressed tamarind block and dried tamarind slices

Tamarind

Although tamarind doesn't have much of an aroma, its flavour is tart, sour, fruity and refreshing. It is used in many South-east Asian curries, chutneys and dhals, and is an essential ingredient of Thai hot and sour soups. Blocks of compressed tamarind and slices of dried tamarind have been available for a while, but it is now also possible to buy jars of fresh tamarind and cartons of tamarind concentrate and paste, which require less preparation time. There really is no substitute for tamarind. Some recipes may suggest using vinegar or lemon or lime juice instead, but the results will not compare with using the real thing.

Compressed tamarind is sold in a solid block and looks rather like dried dates. To prepare it, tear off a piece that is roughly equivalent to 15ml/1 tbsp and soak it in 150ml/¼ pint/⅔ cup warm water for 10 minutes. Swirl the tamarind around with your fingers so that the pulp is released from the seeds. Using a nylon sieve, strain the juice into a jug (pitcher). Discard the contents of the sieve and use the liquid as required.

Tamarind slices look a little like dried apple slices. Place them in a small bowl, then pour over enough warm water to cover and leave to soak for 30 minutes to extract the flavour, squeeze the tamarind slices with your fingers, then strain the juice into a jug.

Tamarind concentrate or paste is sold in Asian food stores, and is a quick and convenient alternative to compressed tamarind and tamarind slices. To prepare, mix 15ml/1 tbsp concentrate or paste with 60–90ml/4–6 tbsp warm water. Stir briskly until dissolved, then use as required in the recipe. Any leftover liquid can be stored in the refrigerator and used for another recipe.

CURRY POWDERS and PASTES

Curry powders and pastes are spice blends that are used as the basis of a curry. Traditionally, these mixtures would be prepared as needed, using fresh ingredients, but for convenience a wide variety of prepared pastes and powders are now available commercially, and most supermarket shelves carry a wealth of different spice mixtures from all parts of the globe. However, for enthusiastic cooks it is fun and a creative challenge to make up your own curry powders and pastes. Keep experimenting until you find the balance of spicing that suits you and your family. It is perfectly possible to mix ground spices, but it is more satisfying (and much more satisfactory in terms of flavour) to start with whole spices.

Curry powders

The word curry evolved from the Tamil word *kaari*, meaning any food cooked in a sauce. There is little doubt that curry powder, a ready-made blend of spices, was an early convenience food, prepared for merchants, sailors and military men who had served in the East and wished to bring these exotic flavours home.

Simple curry powder

This Malayan Chinese spice mixture is good for poultry, especially chicken, and robust fish curries.

MAKES ABOUT 60ML/4 TBSP

- 2 dried red chillies
- 6 whole cloves
- 1 small cinnamon stick
- 5ml/1 tsp coriander seeds
- 5ml/1 tsp fennel seeds
- 10ml/2 tsp Sichuan peppercorns
- 2.5ml/½ tsp freshly grated nutmeg
- 5ml/1 tsp ground star anise
- 5ml/1 tsp ground turmeric

WATCHPOINTS

- Ensure that you wash your hands, and the chopping board and other utensils thoroughly after preparing chillies.
- If your skin is particularly sensitive, then you should wear rubber gloves while you are preparing the chillies.

1 Remove the seeds from the dried chillies using the point of a knife, and discard any stems. If you prefer a very hot and punchy spice mixture, then retain some or all of the chilli seeds.

2 Put the chillies, cloves, cinnamon, coriander, fennel seeds and Sichuan peppercorns in a wok or large pan. Dry-fry the spices, tossing them around the pan frequently until they start to release a rich, spicy aroma.

3 Grind the spices to a smooth powder in a mortar, using a pestle. Alternatively, use a spice mill, or an electric coffee grinder that is reserved for the purpose.

4 Add the grated nutmeg, star anise and turmeric. Use immediately or store in an airtight jar away from strong light.

SEVEN-SEAS CURRY POWDER

Seven-seas Curry Powder is a mild spice blend used in Indonesian and Malaysian curries. The name refers to the seven seas, including the Andaman and South China Sea, that converge on the shores of Malaysia and the islands of Indonesia.

To make the powder, bruise 6–8 cardamom pods and put them in a wok with 90ml/6 tbsp coriander seeds, 45ml/3 tbsp cumin seeds, 22.5ml/1½ tbsp celery seeds, 5cm/2in piece cinnamon stick, 6–8 cloves and 15ml/1 tbsp chilli powder. Dry-fry until the rich aroma is released.

Curry pastes

On market stalls throughout South-east Asia are mounds of pounded wet spices: lemon grass, chilli, ginger, garlic, galangal, shallots and tamarind. After purchasing meat, chicken or fish, all the cook has to do is to call on the spice seller. He or she will ask a few questions: "What sort of curry is it to be? Hot or mild? How many servings?" Having ascertained the answers and perhaps exchanged a few more pleasantries, the appropriate quantities of each spice will be scooped on to a banana leaf and folded into a neat cone, ready to be taken home.

We may not be able to buy our ingredients in such colourful surroundings, but Western supermarkets now stock some very good ready-made pastes, or you can make your own at home. By experimenting, you will find the balance of flavours you like, and can then make your favourite mixtures in bulk. Store surplus curry paste in in the freezer.

COOK'S TIP

If you grind wet spices a lot, you may find it useful to invest in a traditional Asian mortar, made from granite, with a rough, pitted or ridged bowl, which helps to hold the ingredients while they are being pounded with the pestle. Alternatively, for speed, you can use a food processor or blender instead of a mortar and pestle.

Red curry paste

This Thai paste was named after the colour of the chillies used to prepare it. For a hotter paste, add a few chilli seeds.

MAKES ABOUT 175G/6OZ/¾ CUP

5ml/1 tsp coriander seeds, roasted
2.5ml/½ tsp cumin seeds, roasted
12–15 fresh red chillies, seeded and roughly chopped
4 shallots, thinly sliced
2 garlic cloves, chopped
15ml/1 tbsp peeled and chopped fresh galangal
2 lemon grass stalks, chopped
4 fresh coriander roots
10 black peppercorns
good pinch of ground cinnamon
5ml/1 tsp ground turmeric
2.5ml/½ tsp shrimp paste
5ml/1 tsp salt
30ml/2 tbsp vegetable oil

1 Put all the ingredients except the oil in a mortar or food processor and pound or process to a paste.

2 Add the oil, a little at a time, mixing or processing well after each addition. Transfer to a glass jar, and keep in the refrigerator until ready to use.

VARIATIONS

- For Green Curry Paste, process 12–15 green chillies, 2 chopped lemon grass stalks, 3 sliced shallots, 2 garlic cloves, 15ml/1 tbsp chopped galangal, 4 chopped kaffir lime leaves, 2.5ml/½ tsp grated kaffir rind, 5ml/1 tsp each of chopped coriander root, salt, roasted coriander seeds, roasted cumin seeds and shrimp paste, 15ml/1 tbsp granulated sugar, 6 black peppercorns and 15ml/1 tbsp vegetable oil until a paste forms.
- For Yellow Curry Paste, process 6–8 yellow chillies, 1 chopped lemon grass stalk, 4 sliced shallots, 4 garlic cloves, 15ml/1 tbsp chopped fresh root ginger, 5ml/1 tsp coriander seeds, 5ml/1 tsp each of mustard powder and salt, 2.5ml/½ tsp ground cinnamon, 15ml/1 tbsp light brown sugar and 30ml/2 tbsp vegetable oil until a paste forms.

Mussaman curry paste

This hot and spicy paste is used to make the Thai version of a Muslim curry, which is traditionally made with beef, but can also be made with other meats such as chicken or lamb.

MAKES ABOUT 175G/6OZ/¾ CUP

12 large dried red chillies
1 lemon grass stalk
60ml/4 tbsp chopped shallots
5 garlic cloves, roughly chopped
10ml/2 tsp chopped fresh galangal
5ml/1 tsp cumin seeds
15ml/1 tbsp coriander seeds
2 cloves
6 black peppercorns
5ml/1 tsp shrimp paste, prepared
5ml/1 tsp salt
5ml/1 tsp granulated sugar
30ml/2 tbsp vegetable oil

1 Carefully remove the seeds from the dried chillies and discard. Soak the chillies in a bowl of hot water for about 15 minutes.

2 Trim the root end from the lemon grass stalk and slice the lower 5cm/2in of the stalk into small pieces.

3 Place the chopped lemon grass in a dry wok over a low heat, and then add the chopped shallots, garlic and galangal and dry-fry for 2–3 minutes.

4 Stir in the cumin seeds, coriander seeds, cloves and peppercorns and continue to dry-fry over a low heat for 5–6 minutes, stirring constantly. Spoon the mixture into a large mortar.

5 Drain the chillies and add them to the mortar. Grind finely, using the pestle, then add the prepared shrimp paste, salt, sugar and oil and pound again until the mixture forms a rough paste. Use as required, then spoon any leftover paste into a jar, seal tightly and store in the refrigerator for up to 4 months.

COOK'S TIPS

- Preparing a double or larger quantity of paste in a food processor or blender makes the blending of the ingredients easier and the paste will be smoother.
- For the best results, before you start to process the ingredients, slice them up in the following order: galangal, lemon grass, fresh ginger and turmeric, chillies, nuts, shrimp paste, garlic and shallots. Add some of the oil (or coconut cream if that is to be your frying medium) to the food processor if the mixture is a bit sluggish. If you do this, remember to use less oil or coconut cream when you fry the curry paste to eliminate the raw taste of the ingredients before adding the meat, poultry, fish or vegetables.

PREPARING SHRIMP PASTE

Shrimp paste is a seasoning made from fermented shrimps. It can be bought in Asian food stores. Unless it is to be fried as part of a recipe, it should always be lightly cooked before use.

If you have a gas cooker, simply mould the shrimp paste on to a metal skewer and rotate over a low gas flame, or heat under the grill of an electric cooker, until the outside begins to look crusty but not burnt.

ADDITIONAL INGREDIENTS

Many of the basic ingredients called for in South-east Asian curry recipes will store very well. Others should be bought fresh, as needed.

Peanuts

Also known as groundnuts or monkey nuts, peanuts are eaten as a snack food, and as ingredients in salads and curries . In Indonesia and Malaysia, roasted peanuts, pounded to a paste, are the basis for satay sauce.

Above: *Whole peanuts*

Palm sugar

This strongly flavoured brown sugar is made from the sap of the coconut palm tree. It is sold in Asian food stores. Dark brown sugar can be used as a substitute.

Soy sauce

This is made from fermented soya beans, wheat grain, salt and water. There are two main varieties: thick, sometimes referred to as black or dark, and thin, curiously referred to as white or light. In Indonesia, a soy sauce called kecap manis is preferred, because it is thicker and sweeter.

Brown bean sauce

Made from salted, fermented soy beans, this is a popular flavouring in Asian cooking. Yellow bean sauce is also available.

Rice wine vinegar

Japanese rice wine vinegar is used in South-east Asia for dipping sauces and preserving. Cider vinegar and any mild, plain white vinegar can be used instead.

Shrimp paste

An essential ingredient common to the countries of South-east Asia, this paste is also known as *terasi*, *blachan* and *balachan*. It is made from fermented shrimps or prawns, with salt, pounded into a paste and sold in blocks. Wrap a cube in a foil parcel and place in a dry pan over a low heat for 5 minutes, turning from time to time. This takes away the rawness from the paste and avoids filling the kitchen with the strong smell. If the paste is to be fried, this initial cooking is not needed.

Fish sauce

The most commonly used flavouring in Thai cooking is fish sauce, which is known in Thailand as *nam pla*. It is made from salted anchovies, and may be sold as anchovy sauce in Asian stores. Fish sauce has a strong salty flavour, and is used in the same way as soy sauce.

Salted eggs

This is the traditional way to preserve duck eggs in South-east Asia. The eggs are sold in Asian stores, often covered in a layer of charcoal ash. Rub off the ash under running water, then hard-boil (hard-cook) the eggs.

Below: *Dark and light soy sauce*

Beancurd/tofu and tempeh

These fragile looking 7.5cm/3in cubes are available fresh. Beancurd, which is also known by its Japanese name, tofu, is made in a similar way to soft cheese, but uses soya bean milk instead of dairy milk, set with gypsum, and for this reason it is popular with vegetarians and vegans, who not eat dairy foods. In spite of its bland flavour, beancurd is bursting with protein, and will absorb flavours of other ingredients quickly.

Tempeh is an Indonesian speciality. It is made from fermented soya beans, to give a cake that is packed full of protein, iron and vitamin B. Add it to dishes as directed on the packet.

Below: *Clockwise from left, silken tofu, beancurd skins, firm tofu and deep-fried tofu.*

FRUITS and VEGETABLES

There are several key fruit and vegetable ingredients used in South-east Asian cooking, and most of these are now available from Western supermarkets.

Banana leaves

The large green leaves of the banana tree are South-east Asia's answer to kitchen foil. Make the leaves more pliable by plunging them into boiling water. Place the ingredients for cooking inside, make into a parcel and secure with a skewer. Food wrapped in this way is flavoured by the leaf itself.

Pandan leaves

These leaves impart a warm aroma when cooked. Available fresh, in bunches, pandan (screwpine) leaves are used to flavour rice and desserts. Pull the tines of a fork through a leaf to tear it and release the flavour, and tie the leaf in a knot so that it is easy to remove. Screwpine essence (extract) can be used as an alternative.

Bangkuang (yambean)

These are the same shape as a turnip but with a smooth, light golden skin, which should be peeled thinly. The texture is somewhere between that of an apple and a hard pear. Peel the bangkuang and cut in julienne strips, to use in stir-fries, spring rolls or salads.

Beansprouts

Readily available, beansprouts are widely used in Asian cooking, where they add a crunchy texture and delicate flavour to soups, salads and stir-fries. Most beansprouts come from mung beans, although soya beans are also sold. Both can be sprouted at home. Store beansprouts in the refrigerator in a covered container for 2–3 days.

Bamboo shoots

The edible young shoots of the bamboo plant are sold fresh or canned; fresh shoots take a long time to cook, but taste much better than the canned variety; if buying canned shoots, look for the whole ones, which are better quality than the ready-sliced variety.

Above: *Beansprouts*

Chayote

This pear-shaped vegetable can be eaten raw or cooked, and is often stir-fried or simmered in soups. Chayote has a mild taste not unlike courgette (zucchini). It is usually cooked with strong seasonings such as garlic, ginger and chillies.

Chinese leaves

This versatile vegetable, known as Chinese cabbage in the United States, can be used in stir-fries, stews, curries or soups. It will absorb the flavours of other ingredients, while retaining its own mild, cabbage flavour and crunchy texture.

Sweet potatoes

Several varieties of sweet potatoes are grown all over South-east Asia. After peeling, they are sliced and stir-fried, or braised with seasoning amd spices.

Aubergines

Many varieties of aubergine (eggplant) are grown in South-east Asia, from tiny pea aubergines, which are added at the end of cooking, to white, yellow or green aubergines. When these types are unavailable, use the purple variety.

Onions

The versatile onion is an important flavouring agent in Asian cooking, and an essential ingredient in sauces, curries and stews. Only spring onions (scallions) are usually eaten as a vegetable, although deep-fried onions are a popular garnish. Shallots are used extensively in Thai dishes in place of onions.

Papaya

In South-east Asia, papaya is eaten both as a fruit and a vegetable. Unripe green papayas are served raw in salads or used in pickles, while papayas that are not too ripe are added to soups, curries and seafood dishes. The ripe fruit is eaten as a dessert. Both the juice and skin of papaya are also used to tenderize meat.

Coconut

This versatile fruit is one of the hallmarks of South-east Asian cooking. Coconut milk is used as a cooking medium, in place of stock, and is added at the end of cooking to enrich curries; canned milk is sold commercially, but it can also be made at home, using desiccated (dry, unsweetened, shredded) coconut. If the milk is left to stand, coconut cream will rise to the surface. Creamed coconut is sold in blocks or in powdered form. Small quantities are used to enrich and thicken dishes at the end of cooking.

MAKING COCONUT MILK

Coconut milk can be made at home from desiccated coconut. Make as much or as little as you like, varying the quantities accordingly.

Tip 225g/8oz/2⅔ cups desiccated coconut into the bowl of a food processor and pour over 450ml/¾ pint/scant 2 cups boiling water. Process for 20-30 seconds and allow to cool.

Place a sieve lined with muslin (cheesecloth) over a large bowl in the sink. Ladle some of the softened coconut into the muslin.

Bring up the ends of the cloth and twist it over the sieve to extract as much of the liquid as possible. Discard the spent coconut. Store the coconut milk in the refrigerator. Use as directed in the recipes.

RICE and NOODLES

The unassertive flavour of rice and noodles makes them perfect partners for spicy curry dishes. Rice is the staple grain of the whole of Asia, but noodles also form an important part of the daily diet throughout the region.

Rice

A bowl of rice is eaten at every meal throughout South-east Asia, including breakfast. It is usually served simply boiled or steamed, although in some countries coconut milk is used instead of water for some dishes. There are thousands of varieties of rice in the major rice-growing regions of South-east Asia, although people generally only eat the rice that is grown locally. Types of rice are classified by region, by colour, by cooking properties or even by price, but the most common classification is by the length of grain, which can be long, medium or short. As a general rule, long and medium grain rices are used in South-east Asia for savoury dishes, while short grain rice is used for puddings and desserts.

Right: Thai fragrant rice

Long grain rices

There are many strains of long grain rice, and it is the most common rice in South-east Asia, partly because it can be used in a variety of recipes. White long grain rice has had its husk, bran and germ removed. It is light and fluffy when cooked, with a bland flavour. Brown long grain rice has had only its outer husk removed, which gives it a chewy texture and nutty flavour. It takes longer to cook than white long grain rice, but contains more fibre, vitamins and minerals.

Thai fragrant rice is a long grain rice cultivated in Thailand, and it is widely used throughout South-east Asia. The rice has a distinctive scent of jasmine (it is also known as jasmine rice) and a perfumed flavour, for which it is highly prized. Once cooked, the grains become slightly sticky.

Glutinous rice

This short grain rice is also known as sticky or waxy rice because of the way the grains stick together after cooking. White glutinous rice is the most common type in South-east Asia, but there is also a black glutinous rice, which retains the husk and has a nutty flavour. A pinkish-red variety is cultivated on the banks of the River Yangtze in China.

COOKING BOILED RICE

Always use a tight-fitting lid for your rice pan. If you do not have a lid that fits tightly, wrap a dishtowel around the lid or put some foil between the lid and the pan. Try not to remove the lid until the rice is cooked. (The advantage of using a lid is that you can tell when the rice is ready because steam begins to escape, visibly and rapidly, from underneath.) As a guide, allow 75g/3oz/scant ½ cup rice per person.

Put the dry rice in a colander and rinse it under cold running water until the water runs clear. Then place the rice in a large pan and pour in enough cold water to come 2cm/¾in above the surface of the rice. Add a pinch of salt and, if you like, 5ml/1 tsp vegetable oil, stir once and bring to the boil. Stir once more, reduce the heat to low and cover the pan with the lid. Cook the rice for 12–15 minutes, then turn off the heat and leave the rice to stand, still covered, for 10 minutes. Before serving, fluff up the rice with a fork or a slotted rice spoon.

COOKING FRIED RICE

Fried rice is usually served as a snack on its own, or as part of a special buffet dinner. For best results, use cold, firm, cooked rice.

1 Stir-fry any uncooked meat in oil in a wok, then add chopped onions. Transfer to a plate and set aside.

2 Add beaten egg to the frying pan and scramble with sliced spring onions (scallions). Add spices and flavourings such as soy sauce, rice wine, chopped herbs, fresh chillies, or tomato purée (paste).

3 Tip the cold rice into the wok and mix with the egg. Return any cooked meats or seafood to the wok. Cook until heated through.

Noodles

These are second only to rice as a staple food in South-east Asia. Unlike rice, however, which is served plain to be eaten with cooked dishes, noodles are usually cooked with other ingredients. For this reason, they are seldon served as accompaniments, but are eaten on their own as light meals or snacks. Noodle street vendors are a common sight, particularly in Thailand.

South-east Asian noodles are made from flour pastes, including wheat, rice and mung bean. Some are plain; others are enriched with egg. All are easy to prepare, but see individual recipes for advice as some types benefit from being soaked before cooking. Both fresh and dried noodles have to be cooked in boiling water; they are then served in one of three ways: in a soup, braised in a broth and eaten with a sauce, or fried.

***Above**: Cellophane noodles*

Wheat noodles

Plain noodles are made from strong plain wheat flour, and are available flat or round, in a variety of thicknesses. Egg noodles are far more common than plain wheat noodles, and are sold in various thicknesses, fresh or dried.

Rice noodles

These noodles, sometimes called rice sticks, are derived from a paste made from whole rice grains, and are sold in various widths, fresh and dried. Rice noodles are partly cooked when they are made, and they need only to be soaked to soften them before use.

***Above**: Thick and thin Thai noodles.*

***Below**: Fresh egg noodles come in various thicknesses.*

PREPARING NOODLES

- Add dried egg noodles to a pan of salted boiling water and cook for 3–5 minutes. Stir to prevent the noodles from settling on the base of the pan. Drain and rinse with cold water, to wash out starch. Fresh egg noodles take 1 minute to cook in salted, fast-boiling water. Drain.
- Rice noodles can be soaked ahead of cooking, either in cold water for some time or in warm water for just a few minutes. Plunge into fast-boiling, salted water. Return to the boil, then remove from the heat and leave for 2 minutes, until cooked. Test one piece and then drain and rinse well with cold water.
- Soak cellophane noodles in cold water, cut into lengths and place in boiling water for 1 minute. Drain well and use as required.

Cellophane noodles

These are made with green mung bean flour, the same beans as those used for sprouting. Although thin, the strands are firm and will not become soggy when cooked. Cellophane noodles are almost tasteless, although they are never served solo but are always used as an ingredient in a dish, usually in vegetarian cooking.

EQUIPMENT and UTENSILS

The equipment in the average Western kitchen will be perfectly adequate for most of the recipes in this book, particularly now that the wok has become an indispensable item in many households. There are some items, however, that will make cooking South-east Asian food easier and more pleasurable. The fact that many of these simple pieces of equipment also look good, and instantly establish you as an adventurous cook in the eyes of your friends, is a bonus.

The best way to build up your store of specialist items is to start slowly, with a few basics such as a cleaver, bamboo grater and wok, then gradually add extra pieces as you experiment with different styles of cooking. The design of many utensils has not changed in centuries, and items made from basic materials are often more effective than modern equivalents.

Below: Cleaver

Below: Traditional bamboo grater

Cleaver

To Western cooks, a cleaver can seem rather intimidating. In reality, cleavers are among the most useful pieces of equipment ever invented. They come in several sizes and weights. Number one is the heaviest, with a blade 23cm/9in long and 10cm/4in wide, and weighing up to 1kg/2¼lb. At the other end of the scale, number three has a shorter, narrower blade and is only half as heavy. Number two is the cook's favourite because of its many uses. The back of the blade is used for pounding and tenderizing, and the flat for crushing and transporting. Even the handle has more than one purpose – its end can be used as a pestle.

Cleavers can be made of carbonized steel with wooden handles, or of stainless steel with metal or wooden handles. Choose the one you are comfortable with. Hold it in your hand and feel the weight; it should be neither too heavy nor too light. One point to remember is that a stainless steel cleaver will require frequent sharpening if it is to stay razor sharp. To prevent a carbonized steel blade from rusting, wipe it dry after every use, then give it a thin coating of vegetable oil. Cleavers should always be sharpened on whetstone, never with a steel sharpener. The cleaver is not as dangerous as it looks, if handled with care. Learn to regard it as just another kitchen knife, and you will be rewarded with very satisfactory results.

Chopping block

The traditional chopping block in South-east Asia is simply a cross-section of a tree trunk, usually hardwood. A large rectangular cutting board of hardwood can be used instead, but make sure it is at least 5cm/2in thick or it may not be able to take a blow from a cleaver. Acrylic boards are also available.

Season a chopping block with vegetable oil on both sides to prevent it from splitting. Let it absorb as much oil as it will take, then clean the block with salt and water and dry it thoroughly. After each use, scrape the surface with the back of your cleaver, then wipe it down with a cloth. Never immerse a wooden block in water.

Grater

Traditional graters, used for preparing ginger, galangal and daikon (mooli), are made from wood or bamboo, but a metal cheese grater makes a satisfactory substitute.

Mortar and pestle

South-east Asian cooks prefer granite or stone mortars and pestles, since these have rough surfaces which help to grip the ingredients. Bigger, flat-bowled mortars are good for making spice pastes that contain large amounts of fresh spices, onion, herbs and garlic.

Spice mill

If you are going to grind a lot of spices, a spice mill will prove useful. An electric coffee grinder works well for this purpose, but it is a good idea to reserve the mill for spices only.

Wok

In the Philippines, the traditional cooking pot is made of clay. Modern households, however, prefer to use a wok, known as a *carajay* (pronounced carahai). The wok is also widely used in Indonesia, where it is known as a *wajan*, and in Malaysia, where it is called a *kulai*.

It is not surprising that the wok has become a universal favourite, for it is remarkably versatile. The rounded bottom was originally designed to

Below: Traditional granite mortar and pestle

Left: *Carbonized steel woks*

Below: *Wok lid and utensils*

conduct and retain heat evenly, and because of its shape, the food always returns to the centre where the heat is most intense. This makes it ideally suited for stir frying, braising, steaming, boiling and even for deep-frying.

There are two basic types of wok available. The most common type, the double-handled wok, is suitable for all types of cooking. The single-handled wok is particularly suitable for quick stir-frying, as it can easily be shaken. Both types are available with flattened bases for use on electric or gas stoves. Choose a wok made from lightweight carbonized steel; cast iron woks are too heavy for comfort, and woks made from other materials are not suitable for the South-east Asian style of cooking.

A new wok must be seasoned before use. To do this, place it over a high heat until the surface blackens, then wash it in warm, soapy water. Use a stiff brush to get the wok clean, then rinse it in clean water and place it over a medium heat to dry. Finally, wipe the surface with kitchen paper soaked in vegetable oil. After each use, wash the wok with hot water, but never use detergent as this would remove the seasoning and cause the wok to rust. Any food that sticks to the wok should be scraped off with a non-metal scourer, and the wok should then be rinsed and dried over a low heat. Before being put away, a little oil should always be rubbed into the surface of the wok.

Wok tools

Some wok sets come with a spatula and ladle made from cast iron or stainless steel. A dome-shaped lid is also useful, as is a metal draining rack that fits over the wok. Small items such as deep-fried foods can be placed on the rack to keep warm while more batches are cooked. Other useful accessories include chopsticks and a wok stand, which will help to protect your table when serving.

Strainers

The two most useful types of strainer are the perforated metal scoop or slotted spoon, and the coarse-mesh, wire skimmer, preferably with a long bamboo handle. Wire skimmers come in a variety of sizes and are useful for removing food from oil when deep-frying.

Clay pot

This earthenware cooking utensil is available in several shapes and sizes. It can be used on top of the stove, where it will retain an even heat as the food cooks.

Rice cooker

Electric rice cookers are very well designed and are worth investing in if you cook a lot of rice. However, a deep, heavy-based pan with a tight-fitting lid will make a perfectly adequate substitute.

THAILAND, BURMA AND VIETNAM

To eat a Thai meal is an experience in itself, with subtle spice blends and exquisite flavours. Burmese food is more robust yet equally exciting, while Vietnamese cuisine shows the influence of neighbouring China, and there is evidence of traditions left over from French colonial rule.

BURMESE-STYLE PORK CURRY

The cuisine of Burma is influenced by its two neighbours, China and India. Soy sauce and noodles are obviously the result of a Chinese influence, but curry itself is definitely an Indian invention. Burmese curries are, however, much lighter.

SERVES 4–6

2.5cm/1in piece fresh root ginger, crushed
8 dried red chillies, soaked in warm water for 20 minutes
2 lemon grass stalks, finely chopped
15ml/1 tbsp chopped galangal or chopped fresh root ginger
15ml/1 tbsp shrimp paste
30ml/2 tbsp brown sugar
675g/1½lb pork, with some of its fat
600ml/1 pint/2½ cups water
10ml/2 tsp ground turmeric
5ml/1 tsp dark soy sauce
4 shallots, finely chopped
15ml/1 tbsp chopped garlic
45ml/3 tbsp tamarind juice or 5ml/1 tsp concentrated tamarind pulp
5ml/1 tsp granulated sugar
15ml/1 tbsp fish sauce
fresh red chillies, to garnish
French (green) beans, to serve

1 In a mortar, pound the ginger, chillies, lemon grass and galangal into a coarse paste with a pestle, then add the shrimp paste and brown sugar to produce a dark, grainy purée.

2 Cut the pork into large chunks and place in a wok or large pan. Add the curry purée and stir well to make sure the meat is well coated.

3 Cook the pork over a low heat, stirring occasionally, until the meat has changed colour and rendered some of its fat, and the curry paste has begun to release its aroma.

4 Stir the water, turmeric and soy sauce into the meat in the pan. Simmer gently for about 40 minutes, until the meat is tender. The pan does not need to be kept covered.

5 Add the shallots, garlic, tamarind juice, sugar and fish sauce. If you are using concentrated tamarind pulp, stir until dissolved. Garnish with fresh chillies and serve with French beans.

CHICKEN with GINGER and LEMON GRASS

This quick and easy recipe from Vietnam contains the unusual combination of ginger and lemon grass with mandarin orange and chillies. The dish is served topped with peanuts, which are first roasted, then skinned.

SERVES 4–6

3 chicken legs (thighs and drumsticks)
15ml/1 tbsp vegetable oil
2cm/¾in piece fresh root ginger, finely chopped
1 garlic clove, crushed
1 small fresh red chilli, seeded and finely chopped
5cm/2in piece lemon grass, shredded
150ml/¼ pint/⅔ cup chicken stock
15ml/1 tbsp fish sauce
10ml/2 tsp granulated sugar
2.5ml/½ tsp salt
juice of ½ lemon
50g/2oz raw peanuts
2 spring onions (scallions), shredded
zest of 1 mandarin or satsuma, shredded
plain boiled rice or rice noodles, to serve

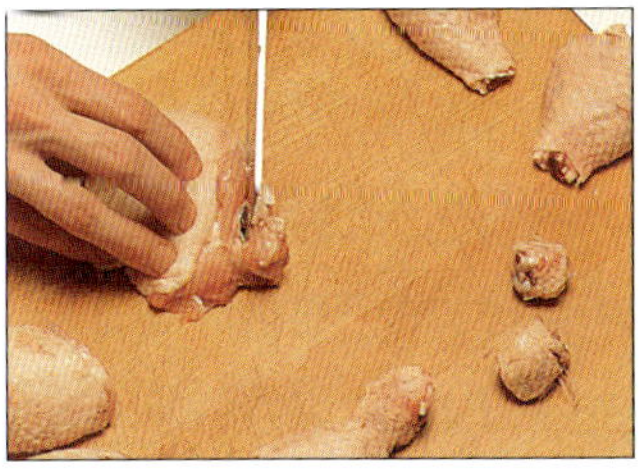

1 With the heel of a knife, chop through the narrow end of each of the chicken drumsticks. Remove the jointed parts of the chicken, then remove the skin. Rinse and pat dry with kitchen paper.

2 Heat the oil in a wok or large pan. Add the chicken, ginger, garlic, chilli and lemon grass and cook for 3–4 minutes. Add the chicken stock, fish sauce, sugar, salt and lemon juice. Cover the pan and simmer for 30–35 minutes.

3 To prepare the peanuts, the red skin must be removed. To do this grill (broil) or roast the peanuts under a medium heat until evenly brown, for 2–3 minutes. Turn the nuts out on to a clean cloth and rub briskly to loosen the skins.

4 Transfer the chicken from the pan to a warmed serving dish, and sprinkle with the roasted peanuts, shredded spring onions and the zest of the mandarin or satsuma. Serve hot with plain boiled rice or rice noodles.

COOK'S TIP

To save yourself time and effort, buy ready-roasted peanuts. These are now available with reduced sodium for a low-salt alternative.

RED CHICKEN CURRY with BAMBOO SHOOTS

Bamboo shoots have a lovely crunchy texture. Try to buy canned whole shoots, which are crisper and of better quality than sliced shoots. It is essential to use chicken breast meat rather than any other cut for this Thai curry, as it is cooked very quickly.

SERVES 4–6

1 litre/1¾ pints/4 cups coconut milk
30ml/2 tbsp red curry paste
450g/1lb chicken breast fillets, skinned and cut into bitesize pieces
30ml/2 tbsp Thai fish sauce
15ml/1 tbsp granulated sugar
225g/8oz canned bamboo shoots, rinsed, drained and sliced
5 kaffir lime leaves, torn
salt and ground black pepper
chopped fresh red chillies and kaffir lime leaves, to garnish
plain boiled rice, to serve

1 Pour half of the coconut milk into a wok or large pan over a medium heat. Bring the coconut milk to the boil, stirring constantly until it has separated.

2 Add the red curry paste and cook the mixture for 2–3 minutes. Stir the paste all the time to prevent it sticking to the base of the pan.

3 Add the chicken pieces, fish sauce and sugar to the pan. Stir well, then cook for 5–6 minutes until the chicken changes colour and is cooked through. Continue to stir to prevent the mixture from sticking to the base of the pan.

4 Pour the remaining coconut milk into the pan, then add the sliced bamboo shoots and torn kaffir lime leaves. Bring back to the boil over a medium heat, stirring constantly to prevent the mixture from sticking, then taste and add salt and pepper if necessary.

5 To serve, spoon the curry into a warmed serving dish and garnish with chopped chillies and kaffir lime leaves.

VARIATION

Instead of, or as well as, bamboo shoots use straw mushrooms. These are available in cans from Asian food stores and good supermarkets. Drain well and then stir into the curry at the end of the recipe.

BEEF CURRY in SWEET PEANUT SAUCE

The consistency of this curry is quite thick, unlike most other Thai curries. Roasted and ground peanuts add a rich taste, and thicken the sauce at the same time. You can grind the peanuts in a coffee grinder or use a pestle and mortar. For a quick alternative, you could use peanut butter, but you will need to reduce the quantity of salt.

SERVES 4–6

600ml/1 pint/2½ cups coconut milk
45ml/3 tbsp red curry paste
45ml/3 tbsp Thai fish sauce
30ml/2 tbsp palm sugar or soft light brown sugar
2 lemon grass stalks, bruised
450g/1lb rump steak cut into thin strips
75g/3oz roasted ground peanuts
2 fresh red chillies, sliced
5 kaffir lime leaves, torn
salt and ground black pepper
10–15 Thai basil leaves, to garnish
2 salted eggs, to serve

1 Put half the coconut milk into a wok or large pan. Heat the milk gently, stirring constantly, until it begins to boil and separate.

2 Add the red curry paste and cook over a medium heat until fragrant. Add the fish sauce, palm or light brown sugar and lemon grass.

3 Continue to cook until the colour of the curry sauce deepens.

4 Add the remaining coconut milk and bring back to the boil. Add the beef and ground peanuts. Cook for 8–10 minutes.

5 Add the sliced chillies and torn kaffir lime leaves and adjust the seasoning. Garnish with the whole Thai basil leaves, and serve with salted eggs, if you like.

GREEN BEEF CURRY with THAI AUBERGINE

Thai cuisine is packed with sensational yet perfectly balanced flavours. This dish, which is cooked in the well-known green curry paste, creates a taste explosion. Thai aubergines are much smaller than the large, purple variety sold in Western supermarkets. You can buy small aubergines from Asian stores or, alternatively, use baby aubergines.

SERVES 4–6

15ml/1 tbsp vegetable oil
45ml/3 tbsp green curry paste
600ml/1 pint/2½ cups coconut milk
450g/1lb beef sirloin
4 kaffir lime leaves, torn
15–30ml/1–2 tbsp Thai fish sauce
5ml/1 tsp palm sugar or soft light brown sugar
150g/5oz small Thai aubergines (eggplant) or baby aubergines, halved
2 fresh green chillies and a small handful of Thai basil, to garnish
plain boiled rice or noodles, to serve

1 Heat the oil in a wok or large pan. Add the green curry paste and fry gently until the paste begins to release its fragrant aromas.

2 Stir in half the coconut milk, a little at a time. Cook over a medium heat for about 5–6 minutes, until the oil begins to separate and an oily sheen appears on the surface.

3 Cut the beef into long thin slices and add to the pan with the kaffir lime leaves, fish sauce, sugar and aubergines. Cook for 2–3 minutes, then stir in the remaining coconut milk.

4 Bring back to a simmer and cook until the meat and aubergines are tender. Finely shred the green chillies and use to garnish the curry, along with the Thai basil leaves.

MUSSAMAN CURRY

Unlike its neighbouring countries, Thailand managed to remain free from colonization by European powers. As a result, its food has no outside influence, although the Thais have borrowed cooking styles from other countries, such as India and China. Mussaman Curry is one such example, which originated within the Muslim community in India.

SERVES 4–6

600ml/1 pint/2½ cups coconut milk (see Cook's Tip)
675g/1½lb stewing beef, cut into 2.cm/1in chunks
250ml/8fl oz/1 cup coconut cream
45ml/3 tbsp mussaman curry paste
30ml/2 tbsp Thai fish sauce
15ml/1 tbsp palm sugar or soft light brown sugar
60ml/4 tbsp tamarind juice or concentrated tamarind pulp
6 cardamom pods
2.5cm/1in piece cinnamon stick
225g/8oz potatoes, cut into even-size chunks
1 onion, cut into wedges
50g/2oz/⅓ cup roasted peanuts
plain boiled rice, to serve

1 Bring the coconut milk to a gentle boil in a wok or large pan. Add the beef and simmer for 40 minutes, until tender.

2 Pour the coconut cream into a small pan, then cook for 5–8 minutes, stirring constantly, until an oily sheen appears on the surface. Add the Thai mussaman curry paste and cook until fragrant.

3 Stir the curry paste into the beef. Add the fish sauce, sugar, tamarind, cardamom pods, cinnamon stick, potatoes and onions. Simmer gently for 10–15 minutes. Add the peanuts and cook for a further 5 minutes. Serve with plain boiled rice.

COOK'S TIP

Coconut milk can be made at home from desiccated coconut. In a food processor, process 225g/8oz/22/3 cups desiccated coconut with 450ml/3/4 pint/scant 2 cups boiling water for 20–30 seconds. Allow to cool a little, then ladle into a sieve (strainer) lined with muslin (cheesecloth) and set over a large bowl. Bring up the ends of the cloth and twist firmly to extract the liquid. Discard the spent coconut and use the milk as directed in recipes. Any unused milk can be stored in the refrigerator for 1–2 days.

BURMESE FISH STEW

Housewives in Burma buy this well-known and delicious one-course meal, known as Mohingha, from hawkers, who can be recognized by a bamboo pole carried across their shoulders. At one end of the pole is a container with a charcoal fire and at the other end is everything else they need to make the meal.

SERVES 8

675g/1½lb huss, cod or mackerel, cleaned but left on the bone
3 lemon grass stalks
2.5cm/1in piece fresh root ginger
30ml/2 tbsp fish sauce
3 onions, roughly chopped
4 garlic cloves, roughly chopped
2–3 fresh red chillies, seeded and chopped
5ml/1 tsp ground turmeric
75ml/5 tbsp groundnut (peanut) oil, for frying
400g/14oz can coconut milk
25g/1oz/¼ cup rice flour
25g/1oz/¼ cup gram flour (besan)
540g/1lb/5oz canned bamboo shoots, rinsed, drained and sliced
salt and ground black pepper
wedges of hard-boiled (hard-cooked) egg, thinly sliced red onions, finely chopped spring onions (scallions), deep-fried prawns (shrimp) and fried chillies, to garnish
rice noodles, to serve

1 Place the fish in a large pan and pour in cold water to cover. Bruise two lemon grass stalks and half the peeled fresh root ginger and add to the pan. Bring to the boil, add the fish sauce and cook for 10 minutes. Lift out the fish with a slotted spoon, and allow to cool. Meanwhile, strain the stock into a large bowl. Discard any skin and bones from the fish and break the flesh into small pieces, using a fork.

2 Cut off the lower 5cm/2in of the remaining lemon grass stalk and discard; roughly chop the remaining lemon grass. Put it in a food processor or blender, along with the remaining ginger, the onions, garlic, chillies and turmeric. Process to a smooth paste. Heat the oil in a wok or large pan, and fry the paste until it gives off a rich, fragrant aroma. Remove the pan from the heat and add the fish pieces.

3 Stir the coconut milk into the reserved fish stock and pour into a large pan. Add water to make up to 2.5 litres/4 pints/10 cups. In a jug (pitcher), mix the rice flour and gram flour (besan) to a thin cream with some of the stock. Stir into the mixture. Bring to the boil, stirring.

4 Add the bamboo shoots to the pan and cook for 10 minutes until tender. Stir in the fish mixture, season to taste, and cook until heated through. Guests pour the soup over the noodles, and add hard-boiled egg, onions, spring onions, prawns and chillies as a garnish.

GREEN PRAWN CURRY

Green Curry has become a firm favourite in the West, and this prawn dish is just one of a range of delicious green curry recipes. Home-made green curry paste has the best flavour, but you can also buy it ready-made from good supermarkets.

SERVES 4–6

30ml/2 tbsp vegetable oil
30ml/2 tbsp green curry paste
450g/1lb raw king prawns (jumbo shrimp), peeled and deveined
4 kaffir lime leaves, torn
1 lemon grass stalk, bruised and chopped
250ml/8fl oz/1 cup coconut milk
30ml/2 tbsp fish sauce
½ cucumber, seeded and cut into thin batons
10–15 basil leaves
4 fresh green chillies, sliced, to garnish

1 Heat the oil in a wok or large pan. Add the green curry paste and fry gently until bubbling and fragrant.

2 Add the prawns, kaffir lime leaves and chopped lemon grass. Fry for 2 minutes, until the prawns are pink.

3 Stir in the coconut milk and bring to a gentle boil. Simmer, stirring occasionally, for about 5 minutes or until the prawns are tender.

4 Stir in the fish sauce, cucumber batons and whole basil leaves, then top with the green chillies and serve from the pan.

VARIATION

Strips of skinned chicken breast fillet can be used in place of the prawns if you prefer. Add them to the pan in step 2 and fry until browned on all sides.

PRAWNS with YELLOW CURRY PASTE

Fish and shellfish, such as prawns, and coconut milk were made for each other. This is a very quick recipe if you make the yellow curry paste in advance, or buy it ready-made. It keeps well in a screw-top jar in the refrigerator for up to four weeks.

SERVES 4–6

600ml/1 pint/2½ cups coconut milk
30ml/2 tbsp yellow curry paste
15ml/1 tbsp fish sauce
2.5ml/½ tsp salt
5ml/1 tsp granulated sugar
450g/1lb raw king prawns (jumbo shrimp), thawed if frozen, peeled and deveined
225g/8oz cherry tomatoes
juice of ½ lime
red (bell) peppers, seeded and cut into thin strips, and fresh coriander (cilantro) leaves, to garnish
plain boiled rice or rice noodles, to serve

1 Put half the coconut milk in a wok or large pan and bring to the boil. Add the yellow curry paste, and stir until it disperses. Lower the heat and simmer gently for about 10 minutes.

2 Add the fish sauce, salt, sugar and remaining coconut milk to the sauce. Simmer for 5 minutes more.

3 Add the prawns and cherry tomatoes. Simmer very gently for about 5 minutes until the prawns are pink and tender.

4 Spoon into a serving dish, sprinkle with lime juice and garnish with strips of pepper and coriander.

VARIATION

Use cooked prawns if preferred. Add in step 3 and heat through.

COOK'S TIP

- Unused coconut milk can be stored in the refrigerator for 1–2 days, or poured into a freezer container and frozen.
- If making your own coconut milk, instead of discarding the spent coconut, it can be reused to make a second batch of coconut milk. This will be of a poorer quality and should only be used to extend a good quality first quantity of milk.
- Leave newly made coconut milk to stand for 10 minutes. The coconut cream will float to the top: skim off with a spoon.

BEANCURD and GREEN BEAN CURRY

These days, beancurd is widely available from supermarkets and Asian stores. It has a silky appearance and an extremely soft texture. Tofu makes an excellent substitute; like beancurd, tofu is made of soya bean paste, but is much firmer. It is also much more easily available and can be found in most supermarkets and health food stores.

SERVES 4–6

600ml/1 pint/2½ cups coconut milk
15ml/1 tbsp red curry paste
45ml/3 tbsp Thai fish sauce
10ml/2 tsp palm sugar or soft light brown sugar
225g/8oz button (white) mushrooms
115g/4oz French (green) beans, trimmed
175g/6oz beancurd, rinsed and cut into 2cm/¾in cubes
4 kaffir lime leaves, torn
2 fresh red chillies, sliced
fresh coriander (cilantro) sprigs, to garnish

1 Put about one-third of the coconut milk in a wok or large pan. Cook until an oily sheen appears on the surface.

2 Add the red curry paste, fish sauce and sugar to the coconut milk. Mix together thoroughly.

3 Add the button mushrooms. Stir well and cook over a medium heat for about 1 minute. Stir in the rest of the coconut milk and bring back to the boil.

4 Add the French beans and cubes of beancurd and allow to simmer gently for another 4–5 minutes.

5 Stir in the kaffir lime leaves and red chillies. Serve garnished with the fresh coriander sprigs.

GREEN PAPAYA SALAD

This salad appears in many guises in South-east Asia. If green papaya is not easy to get hold of, finely grated carrots, cucumber or green apple can be used instead. Alternatively, use very thinly sliced white cabbage.

SERVES 4

I green papaya
4 garlic cloves, roughly chopped
15ml/1 tbsp chopped shallots
3–4 fresh red chillies, seeded and sliced
2.5ml/½ tsp salt
2–3 snake beans or 6 green beans
2 tomatoes, seeded and cut into very thin wedges
45ml/3 tbsp Thai fish sauce
15ml/1 tbsp granulated sugar
juice of 1 lime
30ml/2 tbsp coarsely crushed roasted peanuts
1 fresh red chilli, seeded and sliced, to garnish

1 Cut the papaya in half lengthwise. Scrape out the seeds with a spoon, then peel using a swivel vegetable peeler or a small sharp knife. Shred the flesh finely using a food processor grater.

2 Put the garlic, shallots, chillies and salt in a large mortar and grind to a rough paste with a pestle. Add the shredded papaya, a little at a time, pounding until it becomes slightly limp and soft.

3 Cut the snake beans or green beans into 2cm/¾in lengths. Add the sliced beans and the wedges of tomato to the mortar and crush them very lightly with the pestle.

4 Season the mixture with the Thai fish sauce, sugar and lime juice. Transfer the salad to a serving dish and sprinkle with the crushed peanuts. Garnish with slices of red chilli and serve.

MALAYSIA

The food of Malaysia is a rich blend of some of the world's most exciting cuisines: Malay, Chinese and Indian. The result is a harmonious mixture of flavours, some cool and some famously hot and spicy, such as the dishes cooked in the traditional style known as Nonya.

CHICKEN with SPICES and SOY SAUCE

This simple but delicious dish, known as ayam kecap, *suggests a Chinese influence. Although a significant number of people from China had already settled in Malaysia, by the 15th century Malacca was established as one of the important trading posts in the world, and more Chinese poured into the area. Together with the local Malay people, they developed a unique style of cuisine known as* Nonya.

SERVES 4

1.3–1.6kg/3–3½lb chicken, jointed and cut into 16 pieces
3 onions, sliced
about 1 litre/1¾ pints/4 cups water
3 garlic cloves, crushed
3–4 fresh red chillies, seeded and sliced, or 15ml/1 tbsp chilli powder
45ml/3 tbsp vegetable oil
2.5ml/½ tsp grated nutmeg
6 whole cloves
5ml/1 tsp tamarind pulp, soaked in 45ml/3 tbsp warm water
30–45ml/2–3 tbsp dark or light soy sauce
salt
fresh green and red chilli shreds, to garnish
plain boiled rice, to serve

1 Place the prepared chicken pieces in a large pan with one of the sliced onions. Pour over enough water to just cover. Bring to the boil and then reduce the heat and allow to simmer gently for about 20 minutes.

2 Grind the remaining onions, with the garlic and chillies or chilli powder, to a fine paste in a food processor or with a pestle and mortar. Heat a little of the oil in a wok or frying pan and cook the paste to bring out the flavour. Do not allow the paste to brown.

COOK'S TIP
When adding salt, start with a very small quantity and taste before adding more.

3 When the chicken has cooked for 20 minutes, lift it out of the stock and into the spicy mixture. Toss everything together over a fairly high heat so that the spices permeate the chicken pieces. Reserve 300ml/½ pint/1¼ cups of the chicken stock to add to the pan later.

4 Stir in the nutmeg and cloves. Strain the tamarind and add the tamarind juice and the soy sauce to the chicken. Cook for a further 2–3 minutes, then add the reserved stock.

5 Taste and adjust the seasoning to taste and cook, uncovered, for a further 25–35 minutes, or until the chicken pieces are tender.

6 Transfer the chicken to a bowl, topped with shredded green and red chillies, and serve with plain boiled rice.

COOK'S TIP
Dark soy sauce is thicker and more salty than light. Adding the dark variety will give a deeper colour to the chicken.

CHICKEN with GOLDEN TURMERIC

As turmeric grows abundantly throughout South-east Asia, using it fresh is quite natural for the local people. The fresh version, which is a root like ginger, has a completely different taste and produces a luxurious golden colour in a dish. It is a difficult ingredient to find in the West. A little more than the normal amount of dried ground turmeric will produce an acceptable colour, although the flavour will be somewhat different.

SERVES 4

1.3–1.6kg/3–3½lb chicken, cut into 8 pieces, or 4 chicken quarters, halved
15ml/1 tbsp light brown sugar
3 macadamia nuts or 6 almonds
2 garlic cloves, crushed
1 large onion, quartered
2.5cm/1in piece fresh galangal or 1cm/½in piece fresh root ginger, sliced, or 5ml/1 tsp galangal powder
1–2 lemon grass stalks, lower 5cm/2in sliced, top bruised
1cm/½in cube shrimp paste
4cm/1½in piece fresh turmeric, sliced, or 10ml/2 tsp ground turmeric
15ml/1 tbsp tamarind pulp, soaked in 150ml/¼ pint/⅔ cup warm water
60–90ml/4–6 tbsp vegetable oil
400g/14oz can coconut milk
salt and ground black pepper
Deep-fried Onions, to garnish

1 Rub each of the chicken joints with a little sugar and set them aside.

2 Grind the nuts and garlic in a food processor with the onion, galangal or ginger, sliced lemon grass, shrimp paste and turmeric. Alternatively, pound the ingredients to a paste with a pestle and mortar. Strain the tamarind pulp and reserve the juice.

COOK'S TIP

In step 3, start with a medium heat and reduce it to low after 1 minute.

3 Heat the oil in a wok or large pan, and cook the paste, without browning, until it gives off a spicy aroma. Add the pieces of chicken and toss well in the spices. Add the strained tamarind juice. Spoon the coconut cream off the top of the milk and set it to one side.

4 Add the coconut milk to the pan. Cover and cook for 45 minutes, or until the chicken is tender.

5 Before serving, stir in the coconut cream. Season to taste and serve, garnished with Deep-fried Onions.

SPICED CHICKEN SAUTE

This makes a wonderfully simple supper dish. If you wish to prepare it in advance, bake the chicken and make the sauce following the recipe, then allow to cool, and store in the refrigerator until needed.

SERVES 4

1.3–1.6kg/3–3½lb chicken breast fillets, skinned and cut into in 8 pieces
5ml/1 tsp each salt and ground black pepper
2 garlic cloves, crushed
150ml/¼ pint/⅔ cup vegetable oil

For the sauce
25g/1 oz butter
30ml/2 tbsp vegetable oil
1 onion, sliced
4 garlic cloves, crushed
2 large, ripe beefsteak tomatoes, chopped
600ml/1 pint/2½ cups water
50ml/2fl oz/¼ cup dark soy sauce
salt and ground black pepper
fresh red chilli, sliced, and Deep-fried Onions, to garnish
plain boiled rice, to serve

1 Preheat the oven to 190°C/375°F/ Gas 5. Make two slashes in each chicken piece and rub with salt, pepper and garlic. Drizzle with oil and bake for about 30 minutes, until browned.

2 To make the sauce, heat the butter and oil and fry the onion and garlic. Add the tomatoes, water, soy sauce and seasoning. Boil for 5 minutes to reduce.

3 Add the chicken pieces to the sauce in the wok, turning the pieces over to coat them well. Continue cooking slowly for about 20 minutes until the chicken is tender. Stir the mixture occasionally.

4 Arrange the chicken on a serving platter and garnish with the chilli and Deep-fried Onions. This dish is usually served with plain boiled rice.

STIR-FRIED CHICKEN with PINEAPPLE

In this Indonesian-influenced dish, chicken fillets benefit from the wonderful tenderizing qualities of pineapple. If you use dark soy sauce, which is quite salty, use only a sprinkling of salt. A dash of sugar will achieve the flavour imparted by the local kecap manis.

SERVES 4–6

500g/1¼lb chicken breast fillets, skinned and thinly sliced at an angle
30ml/2 tbsp cornflour (cornstarch)
60ml/4 tbsp vegetable oil
1 garlic clove, crushed
5cm/2in piece fresh root ginger, cut into thin batons
1 small onion, thinly sliced
1 fresh pineapple, peeled, cored and cubed, or 400g/14oz can pineapple chunks in natural juice
30ml/2 tbsp dark soy sauce or 15ml/1 tbsp kecap manis
1 bunch spring onions (scallions), white bulbs left whole, green tops sliced
salt and ground black pepper
plain boiled rice or noodles, to serve

1 Toss the strips of chicken in the cornflour with a little seasoning. Fry in hot oil until tender.

2 Lift the chicken strips out of the wok or frying pan and keep warm. Reheat the oil and fry the garlic, ginger and onion until soft, but not browned. Add the fresh pineapple and 120ml/4fl oz/ ½ cup water, or the canned pineapple pieces together with their juice.

3 Stir in the soy sauce or kecap manis and return the chicken to the pan to heat through.

4 Taste the chicken and adjust the seasoning. Stir in the whole spring onion bulbs and half the sliced green tops. Toss well together and then turn the chicken stir-fry on to a serving platter. Garnish with the remaining sliced green spring onions. Serve with plain rice or noodles.

CLAY-POT CHICKEN

This deliciously spiced dish is a refined version of the ancient cooking method, whereby the food was placed in a clay pot and buried in the dying embers of an open fire. Today, it is cooked in a low oven and the gentle heat is evenly distributed and retained by the clay pot, resulting in tender meat that melts in the mouth.

SERVES 4–6

1 × 1.3–1.6kg/3–3½lb oven-ready chicken
45ml/3 tbsp grated fresh coconut
30ml/2 tbsp vegetable oil
2 shallots or 1 small onion, finely chopped
2 garlic cloves, crushed
5cm/2in piece lemon grass
2.5cm/1in piece fresh galangal or fresh root ginger, thinly sliced
2 fresh green chillies, seeded and chopped
12mm/½in cube shrimp paste
400g/14oz can coconut milk
300ml/½ pint/1¼ cups chicken stock
2 kaffir lime leaves (optional)
15ml/1 tbsp granulated sugar
15ml/1 tbsp rice or white wine vinegar
2 ripe tomatoes
30ml/2 tbsp chopped fresh coriander leaves (cilantro), to garnish

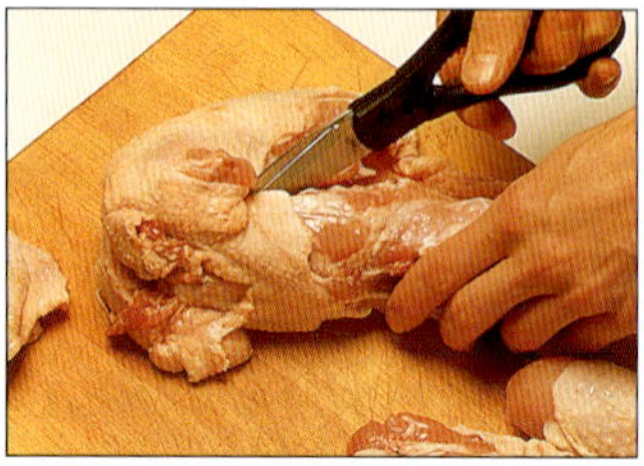

1 To joint the chicken, remove the legs and wings with a sharp knife. Skin the pieces, divide the drumsticks from the thighs and, using kitchen scissors, remove the lower part of the chicken, leaving only the breast piece. Remove as many of the bones as you can, to make the dish easier to eat. Cut the breast piece into four or six and set aside.

2 Dry-fry the coconut in a large wok until evenly browned. Add the vegetable oil, shallots or onion, garlic, lemon grass, galangal or ginger, chillies and shrimp paste. Fry for 2–4 minutes to release the flavours. Preheat the oven to 180°C/350°F/Gas 4. Add the chicken joints to the wok and brown evenly with the spices for 2–3 minutes.

3 Strain the coconut milk, and add the thin part with the chicken stock, lime leaves, if using, sugar and vinegar. Transfer to a glazed clay pot, cover and bake in the centre of the oven for 50 minutes, or until the chicken is tender. Stir in the thick part of the coconut milk and return to the oven for 5–10 minutes.

4 Place the tomatoes in a bowl and cover with boiling water to loosen and remove the skins. Halve the tomatoes, then remove the seeds and chop into large dice. Add the chopped tomatoes to the finished dish, sprinkle with the chopped coriander and serve. Plain rice would make a good accompaniment.

BEEF and AUBERGINE CURRY

The flavour of this versatile dish is subtle yet complex. As well as the fine combination of beef and aubergine, the dish successfully unites the mellow flavour of coconut milk with the pungency of fresh chillies, and the flavours of lemon grass and tamarind. The result is a dish that is equally suitable for a family meal or a dinner party.

SERVES 6

120ml/4fl oz/½ cup vegetable oil
2 onions, thinly sliced
2.5cm/1in piece fresh root ginger, sliced and cut into thin batons
1 garlic clove, crushed
2 fresh red chillies, seeded and finely sliced
2.5cm/1in piece fresh turmeric, crushed, or 5ml/1 tsp ground turmeric
1 lemon grass stalk, lower part sliced finely, top bruised
675g/1½lb braising steak, cut into even-size strips
400g/14oz can coconut milk
300ml/½ pint/1¼ cups water
1 aubergine (eggplant), sliced and patted dry
5ml/1 tsp tamarind pulp, soaked in 60ml/4 tbsp warm water
salt and ground black pepper
finely sliced fresh chilli (optional) and Deep-fried Onions, to garnish
plain boiled rice, to serve

1 Heat half the oil in a wok or large pan, and fry the onions, ginger and garlic until they give off a rich aroma. Add the chillies, turmeric and the lower part of the lemon grass stalk. Push the contents of the pan to one side, then turn up the heat and add the steak, stirring until the meat changes colour.

2 Add the coconut milk, water and lemon grass top, with seasoning. Cover the pan or wok and simmer gently for 1½ hours, or until the meat is tender.

3 Towards the end of the cooking time heat the remaining oil in a frying pan. Fry the aubergine slices until they are brown on both sides.

COOK'S TIP

If you want to make this curry in advance, prepare to the end of step 2, then chill and store in the refrigerator until required.

4 Add the browned aubergine slices to the beef curry and cook for a further 15 minutes. Stir gently from time to time. Strain the tamarind and stir the juice into the curry. Taste and adjust the seasoning. Put into a warm serving dish. Garnish with the sliced chilli, if using, and Deep-fried Onions, and serve with plain boiled rice.

PRAWNS and CHAYOTE in COCONUT MILK

This delicious dish features chayote, which belongs to the squash family. Widely used in South-east Asia and some parts of India, it is pear-shaped, and generally pale yellow in colour. Larger supermarkets usually sell chayote, but you can use courgettes instead.

SERVES 4

1–2 chayotes or 2–3 courgettes (zucchini)
2 fresh red chillies, seeded
1 onion, quartered
5mm/¼in piece fresh galangal or 1cm/½in piece fresh root ginger, sliced
1 lemon grass stalk, lower 5cm/2in sliced, top bruised
2.5cm/1in piece fresh turmeric or 5ml/1 tsp ground turmeric
200ml/7fl oz/scant 1 cup water
lemon juice, to taste
400g/14oz can coconut milk
450g/1lb cooked, peeled prawns (shrimp)
salt
fresh red chilli shreds, to garnish
plain boiled rice or noodles, to serve

1 Peel the chayotes, remove the seeds and cut into strips. If using courgettes, cut into 5cm/2in strips.

2 Grind the fresh red chillies, onion, sliced galangal or root ginger, sliced lemon grass and the turmeric to a paste in a food processor or with a pestle and mortar. Add the water to the paste mixture, with a squeeze of lemon juice and salt to taste.

3 Pour into a pan. Add the top of the lemon grass stalk. Bring to the boil and cook for 1–2 minutes. Add the chayote or courgette pieces and then cook for 2 minutes. Stir in the coconut milk. Taste and adjust the seasoning.

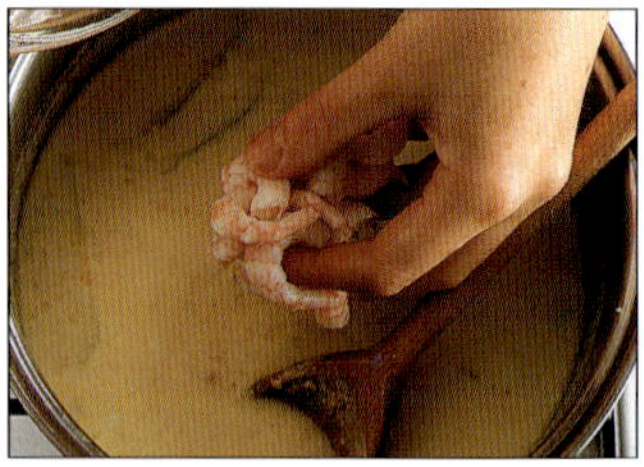

4 Add the peeled prawns and cook gently for 2–3 minutes. Remove the lemon grass stalk. Garnish with shreds of fresh red chilli, if using. This dish is usually served with plain boiled rice, but would taste equally good with rice noodles or egg noodles.

FRIED FISH with a SPICY SAUCE

Although this is not strictly a curry, it is one of the popular styles of cooking used in Malaysia. Locally known as ikan kecap, *it comes from a small range of Eurasian recipes that combine Western techniques with Eastern flavours.*

SERVES 3–4

450g/1lb fish fillets, such as mackerel, cod or haddock
30ml/2 tbsp plain (all-purpose) flour
groundnut (peanut) oil, for frying
1 onion, roughly chopped
1 small garlic clove, crushed
4cm/1½in piece fresh root ginger, grated
1–2 fresh red chillies, seeded and sliced
1cm/½ in cube shrimp paste, prepared
60ml/4 tbsp water
juice of ½ lemon
15ml/1 tbsp brown sugar
30ml/2 tbsp dark soy sauce
salt
roughly torn lettuce leaves, to serve

1 Rinse the fish fillets under cold water and dry on kitchen paper. Cut into serving portions and remove any bones.

2 Season the flour and use it to dust the fish. Heat some oil and fry the fish on both sides for 3–4 minutes, or until cooked. Transfer to a plate and set aside.

3 Rinse out and dry the pan. Heat a little more oil in the clean frying pan and fry the onion, garlic, ginger and chillies to bring out the flavour. Do not brown.

4 Blend the shrimp paste with the water to make a smooth paste. Add it to the onion mixture, with a little extra water if necessary. Cook for 2 minutes and then stir in the lemon juice, brown sugar and soy sauce.

5 Pour the sauce over the fish and serve, hot or cold, with roughly torn lettuce leaves.

COOK'S TIP

If serving this dish as part of a buffet menu, cut the fish into bitesize pieces.

MALAYSIAN FISH CURRY

The cooking styles of Malaysia have been greatly influenced by neighbouring countries such as India, Indonesia, China and the Middle East. The Malay people thrive on fish curry and rice. This is a superbly flavoured coconut-rich fish curry known as ikan moolee, which is best served with a bowl of steaming hot boiled rice.

SERVES 4

500g/1¼lb monkfish or other firm-textured fish fillets, skinned and cut into 2.5cm/1in cubes
2.5ml/½ tsp salt
50g/2oz/⅔ cup desiccated (dry, unsweetened, shredded) coconut
6 shallots or small onions, chopped
6 blanched almonds
2–3 garlic cloves, roughly chopped
2.5cm/1in piece fresh root ginger, sliced
2 lemon grass stalks, trimmed
10ml/2 tsp ground turmeric
45ml/3 tbsp vegetable oil
2 × 400g/14oz cans coconut milk
1–3 fresh red and green chillies, seeded and sliced
salt and ground black pepper, to taste
fresh chives, to garnish
plain boiled rice, to serve

1 Spread out the pieces of fish in a shallow dish and sprinkle them with the salt. Dry-fry the coconut in a wok over a gentle heat, turning all the time until it is crisp and golden (see Cook's Tip).

2 Transfer the coconut to a food processor and process to an oily paste. Scrape into a bowl and reserve.

3 Add the shallots or onions, almonds, garlic and ginger to the food processor. Cut off the lower 5cm/2in of the lemon grass stalks, chop them roughly and add to the processor. Process to a paste.

4 Add the turmeric to the mixture in the food processor and process briefly. Bruise the remaining lemon grass and set the stalks aside.

5 Heat the oil in a wok. Add the onion mixture and cook for a few minutes without browning. Stir in the coconut milk and bring to the boil, stirring constantly to prevent curdling.

6 Add the cubes of fish to the wok, along with most of the sliced fresh chillies and the bruised lemon grass stalks. Cook for 3–4 minutes. Stir in the coconut paste (this can be moistened with some of the sauce if necessary) and cook for a further 2–3 minutes only. Do not overcook the fish. Taste the curry and adjust the seasoning, as required.

7 Remove the lemon grass. Transfer to a hot serving dish and sprinkle with the remaining slices of chilli. Garnish with chopped and whole chives and serve with plain boiled rice.

COOK'S TIP

Dry-frying is a feature of Malay cooking. When dry-frying do not be distracted. The coconut must be constantly on the move so that it becomes crisp and of a uniform golden colour.

CUCUMBER and PINEAPPLE SAMBAL

Sambals are the little side dishes served at almost every Malay meal. In poorer societies, a main meal may simply be a bowl of rice and a sambal made from pounded shrimp paste, chillies and lime juice: the sambal is poured over the rice to give it flavour. This recipe is known as sambal nanas. *Use sparingly, as it is quite fiery.*

SERVES 8–10

1 small or ½ large fresh ripe pineapple
½ cucumber, halved lengthways
50g/2oz dried shrimps
1 large fresh red chilli, seeded
1.25cm/½ in cube shrimp paste, prepared
juice of 1 large lemon or lime
light brown sugar, to taste (optional)
salt

1 Cut off the top and the bottom of the pineapple. Stand it upright on a board, then slice off the skin from top to bottom, cutting out the spines. Slice the pineapple, removing the central core. Cut into thin slices and set aside.

2 Trim the ends from the cucumber and slice thinly. Sprinkle with salt and set aside. Place the dried shrimps in a food processor and chop finely. Add the chilli, prepared shrimp paste and lemon or lime juice, and process again to a paste.

3 Rinse the cucumber, drain and dry on kitchen paper. Mix the pineapple and chill. Just before serving, spoon in the spice mixture with sugar to taste, if liked. Mix well and serve.

COOK'S TIP

The pungent shrimp paste, also called blachan and terasi, is popular in many South-east Asian countries, and is available in Asian food markets. Since it can taste a bit raw in a sambal, dry fry it by wrapping it in foil and heating it in a frying pan over a low heat for 5 minutes, turning from time to time. If the shrimp paste is to be fried with other spices, this preliminary cooking can be eliminated.

INDONESIA

Numerous cultures have flourished among the 13,000 islands of this lush tropical archipelago, including the Dutch, Portuguese and British. The result is a rich culinary heritage that makes use of an abundance of indigenous ingredients, such as rice, chillies, limes, tamarind and spices.

CHICKEN COOKED in COCONUT MILK

Traditionally, the chicken pieces in this dish would be part-cooked by frying, but roasting in the oven can be a better option. This is an unusual recipe in that the sauce is white, as it does not contain chillies or turmeric, unlike many other Indonesian dishes. The dish is usually sprinkled with crisp Deep-fried Onions before serving.

SERVES 4

1.3–1.6kg/3–3½lb chicken or 4 chicken quarters
4 garlic cloves
1 onion, sliced
4 macadamia nuts or 8 almonds
15ml/1 tbsp coriander seeds, dry-fried, or 5ml/1 tsp ground coriander
45ml/3 tbsp vegetable oil
2.5cm/1in piece fresh galangal or 4cm/1½in piece fresh root ginger, bruised
2 lemon grass stalks, fleshy part bruised
3 lime leaves
2 bay leaves
5ml/1 tsp granulated sugar
600ml/1 pint/2½ cups coconut milk
salt
Deep-fried Onions, to garnish
plain boiled rice, to serve

1 Preheat the oven to 190°C/375°F/Gas 5. Cut the chicken into four or eight pieces. Season with salt. Put in an oiled roasting pan. Bake for 25–30 minutes.

COOK'S TIP

For fan assisted ovens, reduce the temperature by at least 10°C/20°F/Gas 1 when cooking the chicken in step 1. Check the chicken from time to time.

2 To make the sauce, grind the garlic, onion, nuts and coriander to a fine paste in a food processor or with a pestle and mortar. Heat the oil in a wok and lightly fry the paste to bring out the flavour.

3 Add the chicken pieces to the wok together with the galangal or ginger, lemon grass, lime and bay leaves, sugar, coconut milk and salt. Mix wel.

4 Bring to the boil and then reduce the heat and allow to simmer gently for 30–40 minutes, uncovered, until the chicken is tender and the coconut sauce is reduced and thickened. Stir the mixture occasionally during cooking.

5 Just before serving, remove the bruised galangal or ginger and lemon grass. Serve with plain boiled rice, sprinkled with Deep-fried Onions.

VARIATION

Instead of deep-frying the onions, coat them with oil, and bake until browned at the same time as the chicken.

MADURA CHICKEN with AROMATIC SPICES

Spices, such as the coriander and cumin used in this recipe, are added to a dish mainly for their taste. With the inclusion of nutmeg and cloves, magadip, as it is known in Indonesia, combines both taste and aroma. It is best cooked a day or two in advance to allow the flavours to mellow and permeate the flesh of the chicken.

SERVES 4

1.3–1.6kg/3–3½lb chicken, cut into quarters, or 4 chicken quarters
5ml/1 tsp granulated sugar
30ml/2 tbsp coriander seeds
10ml/2 tsp cumin seeds
6 whole cloves
2.5ml/½ tsp grated nutmeg
2.5ml/½ tsp ground turmeric
1 small onion
2.5cm/1in piece fresh root ginger, thinly sliced
300ml/½ pint/1¼ cups chicken stock or water
salt and ground black pepper
Deep-fried Onions, to garnish
plain boiled rice, to serve

1 Cut each chicken quarter in half to make eight pieces. Place the pieces in a flameproof casserole, sprinkle with the sugar and season to taste with salt and pepper. Toss the chicken pieces and seasoning together. This helps release the juices in the chicken. Use the chicken backbone and any remaining carcass, if using, to make chicken stock for use later in the recipe, if you like (see Cook's Tip).

2 In a preheated wok or large pan, dry-fry the coriander and cumin seeds and the whole cloves until the spices give off a good aroma. Add the nutmeg and turmeric and heat briefly. Remove and cool. Grind in a spice mill or food processor or use a pestle and mortar.

3 In a food processor, process the onion and ginger until finely chopped. Otherwise, finely chop the onion and ginger and pound to a paste with a pestle and mortar. Add the spices and stock or water and mix well.

4 Pour the spice mixture over the chicken in the flameproof casserole, and stir to ensure the pieces are well coated. Cover the casserole with a lid and cook over a gentle heat for 45–50 minutes until the chicken pieces are tender.

5 Serve the chicken with the sauce on plain boiled rice, sprinkled with crisp Deep-fried Onions.

COOK'S TIP

Add a large piece of bruised fresh root ginger, a small onion studded with a clove, a carrot and a stick of celery and a few peppercorns to the chicken stock to ensure a good flavour.

BEEF RENDANG with DEEP-FRIED ONIONS

In Indonesia, Rendang would be made of prime quality beef, but it can be made with other meats such as lamb, pork or even venison. The flavour of this dish improves significantly if it is cooked a day or two in advance and reheated.

SERVES 6–8

1kg/2¼lb prime beef in one piece
2 onions or 5–6 shallots, sliced
4 garlic cloves, crushed
2.5cm/1in piece fresh galangal, sliced, or 5ml/1 tsp galangal powder
2.5cm/1in piece fresh root ginger, sliced
4–6 fresh red chillies, seeded and sliced
1 lemon grass stalk, lower part, sliced
2.5cm/1in piece fresh turmeric, sliced, or 5ml/1 tsp ground turmeric
5ml/1 tsp coriander seeds, dry-fried and ground
5ml/1 tsp cumin seeds, dry-fried and ground
2 lime leaves
5ml/1 tsp tamarind pulp, soaked in 60ml/4 tbsp warm water
2 × 400g/14oz cans coconut milk
300ml/½ pint/1¼ cups water
30ml/2 tbsp dark soy sauce
8 small new potatoes, scrubbed
salt
plain boiled rice, to serve (optional)

For the deep-fried onions
450g/1lb onions
vegetable oil, for deep-frying

1 Cut the meat into long strips and then into even-size pieces. Place in a large mixing bowl and set aside.

2 Grind the onions or shallots, garlic, fresh galangal or galangal powder, ginger, chillies, sliced lemon grass and turmeric to a fine paste in a food processor or with a pestle and mortar.

3 Add the paste to the meat with the coriander and cumin and mix well. Tear the lime leaves and add them to the mixture. Cover and leave in a cool place to marinate while you prepare the rest of the ingredients.

4 Strain the tamarind and reserve the juice. Place the spiced meat and soy sauce into a wok or large pan, and stir in the coconut milk, water and tamarind juice. Season to taste with salt.

COOK'S TIPS

- If you cannot find either fresh or dried galangal (sold in Asian food stores), use extra fresh root ginger.
- Deep-fried Onions, known as Bawang Goreng, are a traditional Indonesian garnish used to accompany many dishes. They are available ready-prepared from Asian food stores. If preparing them yourself, try to find the small red onions, as they contain less water and are more suitable for this recipe.
- Deep-fried onions may be made in advance and stored in a cool, dark place in an airtight container.

5 Stir until the liquid comes to the boil and then reduce the heat and simmer gently, half-covered, for 1½–2 hours or until the meat is tender and the liquid is reduced.

6 Add the potatoes 20–25 minutes before the end of the cooking time. They will absorb some of the sauce, so add a little more water to compensate for this if you prefer the Rendang to be rather moister than it would be in Indonesia. Adjust the seasoning and keep warm.

7 To make the Deep-fried Onions, slice the onions as finely as possible, then spread out in a single layer on kitchen paper, and leave to dry in an airy place for 30 minutes–2 hours. Heat the oil in a deep-fryer or wok to 190°C/375°F. Fry the onions in batches, until crisp and golden, turning all the time. Drain on kitchen paper and allow to cool.

8 Transfer the Beef Rendang to a warmed serving bowl and sprinkle with the Deep-fried Onions. Plain boiled rice would make a good accompaniment.

GINGER-FLAVOURED DUCK with CHINESE MUSHROOMS

Ducks are often seen, comically herded in single file, along the water channels between the rice paddies throughout Indonesia. There is a substantial Chinese population in Indonesia, among whom duck is a particular favourite. The delicious ingredients in this recipe give it an unmistakable flavour.

SERVES 4

2.5kg/5½lb duck
5ml/1 tsp granulated sugar
50ml/2fl oz/¼ cup light soy sauce
2 garlic cloves, crushed
8 dried Chinese mushrooms, soaked in warm water for 15 minutes
5cm/2in piece fresh root ginger, sliced
1 onion, sliced
200g/7oz baby corn cobs
½ bunch spring onions (scallions)
15–30ml/1–2 tbsp cornflour (cornstarch), mixed with 60ml/4 tbsp water
salt and ground black pepper
plain boiled rice, to serve

1 Cut the duck along the breastbone, open it up and cut along each side of the backbone. Use the backbone, wings and giblets to make a stock to use later in the recipe. Any trimmings of fat can be rendered in a wok or large pan to use later. Cut each leg and each breast in half. Place in a bowl, rub with sugar and pour over the soy sauce and garlic.

2 Drain the mushrooms, reserving the soaking liquid. Trim, discarding the stalks.

VARIATION

Replace the corn with chopped celery and slices of canned water chestnuts.

3 Cut the slices of fresh root ginger into thin batons and fry with the onion in the duck fat, until they give off a good aroma. Set aside the ginger and onion. Lift the duck pieces out of the soy sauce marinade and transfer to the pan. Fry them until browned on both sides. Add the mushrooms and reserved liquid.

4 Add 600ml/1 pint/2½ cups of stock or water to the browned duck pieces in the pan. Add the onion and ginger and season to taste with salt and ground black pepper. Cover the pan with a lid and cook over a gentle heat for about 1 hour, until the duck is tender.

5 Slice the spring onion tops and set aside. Add the corn cobs and the white part of the spring onions and cook for a further 10 minutes. Remove from the heat and add the cornflour paste. Return to the heat and bring to the boil, stirring. Cook for 1 minute until glossy. Sprinkle with the spring onion tops, and serve with plain boiled rice.

BALINESE FISH CURRY

On the beautiful island of Bali, along with neighbouring Java and Sumatra, fish curry and rice constitute the population's dietary staples. Food here has simple, uncomplicated yet delicious flavours. Handle the fish carefully as both cod and haddock flake easily. Alternatively, use a firm-textured fish such as monkfish, swordfish or fresh tuna.

SERVES 4–6

675g/1½lb cod or haddock fillet
1cm/½in cube shrimp paste
2 red or white onions, roughly chopped
2.5cm/1in piece fresh root ginger, sliced
1cm/½in piece fresh galangal, sliced, or 5ml/1 tsp galangal powder
2 garlic cloves
1–2 fresh red chillies, seeded, or 10ml/2 tsp Chilli Sambal, or 5–10ml/1–2 tsp chilli powder
90ml/6 tbsp vegetable oil
15ml/1 tbsp dark soy sauce
5ml/1 tsp tamarind pulp, soaked in 30ml/2 tbsp warm water
250ml/8fl oz/1 cup water
celery leaves or chopped fresh chilli, to garnish
plain boiled rice, to serve

1 Skin the fish and remove any bones, if necessary. Cut the flesh into bitesize pieces. Pat dry with kitchen paper and set aside.

2 Grind the shrimp paste, onions, ginger, fresh galangal, if using, garlic and fresh chillies, if using, to a paste in a food processor or with a pestle and mortar. Stir in the Chilli Sambal or chilli powder and galangal powder, if using.

VARIATION
Substitute 450g/1lb cooked tiger prawns (shrimp) for the fish. Add them to the sauce 3 minutes before the end of cooking and heat through thoroughly.

3 Heat 30ml/2 tbsp of the oil and fry the spice mixture, stirring, until it gives off a rich aroma. Add the soy sauce. Strain the tamarind and add the juice and water. Cook for 2–3 minutes.

4 In a separate pan, fry the fish in the remaining oil for 2–3 minutes. Turn once only so that the pieces stay whole. Lift out with a slotted spoon and put into the sauce.

5 Cook the fish in the sauce for a further 3 minutes. Garnish the dish with feathery celery leaves or a little chopped fresh chilli. Serve with plain boiled rice.

COOK'S TIP
Galangal paste is sold in Asian stores and can be used in place of galangal powder. It is worth buying a jar as it will keep in the refrigerator for several weeks.

SAMBAL GORENG with PRAWNS

This is an immensely useful and adaptable sauce. Here it is combined with prawns and green pepper, but you could use fine strips of calf's liver or chicken livers in place of the prawns, and tomatoes and green beans in place of the pepper.

SERVES 4–6

350g/12oz peeled cooked prawns (shrimp)
1 green (bell) pepper, seeded and thinly sliced
60ml/4 tbsp tamarind juice
pinch of granulated sugar
45ml/3 tbsp coconut milk or cream
lime strips and sliced red onion, to garnish
plain boiled rice, to serve

For the Sambal Goreng

2.5cm/1in cube shrimp paste
2 onions, roughly chopped
2 garlic cloves, roughly chopped
2.5cm/1in piece fresh galangal, sliced
2 fresh red chillies, seeded and sliced
1.5ml/¼ tsp salt
30ml/2 tbsp vegetable oil
45ml/3 tbsp tomato purée (paste)
600ml/1 pint/2½ cups vegetable stock or water

1 To make the Sambal Goreng, grind the shrimp paste with the onions and garlic using a mortar and pestle or a food processor. Add the galangal, chillies and salt. Pound or process to a paste.

2 Heat the oil in a wok or large pan and fry the paste for 2 minutes, without browning, until the mixture gives off a rich aroma. Stir in the tomato purée and the stock or water. Cook for 10 minutes. Ladle half the sauce into a bowl and leave to cool. This leftover sauce can be used in another recipe (see Cook's Tip).

VARIATIONS

To make Tomato Sambal Goreng, add 450g/1lb peeled, coarsely chopped tomatoes to the sauce mixture before stirring in the stock or water. To make Egg Sambal Goreng, add 3 or 4 chopped hard-boiled (hard-cooked) eggs, and 2 peeled, chopped tomatoes to the sauce.

3 Add the prawns and green pepper to the remaining sauce in the wok. Cook gently for 3–4 minutes, then stir in the tamarind juice, sugar and coconut milk or cream. Spoon into serving bowls and garnish with strips of lime rind and sliced red onion. Serve with plain boiled rice.

COOK'S TIP

Any remaining sauce can be stored in the refrigerator for up to 3 days. It can also be frozen for up to 3 months.

PRAWN CURRY with QUAIL'S EGGS

This exotic combination lives up to all the promises of the East. The earthy flavour of ginger is blended with refreshing lemon grass, fiery red chillies and soothing coconut milk to create this exquisite dish. Quail's eggs are now stocked in most supermarkets.

SERVES 4

12 quail's eggs
30ml/2 tbsp vegetable oil
4 shallots or 1 onion, finely chopped
2.5cm/1in piece fresh galangal or 2.5cm/1in piece fresh root ginger, chopped
2 garlic cloves, crushed
5cm/2in piece lemon grass, finely shredded
1–2 small fresh red chillies, seeded and finely chopped
2.5ml/½ tsp ground turmeric
12mm/½in cube shrimp paste or 15ml/1 tbsp fish sauce
900g/2lb raw prawn (shrimp) tails, peeled and deveined
400g/14oz can coconut milk
300ml/½ pint/1¼ cups chicken stock
115g/4oz Chinese leaves, roughly shredded
10ml/2 tsp granulated sugar
2.5ml/½ tsp salt
2 spring onions (scallions), green part only, shredded, and 30ml/2 tbsp shredded coconut, to garnish

1 Boil the quail's eggs for 8 minutes. Refresh in cold water, peel by dipping in cold water to release the shells and set them aside.

2 Heat the vegetable oil in a large wok, add the shallots or onion, galangal or ginger and garlic and cook until the onions have softened, without colouring. Add the lemon grass, chillies, turmeric and shrimp paste or fish sauce and fry briefly to bring out their flavours.

3 Add the prawns to the wok and fry briefly. Pour the coconut milk through a sieve (strainer) over a bowl, then add the thin part of the milk with the chicken stock. Add the Chinese leaves, sugar and salt, and bring to the boil. Simmer for 6–8 minutes.

4 Turn out the prawn curry on to a warmed serving dish. Halve the quail's eggs, using a sharp knife for a clean cut, and toss them in the sauce until they are well coated. Sprinkle with the spring onions and the shredded coconut. Serve with plain boiled rice, if you like.

SQUID in CLOVE SAUCE

The island of Madura, between Bali and Java, makes use of various spices that were originally introduced to Indonesia by Indian and Arab traders. This recipe with cloves and nutmeg, along with tomato and soy sauce, is known as Cumi Cumi Smoor. *It is quite delicious, and not difficult to make.*

SERVES 3–4

675g/1½lb ready-cleaned squid
45ml/3 tbsp groundnut (peanut) oil
1 onion, finely chopped
2 garlic cloves, crushed
1 beefsteak tomato, skinned and chopped
15ml/1 tbsp dark soy sauce
2.5ml/½ tsp grated nutmeg
6 whole cloves
150ml/¼ pint/⅔ cup water
juice of ½ lemon or lime
salt and ground black pepper, to taste
shredded spring onions (scallions) and fresh coriander (cilantro) sprigs, to garnish
plain boiled rice, to serve

1 Wash the squid and pat dry on kitchen paper. Use a sharp kitchen knife to cut the squid into long, thin ribbons. Carefully remove the "bone" from each tentacle, and discard.

2 Heat a wok, toss in the squid and stir constantly for 2–3 minutes, when the squid will have curled into attractive shapes or into firm rings. Lift out and set aside in a warm place.

3 Heat the oil in a clean pan and fry the onion and garlic, until soft and beginning to brown. Add the tomato, soy sauce, nutmeg, cloves, water and lemon or lime juice. Bring to the boil and then reduce the heat and add the squid, with seasoning to taste.

4 Cook the squid in the sauce for 3–5 minutes, uncovered, over a gentle heat, stirring from time to time. Take care not to overcook the squid. Serve hot or warm, with plain rice, or as part of a buffet spread. Garnish with shredded spring onions and fresh coriander.

VARIATION

Instead of squid try using 450g/1lb cooked and peeled tiger prawns (shrimp) in this recipe. Add them to the pan for the final 1–2 minutes.

FRUIT and RAW VEGETABLE GADO-GADO

Banana leaves, which can be bought from Asian markets, lend an authentic touch to all types of South-east Asian dishes. They are most frequently used as wrappers in which to cook small parcels of food, but if you are serving this salad for a special occasion, you could use a single banana leaf instead of the mixed salad leaves to line the platter.

SERVES 6

½ cucumber
2 pears (not too ripe) or 175g/6oz wedge of yam bean
1–2 eating apples
juice of ½ lemon
mixed salad leaves or 1–2 banana leaves
6 tomatoes, seeded and cut into wedges
3 fresh pineapple slices, cored and cut into wedges
3 eggs, hard-boiled (hard-cooked) and shelled
175g/6oz egg noodles, cooked, cooled and chopped
Deep-fried Onions, to garnish

For the peanut sauce
2–4 fresh red chillies, seeded and ground, or 15ml/1 tbsp Hot Tomato Sambal
300ml/½ pint/1¼ cups coconut milk
350g/12oz/1¼ cups crunchy peanut butter
15ml/1 tbsp dark soy sauce or dark brown sugar
5ml/1 tsp tamarind pulp, soaked in 45ml/3 tbsp warm water
coarsely crushed peanuts
salt

VARIATION
Quail's eggs can be used in place of hen's eggs. Hard boil for 3 minutes.

1 Make the peanut sauce. Put the ground chillies or Hot Tomato Sambal in a pan. Pour in the coconut milk, then stir in the peanut butter. Heat gently, stirring, until well blended.

2 Simmer gently until the sauce thickens, then stir in the soy sauce or sugar. Strain in the tamarind juice, add salt to taste and stir well. Spoon into a bowl and sprinkle with coarsely crushed peanuts.

3 To make the salad, core the cucumber and peel the pears or yam bean. Cut the flesh into fine matchsticks. Finely shred the apples and sprinkle them with the lemon juice. Spread a bed of mixed salad leaves on a flat platter and pile the cucumber, pear or yam bean, apple, tomato and pineapple on top.

4 Add the sliced or quartered hard-boiled eggs, the chopped noodles and garnish with the Deep-fried Onions. Serve the salad at once, with the peanut sauce.

SAMBAL KECAP, HOT TOMATO SAMBAL and CUCUMBER SAMBAL

Piquant sambals are placed on the table as a condiment for dipping meat and fish.

SAMBAL KECAP

MAKES ABOUT 150ML/¼ PINT/⅔ CUP

1 fresh red chilli, seeded and finely chopped
2 garlic cloves, crushed
60ml/4 tbsp dark soy sauce
20ml/4 tsp lemon juice, or 15–25ml/1–1½ tbsp prepared tamarind juice or 5ml/1 tsp concentrated tamarind pulp
30ml/2 tbsp hot water
30ml/2 tbsp Deep-fried Onions

1 Mix the chilli, garlic, soy sauce, lemon juice or tamarind juice or pulp and hot water together in a bowl.

2 Stir in the Deep-fried Onions and then leave the sambal to stand for 30 minutes before serving.

HOT TOMATO SAMBAL

MAKES 120ML/4FL OZ/½ CUP

3 ripe tomatoes
2.5ml/½ tsp salt
5ml/1 tsp chilli sauce
60ml/4 tbsp fish sauce or soy sauce
15ml/1 tbsp chopped fresh coriander (cilantro) leaves

1 Cover the tomatoes with boiling water to loosen the skins. Remove the skins, halve, discard the seeds and chop the flesh finely.

2 Place the chopped tomatoes in a large bowl, add the salt, chilli sauce, fish sauce or soy sauce and chopped coriander.

3 Mix together well. Leave the sambal to stand for 30 minutes before serving.

CUCUMBER SAMBAL

MAKES 150ML/5FL OZ/⅔ CUP

1 clove garlic, crushed
5ml/1 tsp fennel seeds
10ml/2 tsp granulated sugar
2.5ml/½ tsp salt
2 shallots or 1 small onion, finely sliced
100ml/4fl oz/½ cup rice or white wine vinegar
¼ cucumber, finely diced

1 Place the garlic, fennel seeds, sugar and salt in a pestle and mortar and pound finely. Alternatively, grind the ingredients thoroughly in a food processor.

2 Stir in the shallots or onion, vinegar and cucumber. Leave to stand for 6–8 hours to allow the flavours to combine.

COCONUT and PEANUT RELISH and HOT CHILLI AND GARLIC DIPPING SAUCE

These flavoursome accompaniments can be served with many Indonesian dishes.

COCONUT AND PEANUT RELISH

MAKES 120ML/4FL OZ/½ CUP

115g/4oz fresh coconut, grated, or desiccated (dry, unsweetened, shredded) coconut
175g/6oz/1 cup salted peanuts
5mm/¼in cube shrimp paste
1 small onion, quartered
2–3 garlic cloves, crushed
45ml/3 tbsp vegetable oil
2.5ml/½ tsp tamarind pulp, soaked in 30ml/2 tbsp warm water
5ml/1 tsp coriander seeds, roasted and ground
2.5ml/½ tsp cumin seeds, roasted and ground
5ml/1 tsp dark brown sugar

1 Dry-fry the coconut in a wok or large pan over a medium heat, stirring the coconut constantly until crisp and golden colour. Allow to cool and add half to the peanuts in a bowl. Toss together to mix.

2 Process the shrimp paste, the onion and garlic in a food processor or with a pestle and mortar to form a paste. Fry the paste in hot oil, without browning.

3 Strain the tamarind and reserve the juice. Add the coriander, cumin, tamarind juice and brown sugar to the fried paste in the pan. Cook for 3 minutes, stirring.

4 Stir in the remaining toasted coconut and leave to cool. When cold, mix with the peanut and coconut mixture. Leave to stand for 30 minutes before serving.

HOT CHILLI AND GARLIC DIPPING SAUCE

MAKES 120ML/4FL OZ/½ CUP

1 garlic clove
2 fresh Thai red chillies, seeded and roughly chopped
10ml/2 tsp granulated sugar
5ml/1 tsp tamarind juice
60ml/4 tbsp soy sauce
juice of ½ lime

1 Process the garlic, chillies and sugar in a food processor or with a pestle and mortar to create a smooth paste.

2 Add the tamarind juice, soy sauce and lime juice, and mix together. Leave to stand for 30 minutes before serving.

THE PHILIPPINES

Filipino cuisine shows the influence of neighbouring China, Malaysia, Japan and Indonesia, but by far the strongest influence came from the Spanish settlers who arrived to colonize the islands in the 16th century, and stayed for nearly 400 years.

MIXED MEAT SOUP

A Filipino pot-au-feu with Spanish connections, this dish is known as Puchero. Sometimes it is served as two courses, first soup, then meat and vegetables with rice, but it can happily be served as is, on rice in a wide soup bowl. Either way it is very satisfying, and a siesta afterwards is highly recommended.

SERVES 6–8

225g/8oz/generous 1 cup chickpeas, soaked overnight in water to cover
1.3kg/3lb chicken, cut into 8 pieces
350g/12oz belly of pork, rinded, or pork fillet, cubed
2 chorizo, thickly sliced
2 onions, chopped
2.5 litres/4 pints/10 cups water
60ml/4 tbsp vegetable oil
2 garlic cloves, crushed
3 large tomatoes, peeled, seeded and chopped
15ml/1 tbsp tomato purée (paste)
1–2 sweet potatoes, cut into 1cm/½in cubes
2 plantains or unripe bananas, sliced (optional)
salt and ground black pepper
chives or chopped spring onions (scallions), to garnish
½ head Chinese leaves (Chinese cabbage), shredded, to serve

For the aubergine sauce
1 large aubergine (eggplant)
3 garlic cloves, crushed
60–90ml/4–6 tbsp wine or cider vinegar

1 Drain the chickpeas and put them in a pan. Cover with water, bring to the boil and boil rapidly for 10 minutes. Reduce the heat and simmer for 30 minutes until the chickpeas are half tender. Drain.

2 Put the chicken pieces, pork, chorizo and half of the onions in a pan. Add the chickpeas and pour in the water. Bring to the boil and lower the heat, cover and simmer for 1 hour or until the meat is just tender when tested with a skewer.

3 Meanwhile, make the aubergine sauce. Preheat the oven to 200°C/400°F/Gas 6. Prick the aubergine in several places, then place it on a baking sheet and bake for 30 minutes or until very soft.

4 Cool slightly, then peel away the aubergine skin and scrape the flesh into a bowl. Mash the flesh with the crushed garlic, season to taste and add enough vinegar to sharpen the sauce, which should be quite piquant. Set aside.

5 Heat the oil in a wok or large pan and fry the remaining onion and garlic for 5 minutes, until soft but not brown. Add the tomatoes and tomato purée and cook for 2 minutes, then add this mixture to a pan with the diced sweet potato. Add the plantains or unripe bananas, if using. Cook over a gentle heat for 20 minutes until the sweet potato is cooked. Add the Chinese leaves for the last minute or two.

6 Spoon the thick meat soup into a soup tureen, and put the vegetables in a separate serving bowl. Garnish both with whole or chopped chives or spring onions and serve with Chinese leaves and the aubergine sauce. Plain boiled rice goes very well with this dish.

SWEET and SOUR PORK with COCONUT SAUCE

This is known as adobo *in the Philippines, which refers to a cooking style rather than the name of the dish. There are many variations of the recipe, and this version includes papaya, because the enzymes in the unripe fruit are excellent for tenderizing meat.*

SERVES 4–6

675g/1½lb lean pork, diced
1 garlic clove, crushed
5ml/1 tsp paprika
5ml/1 tsp crushed black peppercorns
15ml/1 tbsp granulated sugar
175ml/6fl oz/¾ cup palm or cider vinegar
2 small bay leaves
425ml/15fl oz/1¾ cups chicken stock
50g/2oz creamed coconut (coconut cream)
150ml/¼ pint/¾ cup vegetable oil, for frying
1 under-ripe papaya, peeled, seeded and chopped
salt
½ cucumber, peeled and cut into batons, 2 firm tomatoes, skinned, seeded and chopped, and 1 small bunch chives, chopped, to garnish

1 Marinate the pork with the garlic, paprika, black pepper, sugar, vinegar and bay leaves in a cool place for 2 hours. Add the chicken stock and coconut.

2 Transfer to a wok and simmer gently for 30–35 minutes, then remove the pork and drain. In a frying pan, heat the oil and brown the pork. Remove and drain.

3 Return the pork to the sauce with the papaya, season with salt and simmer for 15–20 minutes. Garnish with the cucumber batons, chopped tomatoes and chives and serve.

COOK'S TIP

If creamed coconut is not available, use 50ml/2fl oz/10 tsp coconut cream.

BRAISED BEEF in a RICH PEANUT SAUCE

Like many dishes brought to the Philippines by Spanish settlers, this slow-cooking estofado, renamed kari kari, retains much of its original charm. Rice and peanuts are used to thicken the juices, yielding a rich glossy sauce.

SERVES 4–6

900g/2lb stewing beef, chuck, shin or blade steak
30ml/2 tbsp vegetable oil
15ml/1 tbsp annatto seeds, or 5ml/1 tsp paprika and a pinch of ground turmeric
2 onions, chopped
2 garlic cloves, crushed
275g/10oz celeriac or swede (rutabaga), peeled and roughly chopped
425ml/15fl oz/1¾ cups beef stock
350g/12oz new potatoes, peeled and cut into large dice
15ml/1 tbsp fish sauce
30ml/2 tbsp tamarind sauce
10ml/2 tsp granulated sugar
1 bay leaf
1 sprig thyme
45ml/3 tbsp long grain rice
50g/2oz/⅓ cup peanuts or 30ml/2 tbsp peanut butter
15ml/1 tbsp white wine vinegar
salt and ground black pepper

1 Cut the beef into 2.5cm/1in cubes and set aside.

2 Heat the vegetable oil in a wok or large pan. Add the annatto seeds, if using, and stir to colour the oil a dark red. Remove the seeds with a slotted spoon and discard. If you are not using annatto seeds, paprika and turmeric can be added later.

3 Soften the onions, garlic and the celeriac or swede in the oil without letting them colour. Add the beef cubes and fry over a high heat to seal. If you are not using annatto seeds to redden the sauce, stir in the paprika and ground turmeric with the beef.

4 Add the beef stock, potatoes, fish sauce and tamarind sauce, granulated sugar, bay leaf and thyme. Bring to a simmer and allow to cook on the top of the stove for about 2 hours.

5 Cover the rice with cold water and leave to stand for 30 minutes. Roast the peanuts under a hot grill (broiler), if using, then rub the skins off in a clean cloth. Drain the rice and grind with the peanuts or peanut butter, using a pestle and mortar, or food processor.

6 When the beef is tender, add 60ml/4 tbsp of the cooking liquid to the ground rice and nuts. Blend smoothly and stir into the contents of the pan. Simmer gently on the stove to thicken, for about 15–20 minutes. To finish, stir in the wine vinegar and season well.

FISH in SPICED VINEGAR

This fish dish, cooked in the pickling style, is served hot and is known as escabeche. It is eaten wherever there are or have been Spanish settlers. In the Philippines, palm vinegar is commonly used as a souring agent, but herb or cider vinegars will work just as well.

SERVES 6

675–900g/1½–2lb white fish fillets, such as sole, plaice or flounder
45–60ml/3–4 tbsp seasoned flour
vegetable oil, for shallow frying

For the sauce
30ml/2 tbsp vegetable oil
2.5cm/1in piece fresh root ginger, thinly sliced
2–3 garlic cloves, crushed
1 onion, cut into thin rings
½ large green (bell) pepper, seeded and cut into small neat squares
½ large red (bell) pepper, seeded and cut into small neat squares
1 carrot, cut into thin batons
25ml/1½ tbsp cornflour (cornstarch)
450ml/¾ pint/scant 2 cups water
45–60ml/3–4 tbsp herb or cider vinegar
15ml/1 tbsp light soft brown sugar
5–10ml/1–2 tsp fish sauce
salt and ground black pepper
1 small fresh chilli, seeded and sliced and spring onions (scallions), finely shredded, to garnish
plain boiled rice, to serve

1 Wipe the fish fillets and leave them whole, or cut into serving portions, if you like. Pat dry on kitchen paper then dust lightly with the seasoned flour.

2 Heat oil for shallow frying in a frying pan and fry the fish in batches until golden and almost cooked. Transfer the fried fish to a large ovenproof dish and keep warm while you prepare the other ingredients.

3 Make the sauce in a wok or large pan. Fry the ginger, garlic and onion in the oil for 5 minutes or until the onion is softened but not browned.

4 Add the pepper squares and carrot strips and stir-fry for 1 minute.

5 Put the cornflour in a small bowl and add a little of the water to make a paste. Stir in the remaining water, the vinegar and the sugar. Pour the cornflour mixture over the vegetables in the wok and stir until the sauce boils and thickens a little. Season with fish sauce and salt and pepper if needed.

6 Add the fish to the sauce and reheat without stirring. Transfer to a serving platter and garnish with chilli and spring onions. Serve with plain boiled rice.

COOK'S TIP

Red snapper or small sea bass could be used for this recipe, in which case ask your fishmonger to cut it into fillets.

FISH STEW with VEGETABLES

Sinigang, as it is known in the Philippines, is a soured soup-like stew, which many Filipinos consider to be their national dish. It is always served with noodles or rice, and seafood – either prawns or thin slivers of fish fillet – is often added for good measure.

SERVES 4–6

15ml/1 tbsp tamarind pulp or 5ml/1 tsp concentrated tamarind pulp
150ml/¼ pint/⅔ cup warm water
2 tomatoes, roughly chopped
115g/4oz spinach or Chinese kangkong leaves
115g/4oz peeled, cooked large prawns (jumbo shrimp), thawed if frozen
1.2 litres/2 pints/5 cups prepared fish stock (see Cook's Tip)
½ mooli (daikon), peeled and finely diced
115g/4oz/¾ cup French (green) beans, cut into 1cm/½in lengths
225g/8oz piece of cod or haddock fillet, skinned and cut into strips
fish sauce, to taste
squeeze of lemon juice, to taste
salt and ground black pepper
plain boiled rice or noodles, to serve

1 Put the tamarind pulp in a large bowl, if using, and pour over the warm water. Set aside. Peel and chop the tomatoes, and discard the seeds. Strip the spinach or kangkong leaves from the stems and tear into small pieces. Set aside.

2 Using your hands, remove the heads and shells from the prawns, if necessary, leaving the tails intact.

3 Pour the prepared fish stock into a large pan and add the finely diced mooli. Cook the mooli for 5 minutes, then add the chopped green beans. Continue to cook the stew gently for 3–5 minutes more.

4 Add the fish strips, tomatoes and spinach or kangkong leaves. Strain in the tamarind juice or add the concentrated tamarind, stir until dissolved, and cook for 2 minutes. Stir in the prawns and cook for 1–2 minutes to heat through.

5 Season the stew with salt and freshly ground black pepper, and add a little fish sauce and lemon juice to taste. Transfer the stew to individual warmed serving bowls, and serve with either plain boiled rice or noodles.

COOK'S TIP

A good fish stock is essential for Sinigang. Ask your fishmonger for about 675g/1½lb fish bones. Wash them, then place in a pan with 2 litres/3½ pints/8 cups water. Add half a peeled onion, a 2.5cm/1in piece of bruised fresh root ginger, and a little salt and pepper. Bring to the boil, skim, then simmer for 20 minutes. Cool slightly, then strain. Freeze any unused stock.

RICE AND NOODLES

The unassertive flavours of rice and noodles make them perfect partners for the fragrant, aromatic foods of South-east Asia. Rice grows in abundance throughout the region. Like noodles, it is a staple food, and is eaten with every meal on a daily basis.

FESTIVE RICE

Rice is the staple food throughout South-east Asia. There are numerous varieties, but the two commonly used ones are polished white long grain and glutinous rice. Generally, any long grain rice will produce good results, but Thai fragrant rice is particularly delicious.

SERVES 8

450g/1lb/2⅓ cups Thai fragrant rice or other long grain rice
60ml/4 tbsp vegetable oil
2 garlic cloves, crushed
2 onions, finely sliced
5cm/2in piece fresh turmeric, crushed
750ml/1¼ pints/3 cups water
400g/14oz can coconut milk
1–2 lemon grass stalks, bruised
1–2 pandan (screwpine) leaves (optional)
salt

For the accompaniments
omelette strips
2 fresh red chillies, shredded
cucumber chunks
tomato wedges
Deep-fried Onions
Coconut and Peanut Relish
prawn (shrimp) crackers

1 Wash the rice thoroughly in several changes of water. Drain well.

2 Heat the vegetable oil in a wok or frying pan and gently fry the crushed garlic, finely sliced onions and crushed fresh turmeric for a few minutes until soft but not browned.

3 Add the rice and stir well so that each grain is coated in oil, and the rice mixes with the garlic, onion and turmeric. Pour in the water and coconut milk and add the bruised lemon grass, pandan leaves, if using, and add salt to taste.

4 Bring to the boil, stirring well. Cover the pan and cook gently for about 15–20 minutes, until all of the liquid has been absorbed.

5 Remove the pan from the heat. Cover with a clean dishtowel, put on the lid and leave the pan to stand in a warm place for 15 minutes. Remove the lemon grass and pandan leaves, if used.

6 Turn out the rice on to a warmed serving platter and garnish with the accompaniments before serving.

COOK'S TIP
It is the custom to shape the rice into a cone (to represent a volcano) and then surround it with the accompaniments. Shape the rice with oiled hands or use a conical sieve.

COCONUT RICE

This is a very popular way of cooking rice throughout the whole of South-east Asia. Nasi uduk*, as it is known in Indonesia, makes a wonderful accompaniment to any meat dish, and goes particularly well with fish, chicken and pork.*

SERVES 4–6

350g/12oz Thai fragrant rice
400g/14oz can coconut milk
300ml/½ pint/1¼ cups water
2.5ml/½ tsp ground coriander
2.5cm/1in piece cinnamon stick
1 lemon grass stalk, bruised
1 pandan (screwpine) or bay leaf or 2–3 drops screwpine essence
salt
fresh coriander (cilantro) sprigs and Deep-fried Onions, to garnish

1 Wash the rice in several changes of water and then put in a large pan with the coconut milk, water, coriander, cinnamon stick, lemon grass and pandan, bay leaf or screwpine essence, if using, and salt. Bring to the boil, stirring constantly to prevent the rice from settling on the base of the pan. Cover with a lid and cook over a very low heat for 12–15 minutes, or until the coconut milk has been absorbed.

2 Fork through and remove the lemon grass, cinnamon, and pandan or bay leaf. Cover and cook for 3 minutes more.

3 Cover the pan with a tight-fitting lid and continue to cook over the lowest possible heat for 3–5 minutes more.

4 When the rice is ready, pile on to a warm serving dish and garnish with the coriander sprigs and crisp Deep-fried Onions. Serve immediately.

COOK'S TIP

If you wish to use fresh coconut milk, crack open the coconut and remove the clear water (this makes an excellent cooling drink). Using a small, sharp knife, remove the flesh in sections, then peel off the brown skin. Process the flesh in a food processor, and squeeze out the milk through a muslin (cheesecloth) cloth.

MALACCA FRIED RICE

Using leftover rice to make up a new dish is a common practice all over the East. In most Eastern countries, rice is equivalent to wealth and it is never thrown away. It is believed that if you throw away wealth it will never return to you.

SERVES 4–6

2 eggs
45ml/3 tbsp vegetable oil
4 shallots or 1 onion, finely chopped
5ml/1 tsp grated fresh root ginger
1 garlic clove, crushed
225g/8oz peeled prawn (shrimp) tails, raw or cooked
5–10ml/1–2 tsp chilli sauce (optional)
3 spring onions (scallions), green part only, roughly chopped
225g/8oz/2 cups frozen peas, thawed
225g/8oz thickly sliced roast pork, diced
45ml/3 tbsp light soy sauce
350g/12oz long grain rice, cooked and allowed to become completely cold
salt and ground black pepper

1 In a bowl, beat the eggs well, and season to taste with salt and ground black pepper.

2 Heat 15ml/1 tbsp of the vegetable oil in a wok or large pan, pour in the eggs and allow them to set, without stirring, for less than a minute.

3 Roll up the pancake with your hands, then cut it into thin strips and set aside. The pancake can be allowed to cool down to room temperature, although it can also be served hot, if you like.

COOK'S TIP
Store cooked, cooled rice in an airtight container in the refrigerator. Heat the rice thoroughly, and make sure the grains are piping hot when using precooked and cooled rice in any recipe.

4 Heat the remaining vegetable oil in the wok, add the shallots or onions, chopped ginger, garlic and prawn tails and cook gently for 1–2 minutes. Keep stirring the contents of the wok to ensure that the garlic doesn't burn.

5 Add the chilli sauce, if using, spring onions, peas, pork and soy sauce. Stir to heat through, then add the rice. Fry the rice over a moderate heat for 6–8 minutes. Turn into a warmed serving dish and decorate with the pancake.

INDONESIAN FRIED RICE

One of the most familiar and well-known Indonesian dishes, Nasi Goreng is a marvellous way to use up leftover rice, chicken and meats such as pork. It is important that the rice is quite cold and the grains are separate before adding the other ingredients.

SERVES 4–6

350g/12oz/1¾ cups dry weight long grain rice, such as basmati, cooked and allowed to become completely cold
2 eggs
30ml/2 tbsp water
105ml/7 tbsp vegetable oil
225g/8oz pork fillet or fillet of beef
115g/4oz peeled, cooked prawns (shrimp)
175–225g/6–8oz cooked chicken, chopped
2–3 fresh red chillies, seeded and sliced
1cm/½in cube shrimp paste
2 garlic cloves, crushed
1 onion, sliced
30ml/2 tbsp dark soy sauce or 45–60ml/3–4 tbsp tomato ketchup
salt and ground black pepper
celery leaves, fresh coriander (cilantro) sprigs, to garnish

1 Once the rice is cooked and cooled, fork it through to separate the grains and keep it in a covered pan or dish until required.

2 Beat the eggs with seasoning and the water and make two or three omelettes in a frying pan, with a minimum of oil. Roll up each omelette and cut into strips when cold. Set aside.

3 Cut the pork or beef into neat strips and put the meat, prawns and chicken pieces in separate bowls. Shred one of the chillies and reserve it.

COOK'S TIP
Always store cooked and cooled rice in the refrigerator.

4 Put the shrimp paste, with the remaining chilli, garlic and onion, in a food processor and grind to a paste, or pound using a pestle and mortar.

5 Fry the paste in the remaining hot oil, without browning, until it gives off a rich, spicy aroma. Add the strips of pork or beef and fry over a high heat to seal in the juices. Stir constantly to prevent the meat sticking to the bottom of the pan.

6 Add the prawns, cook for 2 minutes and then stir in the chicken, cold rice, dark soy sauce or ketchup and seasoning to taste. Stir constantly to keep the rice light and fluffy and prevent it from sticking to the base of the pan.

7 Turn on to a hot platter and garnish with the omelette strips, celery leaves, reserved shredded fresh chilli and coriander sprigs.

PINEAPPLE FRIED RICE

When buying a pineapple, look for a sweet-smelling fruit with an even brownish/yellow skin. To test for ripeness, tap the base – a dull sound indicates that the fruit is ripe. The flesh should also give slightly when pressed.

SERVES 4–6

1 pineapple
30ml/2 tbsp vegetable oil
1 small onion, finely chopped
2 fresh green chillies, seeded and chopped
225g/8oz lean pork, cut into strips
115g/4oz cooked, peeled prawns (shrimp)
675–900g/1½–2lb/3–4 cups plain boiled rice, cooked and completely cold
50g/2oz/⅓ cup roasted cashew nuts
2 spring onions (scallions), chopped
30ml/2 tbsp fish sauce
15ml/1 tbsp soy sauce
2 fresh red chillies, sliced, and 10–12 fresh mint leaves (optional), to garnish

1 Using a sharp knife, cut the pineapple into quarters. Remove the flesh from both halves by cutting around inside the skin. Reserve the pineapple skin shells for serving the rice.

2 Slice the pineapple flesh and chop it into small even-size cubes. You will need about 115g/4oz of pineapple in total. Any remaining fruit can be reserved for use in a dessert.

3 Heat the oil in a wok or large pan. Add the onion and chillies and fry for about 3–5 minutes until softened. Add the strips of pork and cook until they have browned on all sides.

4 Stir in the prawns and rice and toss well together. Continue to stir-fry until the rice is thoroughly heated.

5 Add the chopped pineapple, cashew nuts and spring onions. Season to taste with fish sauce and soy sauce.

6 Spoon into the pineapple skin shells. Garnish with sliced red chillies, and with shredded mint leaves, if you like.

COOK'S TIP

This dish is ideal to prepare for a special occasion meal. Served in the pineapple skin shells, it is sure to be the talking point of the dinner.

THAI FRIED NOODLES

Phat Thai, as this dish is known, has a fascinating flavour and texture. It is made with rice noodles, combined with shellfish and beancurd, a range of vegetables and ground peanuts, and is considered one of the national dishes of Thailand.

SERVES 4–6

350g/12oz rice noodles
45ml/3 tbsp vegetable oil
15ml/1 tbsp chopped garlic
16 raw king prawns (jumbo shrimp), peeled, tails left intact and deveined
2 eggs, lightly beaten
15ml/1 tbsp dried shrimps, rinsed
30ml/2 tbsp pickled white radish
50g/2oz fried beancurd or tofu, chopped
2.5ml/½ tsp dried chilli flakes
115g/4oz garlic chives, cut into 5cm/2in lengths
225g/8oz/1 cup beansprouts
50g/2oz/⅓ cup roasted peanuts, coarsely ground
5ml/1 tsp granulated sugar
15ml/1 tbsp dark soy sauce
30ml/2 tbsp fish sauce
30ml/2 tbsp tamarind juice or 5ml/1 tsp concentrated tamarind pulp
30ml/2 tbsp fresh coriander (cilantro) leaves and 1 kaffir lime, to garnish

1 Soak the noodles in a bowl of warm water for 20–30 minutes, then drain.

2 Heat 15ml/1 tbsp of the oil in a wok or large pan. Add the garlic and fry until golden. Stir in the prawns and cook for 1–2 minutes until pink, tossing from time to time. Remove and set aside.

3 Heat another 15ml/1 tbsp of oil in the pan. Add the eggs and tilt the wok to spread them into a thin sheet. Stir to scramble and break the egg into small pieces. Remove from the pan and set aside with the prawns.

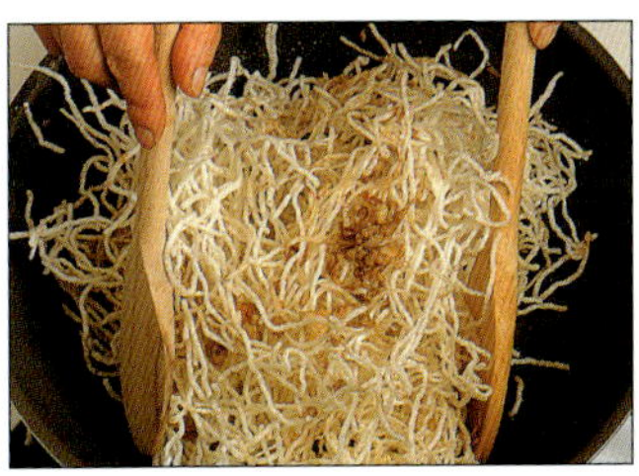

4 Heat the remaining oil in the same pan. Add the dried shrimps, pickled radish, beancurd or tofu and dried chillies. Stir-fry briefly. Add the soaked noodles and stir-fry for 5 minutes.

5 Add the garlic chives, half the beansprouts and half the peanuts. Season with the granulated sugar, soy sauce, fish sauce and tamarind juice or pulp. Mix well and cook until the noodles are completely heated through.

6 Return the prawn and egg mixture to the pan and mix with the noodles. Serve garnished with the rest of the beansprouts, peanuts, coriander leaves and kaffir lime wedges, if using.

COOK'S TIP
Pickled white radish is available in jars from Asian food stores and markets.

MIXED MEAT FRIED NOODLES with PRAWNS

This fried noodle dish, known as bamie goreng, *is wonderfully accommodating. To the basic recipe you can add other vegetables, such as mushrooms, tiny pieces of chayote, broccoli, leeks or beansprouts. As with fried rice, you can use whatever you have to hand.*

SERVES 6–8

450g/1lb dried egg noodles
115g/4oz chicken breast fillets, skinned
115g/4oz pork fillet
115g/4oz calf's liver (optional)
2 eggs, beaten
90ml/6 tbsp vegetable oil
25g/1oz butter or margarine
2 garlic cloves, crushed
115g/4oz peeled, cooked prawns (shrimp)
115g/4oz spinach or Chinese leaves (Chinese cabbage)
2 celery sticks, finely sliced
4 spring onions (scallions), shredded
about 60ml/4 tbsp chicken stock
dark soy sauce and light soy sauce
salt and ground black pepper
Deep-fried Onions and celery leaves, to garnish (optional)

1 Cook the noodles in salted, boiling water for 3–4 minutes. Drain, rinse with cold water and drain again. Set aside until required.

2 Finely slice the chicken, pork fillet and calf's liver, if using.

3 Season the eggs. Heat 5ml/1 tsp oil with the butter or margarine in a small pan until melted and then stir in the eggs and keep stirring until scrambled. Set them aside.

4 Heat the remaining oil in a wok or large pan and fry the garlic with the chicken, pork and liver, if using, for 2–3 minutes, until they change colour. Add the prawns, spinach or Chinese leaves, celery and spring onions, tossing well.

5 Add the cooked, drained noodles and toss well again so that all the ingredients are well mixed. Add enough stock just to moisten, and dark and light soy sauce to taste. Stir in the beaten eggs. Garnish the dish with Deep-fried Onions and celery leaves.

COOK'S TIP

When choosing ingredients for this dish, bear in mind the need to achieve a balance of colour, flavour and texture.

CRISPY FRIED RICE VERMICELLI

Mee krob is usually served at celebration meals. It is a crisp tangle of fried rice vermicelli, with minced pork, prawns, dried shrimp and beansprouts, tossed in a piquant sweet-and-sour sauce and garnished with strips of omelette.

SERVES 4–6

vegetable oil, for frying
175g/6oz rice vermicelli
15ml/1 tbsp chopped garlic
4–6 dried chillies, seeded and chopped
30ml/2 tbsp chopped shallot
15ml/1 tbsp dried shrimps, rinsed
115g/4oz minced (ground) pork
115g/4oz peeled, raw prawns (shrimp), chopped
30ml/2 tbsp brown bean sauce
30ml/2 tbsp rice wine vinegar
45ml/3 tbsp fish sauce
75g/3oz palm sugar or light brown sugar
30ml/2 tbsp tamarind or lime juice
115g/4oz/½ cup beansprouts
salt and ground black pepper

For the garnish
2 spring onions (scallions), shredded
30ml/2 tbsp fresh coriander (cilantro) sprigs
2 heads pickled garlic (optional)
2-egg omelette, rolled and sliced
2 fresh red chillies, chopped

1 Heat the oil in a wok or large pan. Cut the vermicelli into handfuls about 7.5cm/3in long, and deep-fry until they puff up. Remove. Drain on kitchen paper.

2 Leave 30ml/2 tbsp of the hot oil in the pan. Add the garlic, chillies, shallot and shrimps and fry for 2–3 minutes.

3 Add the pork and stir-fry for about 3–4 minutes, until it is no longer pink. Add the prawns and fry for 2 minutes. Remove the mixture and set aside.

4 To the same pan, add the brown bean sauce, vinegar, fish sauce and palm sugar or brown sugar. Bring to a gentle boil, stir to dissolve the sugar and cook until thick and syrupy.

5 Add the tamarind or lime juice and adjust the seasoning. It should be sweet, sour and salty.

6 Reduce the heat. Add the pork and prawn mixture and the beansprouts to the sauce; stir to mix.

7 Add the rice noodles and toss gently to coat them with the sauce. Transfer the noodles to a platter. Garnish with spring onions, coriander leaves, pickled garlic, omelette strips and red chillies.

COURGETTES with NOODLES

Any vegetable from the same family as courgette or squash can be used in this Indonesian recipe, which is known as oseng oseng. It is very similar to a dish enjoyed in Malaysia, and there are strong links between the cuisines of these two neighbouring countries.

SERVES 4–6

450g/1lb courgettes (zucchini)
1 onion, finely sliced
1 garlic clove, finely chopped
30ml/2 tbsp vegetable oil
2.5ml/½ tsp ground turmeric
2 tomatoes, chopped
45ml/3 tbsp water
115g/4oz peeled, cooked prawns (shrimp)
25g/1oz cellophane noodles
salt

COOK'S TIP
Keep an eye on the time as cellophane noodles soften very quickly.

1 Use a potato peeler to cut thin strips from the outside of each courgette. Cut the courgettes into neat slices, then set aside. Fry the onion and garlic in hot oil in a pan; do not allow to brown.

2 Add the turmeric, courgette slices, chopped tomatoes, water and the cooked prawns.

3 Put the noodles in a large pan and pour over enough boiling water to cover. Leave the noodles to soak for a minute and then drain. Cut the noodles into 5cm/2in lengths and then add them to the vegetables.

4 Cover the pan with a lid and allow everything to cook in its own steam for 2–3 minutes. Toss well together. Season the noodles with salt to taste, and transfer to a warmed serving bowl.

NOODLES with CHICKEN, PRAWNS and HAM

The cuisine of the Philippines is a harmonious blend of Malay, Chinese and Spanish influences. This recipe has Chinese origins, and is known in Malaysia as pansit guisado. *Any kind of meat can be cooked with the prawns.*

SERVES 4–6

285g/10oz dried egg noodles
15ml/1 tbsp vegetable oil
1 onion, chopped
1 garlic clove, crushed
2.5cm/1 in piece fresh root ginger, grated
50g/2oz canned water chestnuts, drained and sliced
15ml/1 tbsp light soy sauce
30ml/2 tbsp fish sauce or chicken stock
175g/6oz cooked chicken breast, sliced
150g/5oz cooked ham, thickly sliced, cut into short fingers
225g/8oz peeled, cooked prawn (shrimp) tails
175g/6oz/¾ cup beansprouts
200g/7oz canned baby corn, drained
2 limes, cut into wedges, and 1 small bunch fresh coriander (cilantro), shredded, to garnish

1 Soak the egg noodles in a large bowl of water, and cook them according to the instructions on the packet. Drain the noodles and set aside.

2 Meanwhile, in a wok or large pan, fry the onion, garlic and ginger until soft. Add the water chestnuts, soy sauce and fish sauce or chicken stock, and the chicken and ham and prawn tails.

3 Add the noodles, beansprouts and corn. Stir-fry for 6–8 minutes. Garnish with the lime wedges and shredded coriander. Serve immediately.

COOK'S TIP

Egg noodles can be prepared in advance. Cook them up to 24 hours before they are needed, and keep them in a large bowl of cold water.

GLOSSARY

Almonds Available whole, flaked (slivered) and ground, these sweet nuts impart a sumptuous richness to curries. They are considered a great delicacy in Pakistan and India, where they are extremely expensive and are generally only used for special occasion dishes.
Asafoetida A resin added to dishes as an anti-flatulent. It has an acrid, bitter taste and only a tiny amount should be used.
Aubergines Numerous aubgergine varieties exist in Asia, where the vegetable has been grown for more than 2,000 years. Aubergine absorbs the flavours of other ingredients like a sponge, and therefore benefits from beign cooked with strongly flavoured foods and seasonings.
Banana leaves Traditionally used in Indian and Asian cooking as containers to steam foods, banana leaves are sold in Indian and Asian food stores. If unavailable, squares of lightly oiled kitchen foil or buttered greaseproof paper may be used instead.
Bangkuang (yambean) A major vegetable crop in South-east Asia, bangkuang, or yambean, is peeled and cut into strips before use in stir-fries, spring rolls and salads.
Basil One of the oldest herbs known to man, basil is thought to have originated in India, although it is much more widely used in South-east Asia, in Laos, Cambodia, Vietnam and especially in Thailand, where a variety known as Thai basil is grown. Add basil to curries and salads as an ingredient and as a garnish. Avoid chopping the leaves, but tear them into pieces or add them to the dish whole.
Basmati rice A slender, long grain rice grown in northern India, in the Punjab, Pakistan and the foothills of the Himalayas. Basmati is famous for its distinctive and beautiful fragrance. It is widely used in Indian cooking, particularly in pilaus and biryanis; it has a cooling effect when eaten with hot, spicy curry dishes.

Bay leaves The large dried leaves of the bay laurel tree are one of the oldest herbs used in India. Bay leaves are used for the distinctive flavour they add to a dish.
Beancurd Fresh beancurd is commonly known in the West by its Japanese name, tofu. Made from soya beans, it is a rich source of protein in vegetarian diets and is a popular ingredient in India and South-east Asia. Beancurd is sold in supermarkets and health food stores as silken or soft tofu, and also in a firmer form. Depsite the bland taste of beancurd, the porous texture will absorb the flavour of ingredients with which it is cooked and, depending on the type used, it can be cooked in almost any way with a vast array of ingredients, sweet and savoury. Yellow beancurd is usually only available from Asian food stores, where it is sold cubed, ready to be deep-fried for use in Asian cooking.
Bengal gram A lentil often used whole in curries. Gram flour, known as *besan*, is made from the Bengal gram lentil, and is used to flavour and thicken Indian curries.
Chapati flour A type of wholemeal (whole-wheat) flour, often sold under its Indian name, *atta*, in Indian food stores. It is used to make chapatis and other breads, but well sifted wholemeal flour can be used if chapati flour is not available.
Chillies All chilli varieties are native to tropical America, and were introduced to Asia by European traders after Christopher Columbus took them home to Spain, and they quickly became an integral part of the cuisine. Fresh and dried chillies are used in India and South-east Asia to add heat and flavour to sauces, sambals and salads, and to cooked dishes, such as stocks, soups, curries, stir-fries, and braised dishes.

Coconut milk An essential ingredient in south and east Indian and South-east Asian cooking. Coconut milk can be made at home from desiccated (dry, unsweetened, shredded) coconut, but it is also available canned. If the milk is left to stand, coconut cream will rise to the surface.
Coriander Fresh coriander is a favourite ingredient in all Asian countries, and its unique delicate flavour and bright green colour makes it a popular garnish for curries. It is also available ground and dried.
Creamed coconut Coconut cream left to solidify and moulded into blocks is used to add richness to savoury and sweet dishes from India and South-east Asia. A small quantity can be cut off the block and stirred into a dish just before serving, or it can be diluted with boiling water to produce coconut milk, with the proportions of creamed coconut to water being altered according to the required consistency of coconut milk.
Curry leaves Fragrant, glossy green leaves that are produced by a hardwood tree indigenous to southern India. Curry leaves are used in curries and rice dishes all over Asia, but especially in India. The leaves are sold fresh or dried in Indian food stores.
Curry pastes Wet blends of spices, herbs and chillies that are used as the basis of a curry. Different spice blends will produce different flavours. As they contain fresh ingredients, curry pastes need to be refrigerated and used as required.
Curry powder These are dry blends of spices and chillies. Different blends and roasting times of the spices and chillies produce different flavoured powders.
Fenugreek Sold in bunches, the fresh herb has very small leaves and is used to flavour both meat and vegetable dishes. Always discard the stalks, which will impart a bitterness to the dish. Flat fenugreek seeds are pungent and slightly bitter. They are widely used in Indian curries and rice dishes.
Fish sauce This is an essential seasoning for savoury dishes in Thai and Vietnamese cooking, and is also used to make dipping sauces. In Vietnam, it is often made using

shrimps, but in Thailand, the sauce is more often made using salted, fermented fish.

Kaffir limes This fruit is not a true lime, but instead belongs to a sub-species of the citrus family. Native to South-east Asia, kaffir limes have dark green knobbly skins. The fruit is inedible, and although the rind is sometimes used in cooking, it is the fragrant leaves that are the most highly prized. Kaffir limes are synonymous with Thai cooking, and are also used in Indonesia, Malaysia, Burma and Vietnam. The leaves are torn or finely shredded and used in soups and curries.

Galangal A flavouring agent used in South-east Asian cooking, especially shellfish and meat dishes. Very similar in appearance to root ginger, with galangal being slightly thinner and paler in colour, the two are used in much the same way. Galangal is pounded with shallots, garlic and chillies to make a spice paste for curries and dipping sauces, and it is sliced for use in soups and dressings.

Garam masala A mild, sweet seasoning from north India, and a very popular curry powder. Recipes for garam masala may vary, but all will contain cardamom, cinnamon, cloves, cumin, coriander and black peppercorns. The name garam masala translates as hot spice, which refers to the fact that these spices are known to heat the body.

Garlic A standard ingredient in most Indian and South-east Asian curries, garlic is used crushed, chopped or as whole cloves.

Ghee The traditional Indian cooking fat, ghee, is clarified butter that can be heated to higher temperatures than other oils without burning. Pure ghee is made from dairy milk, but vegetable ghee is also produced, and nowadays this is often used in place of dairy ghee because of its lower fat content. Many modern Indian households prefer to use vegetable oil in place of ghee as their chosen cooking fat.

Ginger Fresh root ginger is a basic ingredient in Indian and South-east Asian cooking. Ground ginger is a useful standby but it lacks the flavour of the fresh spice.

Lemon grass This long, slim citrus-flavoured bulb is a distinctive ingredient in South-east Asian cooking, especially in Thailand, Malaysia and Indonesia. Lemon grass is the perfect complement to coconut milk, particularly in fish, shellfish and chicken dishes. Whole bulbs can be bruised and added to soups, stews and curries, while the stem can be sliced or chopped for use in stir-fries, salads or braised dishes.

Lentils Small, round dry seeds that should be shelled and cooked before use. Lentils are indigenous to Asia, and are a staple food in many countries.

Mango powder Made from unripe green mangoes that have been left to dry in the hot midday sun and then ground finely, this powder has a sour taste and is used in Indian cooking as a souring agent, to add a tangy flavour curries.

Mung beans Small, round olive-green beans with a delicate, sweetish flavour. Mung beans are used in Indian and South-east Asian curry dishes. Beansprouts are sprouted mung beans.

Mustard seeds Round in shape, with a sharp flavour, mustard seeds are used in Indian cooking to flavour curries and pickles.

Mustard oil Made from mustard seeds, this oil has a pungent taste when raw but becomes sweeter when heated. It is widely used in India, especially in eastern regions, where mustard crops are grown.

Noodles Although rarely found in India, noodles are eaten on a daily basis throughout South-east Asia. Many noodle varieties are available, which can be made from wheat flour, with or without eggs, or from rice and other starches. Cellophane noodles are made from the starch of mung beans. Noodles are sold fresh and dried.

Paneer A white, smooth-textured cheese from northern India. Paneer is excellent used in combination with meat or fish, or on its own in vegetarian dishes.

Poppy seeds Whole seeds from the poppy plant are toasted to bring out their flavour.

Saffron The world's most expensive spice is produced from the dried stigmas of the saffron crocus, which is native to Asia Minor. Only a tiny amount of saffron is needed to flavour or colour a dish, whether sweet or savoury. Saffron is sold as threads and in powder form, and the flavour, which really is unsurpassable, almost justifies the cost.

Sambals South-east Asian sambals are hot, spicy relishes or sauces that have chillies as their key ingredients. Sambals are particularly popular in Indonesia. A typical Thai meal will usually include one or two sambals, while in Vietnam, sambals are used as seasoning, in the same way as salt and pepper are used at the table in the West. Sambals are served in small bowls, and pieces of cooked meat, fish or vegetables are then dipped into the bowl.

Shrimp paste An essential ingredient in South-east Asian savoury dishes, including curries and rice dishes, satay sauces, dipping sauces, dressings, and braised dishes. Shrimp paste is made from tiny shrimps that have been salted, dried, pounded, and left to ferment in hot and humid conditions. The uncooked paste has a pungent aroma, although fortunately this disappears when the paste is cooked. Shrimp paste is one of those ingredients that really does make a difference to a dish, contributing depth, pungency and a distinctive South-east Asian signature.

Tamarind The dried black pods of the tamarind plant are sour in taste and very sticky. Tamarind is used for its flavour, which is refreshingly tart and sour, without being bitter. Lemon juice mat be used a substitute but the resulting flavour will not compare.

Turmeric This bright yellow, bitter-tasting spice is sold ground and fresh, with fresh turmeric being peeled and then grated or sliced in the same way as fresh root ginger. Turmeric is often used as a cheaper alternative to saffron, and is used for its colour, as well as for its peppery aroma and warm, musky flavour. Ground turmeric is a key ingredient in curry powders, and is responsible for the characteristic yellow colour.

INDEX

P

R

S

PICTURE CREDITS

Additional picture material supplied by Life File: page 10, page 11 top, page 12, page 13 top and bottom, p167 top right, p168, 169 top and bottom, page 170, page 171 top and bottom.

Notes

Notes

NOTES

Notes

Notes

Notes

Notes

NOTES